On Animals
Volume One: Systematic Theology

ON ANIMALS

VOLUME ONE
SYSTEMATIC THEOLOGY

David L. Clough

BLOOMSBURY

LONDON • NEW DELHI • NEW YORK • SYDNEY

Bloomsbury T&T Clark
An imprint of Bloomsbury Publishing Plc

50 Bedford Square
London
WC1B 3DP
UK

1385 Broadway
New York
NY 10018
USA

www.bloomsbury.com

Bloomsbury is a registered trade mark of Bloomsbury Publishing Plc

First published 2012
Paperback edition first published 2013

British Library Cataloguing-in-Publication Data
A catalogue record for this book is available from the British Library.

ISBN: HB: 978-0-567-13948-1
PB: 978-0-567-63286-9

Library of Congress Cataloging-in-Publication Data
A catalogue record for this book is available from the Library of Congress.

Typeset by Fakenham Prepress Solutions, Fakenham, Norfolk NR21 8NN
Printed and bound in Great Britain

In memory of my mother
Judith Armstrong Clough
1940–2008
whose love sent me on my way

Contents

ACKNOWLEDGEMENTS

The research leave that allowed me to undertake the bulk of this project was funded by the Higher Eduction Funding Council for England (HEFCE) and involved a partnership with the Department of Theology and Religion at the University of Exeter. I am very grateful to Mike Higton for his willingness to host me at Exeter and to his colleagues and graduate students for reading early chapter drafts and giving feedback on seminar papers: alongside Mike, Esther Reed, David Horrell, Cherryl Hunt, Morwenna Ludlow, Adrian Thatcher, David Grumett, Dominic Coad, Suzannah Cornwall and Jon Morgan were all of help in different ways. Christopher Southgate deserves special mention in engaging graciously and patiently in reading and responding to arguments that diverged from his own. I was helped immensely by questions and comments when presenting draft material from the book at seminars at Aberdeen, Edinburgh, King's College London, Lancaster, St John's College, Nottingham and audiences at papers at the Society for the Study of Theology and the American Academy of Religion (AAR). Paul Nimmo also kindly offered helpful written feedback after one such occasion. I am also grateful to Farm Forward, who provided a scholarship that allowed me to present draft material at the AAR, and to the British Academy for an overseas conference grant allowing further material to be presented at a subsequent AAR meeting. Peter Francis at Gladstone's Library, Hawarden, provided me with a desk and scholarship to support the project and I remain profoundly grateful for his work in sustaining the library's unique oasis of scholarly calm. I would also like to record my debt of gratitude to colleagues at Chester who made my research leave possible by covering various duties, and to Hannah Bacon and Wayne Morris who provided feedback on work in progress. I continue to learn from my doctoral students: conversations with John McKeown and Kris Hiuser were particularly helpful in this work, and I am grateful to Kris for his editorial assistance in the final stages of preparing the manuscript.

Two departing colleagues deserve special mention. Celia Deane-Drummond provided both a generous welcome to the Department of Theology and Religious Studies four years ago and has been an energetic collaborative partner in pursuing issues surrounding animals, theology and ethics, through the Centre for Religion and the Biosciences, the symposium which led to our co-edited volume *Creaturely Theology* and the two international conferences on animals we have recently co-hosted. I have a debt of gratitude to her and will miss her greatly following her move to Notre Dame. Tom Greggs has engaged with the ideas behind this work consistently over the four years we have shared at Chester, and has read and commented on virtually all of what follows. I am grateful for his diligence and committed support, as well as his friendship which will now have to be maintained from distant Aberdeen.

Finally, I am grateful to Tom Kraft at T&T Clark/Continuum for his support and patience, and for the preparedness of Lucy, Rebecca, Matthew and Anna to tolerate the occasional absences of husband and father that pursuing such a passion requires.

Chester
November 2011

FOREWORD

Karl Barth says that theology is prompted by the ethical question 'What shall we do?' and this is certainly true of this work. My original intention was to write a Christian ethics of human relationships with non-human animals, but I did not get far into this work before realizing that the doctrinal foundations for such a project were radically underdetermined. If we are not sure where other animals belong in God's works of creation, reconciliation and redemption, it seems to me, we can make little headway with a plausible account of what our responsibilities might be in relation to them. My second thought, therefore, was to write a monograph in which the first half would focus on doctrinal foundations and the second half theological ethics, but over time it became clear that the lack of previous systematic attention to the being of non-human animals meant that the doctrinal foundations required more expansive engagement than half a book would require. The current two-volume monograph is therefore the third and final draft of the structure of the work, where the first volume examines what it might mean to take animals as a serious object of systematic theological enquiry and the second volume explores what this doctrinal account might mean for how Christians should treat other animals across a diverse range of practices.

I hope it is not too off-putting to a reader to note that I am by no means convinced that what follows is the last word either on the place of animals in Christian doctrine or ethics. Indeed, I very much hope that this is not the case, since much of the territory I cover in these volumes seems so woefully underexplored and I am confident that much more remains to be said. Instead, my hope is that this work will be a stimulus to theologians, ethicists and a wider church to take animals more seriously as a topic of Christian theology and ethics, to debate with and beyond the positions for which I argue, and through such discussion and reflection to come to a clearer sense of the meaning of these other creatures God has set alongside us and the understanding that should shape the norms of our relationships with them. It seems to me, and to many of those with whom I have shared work in progress, that there is much of theological interest in this relatively new locus of theological attention, whatever their relation to ethical issues. I agree with Barth, however, that theology is finally fruitless unless the results of its reflections are brought to bear on questions of practice. Notwithstanding the intrinsic delight of good theological work in this area, therefore, such labours must finally be justified according to how far they help us think better and do better concerning our practice in relation to other animal creatures, which means that the systematic theology in the first volume of this work is incomplete without the theological ethics of the second.

INTRODUCTION

Aim and scope

The argument of this book is simple. Christian theology – among many other schools of thought and often in dependence on them – has come to rely on ill-considered renditions of the distinction between human beings and other animals that are implausible, unbiblical, theologically problematic and ethically misleading. Such accounts of human and other-than-human animals need urgent reconsideration for several reasons: to ensure the coherence of Christian theology, to construct an adequate theological anthropology and to enable an appropriate understanding of God's other animal creatures that will inform our relationships with them. This book attempts this necessary reconsideration and reconstruction of Christian doctrine with regard to the question of how to think theologically about animals.

The question of where animals belong in theology is a relatively novel one within the Christian tradition, which for many reasons has focused its attention for the most part on the relation between God and humanity. It has become a crucial and pressing question for theology in three independent respects. First, at a time in which human relationships with non-human animals have undergone rapid transformation, as a result of the industrialization of meat production, the expansion of human population and new scientific knowledge, there is a need for renewed and theologically informed reflection concerning the ethics of such relations, and this theological ethics of animals will not be viable or persuasive in the absence of a clear doctrinal framework. Second, as theology has become alert to the need to encounter and provide room for those who have previously been excluded from its discussions on grounds of gender, race or social location, a legitimate and disturbing question arises concerning whether such a consciousness should end at the species boundary.[1] Third, as

---

[1] On the emergence of other-than-human animals as theological subjects, see Carol J.

the chapters that follow illustrate, the animal question is a properly theological one in the sense that it raises and illuminates issues concerning the adequacy and coherence of Christian doctrine in the areas of trinity, creation, covenant, incarnation, atonement, eschatology, Christology, pneumatology and beyond.

The newness of our current practices in relation to other animals is breathtaking. In the period of the history of the Christian Church, we have travelled from a time in which the killing of animals was only permitted within religious rituals[2] to a time in which 60 billion animals per year are killed for human consumption, the majority of which are raised, slaughtered and processed in factory conditions far removed from the sight or concern of their consumers.[3] The additional new feature of our relationships with other animals is that the massive growth in human population means that competition for room to live between human beings and other creatures is becoming more intense, and the changes in habitats caused by global climate change will further exacerbate this challenge. Both of these novel features of modern relationships between humans and other animals provoke significant ethical questions.

The difficulty in proceeding with the task of new ethical thinking concerning this new context is the paucity of resources to ground adequate ethical regard for animals. Asking questions about other animals highlights the implausibility of the Kantian tradition of ethics, which begins by recognizing moral duties only towards those who can recognize moral duties themselves, and thus is in danger of neglecting the many humans not in this position, as well as other creatures deserving of moral regard. There have been many noble attempts to modify a Kantian rights-based approach to secure rights for non-human animals, but success or failure here turns on whether this or that animal is sufficiently like a human being to be included, which means both that the theory is failing to answer the question of appropriate moral regard – because the question of which creatures should be given moral protection is still open – and that moral regard is being given on the dubious basis of similarity to human beings.[4] Peter Singer has done admirable work in raising the profile of animal suffering as a moral concern from within a utilitarian framework,

Adams and Marjorie Procter-Smith, 'Taking Life or "Taking on Life"? Table Talk and Animals', in C. J. Adams ed. *Ecofeminism and the Sacred* (New York: Continuum, 1993), 296.

[2] See M.-Z. Petropoulou, 'Animal Sacrifice in Greek Religion, Judaism, and Early Christianity in the Period 100 BC–AD 200'. D.Phil. thesis. University of Oxford, 2004.

[3] Compassion in World Farming, *Global Warning: Climate Change and Farm Animal Welfare* (Godalming, Surrey: Compassion in World Farming, 2008), 6.

[4] See, for example, Paola Cavalieri and Peter Singer (eds), *The Great Ape Project: Equality Beyond Humanity* (New York: St Martin's Press, 1993).

but theologians should question whether finally such a framework is able to
support appropriate moral regard for animals – human, as well as non-human
– since any wrong done to any creature can be justified provided the benefit
to others is sufficiently great.[5] In a theological context, there is also very little
ground to stand on: only occasionally has theological thinking been devoted
to where other animals belong in God's great acts of creation, reconciliation
and redemption, which means that the foundations necessary to construct a
theological ethic are largely absent.[6] It is this preliminary task that this book
seeks to address. Following the unlikely common recommendation of both
Karl Barth and Paul Tillich, the doctrinal theology undertaken in this study is
primarily driven by an ethical question:[7] what should we do in our relationships with other creatures? While this book does not reach as far as answering
ethical questions concerning our human relationships with other animals, the
author is the first to acknowledge that the reflections presented here would be
fruitless if they failed to return to this motivating question in order to inform a
new theological ethics of animals, and the second volume of this work will take
up the ethical implications of this doctrinal study. The reason for deferring an
answer to the ethical questions concerning relationships between humans and
other-than-human animals is not that such questions are less important or less

---

[5] See Peter Singer ed. *In Defence of Animals* (Oxford: Blackwell, 1985); Peter Singer,
  Animal Liberation, 2nd edn (London: Pimlico, 1995); Peter Singer, 'All Animals
  Are Equal', in James Rachels ed. *The Right Thing to Do: Basic Readings in Moral
  Philosophy* (Boston: McGraw-Hill, 1999).

[6] The work of Andrew Linzey is the pre-eminent exception to this rule, especially
  Andrew Linzey, *Christianity and the Rights of Animals* (London: SPCK, 1987);
  Andrew Linzey, *Animal Theology* (London: SCM Press, 1994); Andrew Linzey,
  Animals and Trinitarian Doctrine: A Study of the Theology of Karl Barth (Lampeter:
  Mellen, 1996); Andrew Linzey, *Animal Gospel: Christian Faith as Though Animals
  Mattered* (London: Hodder & Stoughton, 1998); Andrew Linzey and Dorothy
  Yamamoto (eds), *Animals on the Agenda: Questions About Animals for Theology
  and Ethics* (London: SCM Press, 1998). Linzey's theology of animals is best
  understood as a liberation theology for animals, however, rather than a project
  in systematic theology or Christian doctrine. See also Stephen H. Webb, *On God
  and Dogs: A Christian Theology of Compassion for Animals* (New York; Oxford:
  Oxford University Press, 1998) and the essays gathered in Celia Deane-Drummond
  and David Clough (eds), *Creaturely Theology: On God, Humans and Other Animals*
  (London: SCM, 2009).

[7] Karl Barth, *Church Dogmatics*, vol. II/2, (eds) T. F. Torrance and G. W. Bromiley
  (Edinburgh: T. & T. Clark, 1957), 515; Karl Barth, *Church Dogmatics*, vol. III/4, (eds)
  G. W. Bromiley and T. Torrance, trans. W. Bromiley et al. (Edinburgh: T. & T. Clark,
  1961), 3; Paul Tillich, *Systematic Theology* (Chicago: University of Chicago, 1957),
  vol. 1, 36.

urgent, but that they cannot adequately be addressed in the absence of the kind of systematic discussion of animals presented here.

This is not a project in creating a list of heroes and villains among biblical texts and theologians with regard to animals, or of gathering up eccentric animal-friendly texts that have previously gone unnoticed. Instead, my aim is to engage constructively with the heart of biblical and focal theological traditions on the question of where animals belong in our theology. For the most part, the novelty of this project comes from the novelty of the question it asks of the Christian theological tradition rather than the proposal of innovative answers to it. The transformation in our thinking about animals for which the book argues, results, in the main, from looking squarely for the first time at the sum of what we are already committed to believing about our fellow creatures and their place in God's creation. The controversial questions addressed here – most of which concern the relative place of human and non-human animals – are few in number compared with the important implications for our thinking about animals of key doctrinal claims about which there is little serious dispute. What is new and surprising in what follows, results more from unrecognized implications of previously unconnected doctrinal insights than proposals for revisions of orthodox tenets of belief, and so is primarily an exercise in systematic theology: an attempt to trace the implications of doing Christian theology alert to the issue of where animals belong.

Terminology

In addressing theological questions concerning animals, an initial problem is the lack of stability in creatures considered as being under this term. The biggest difficulty is not the problem biologists have in distinguishing reliably between plants and animals in species at their margins, although this issue is relevant to my argument and discussed in Chapter 2. A much more significant issue is the question of whether a different kind of species altogether belongs within the 'animal', that is *Homo sapiens*. In biological usage, this is uncontroversial: according to the Linnaean system, humans belong to the class *mammalia*, in the subphylum *vertebrata*, within the phylum *chordata*, in the kingdom *Animalia*. In English usage, however, matters are less clear.[8] The derivation from Latin is clear enough: *anima* means 'soul' or 'breath of life', so *animal* means any

---

[8] For an informative discussion of the difficulty in translating between biological and common English usage in classifying organisms, see John Dupré, 'Are Whales Fish?', in Douglas L. Medin and Scott Atran (eds), *Folkbiology* (Cambridge, MA: MIT, 1999).

creature with the breath of life.[9] Human beings are, then, a particular kind of animal: 'the rational animal' being a common Greek summary of philosophical anthropology. The word hardly appears in English until the end of the sixteenth century, and is absent from the 1611 King James Bible. The *Oxford English Dictionary* makes it clear that in English usage the word has been ambiguous in its inclusion of the human from the outset, with Shakespearean examples on both sides.[10] This radical ambiguity is an apt representation of human ambivalence about whether we belong in the same category as other animals, but causes difficulty when the topic under discussion is the relationship between other creatures. In the title of this book and throughout the text, therefore, 'animal' is used in its original and etymologically natural sense to include *Homo sapiens*, together with all the other millions of species of fleshy creatures with the breath of life. I take this to be both true to biblical thinking about animals and largely synonymous with membership of the biological kingdom of *Animalia*, although boundary cases, such as sponges and slime moulds, mean this can only be approximate.[11] Fortunately, therefore, I have no stake in establishing any absolute boundary between animals and other creatures: rather, I am suggesting only that the kind of life most animals share, in diverse ways, merits theological attention. Using 'animal' to include the human has the disadvantage of necessitating references to 'other-than-human animals' or 'non-human animals' more frequently than is desirable, but this circumlocution at least draws attention to the issue, whereas the alternative of resolving the ambiguity to exclude the human hinders the project of opening boundary questions to scrutiny.

Interpreting Anthropocentrism

A related issue concerns anthropocentrism – viewing the world with human beings as central – which has been a point of dispute at least as far back as Xenophanes in the sixth century BC, debated by philosophers of the Middle Academy in the third century BC, and later taken up by the Academics and

---

[9] This leaves aside the question of whether all animals have souls: see the discussion in Chapter 6.

[10] For example, 'What a piece of work is a man! ... the Paragon of Animals' (*Hamlet*, II.ii.20); 'his Animals on his dunghills are as much bound to him as I' (*As You Like It*, I.i.16).

[11] On the resemblance of the latter to animals, see Jan Klein and Naoyuki Takahata, *Where Do We Come From? The Molecular Evidence for Human Descent* (Berlin; Heidelberg; New York: Springer, 2002), 156. See Chapter 2 for further discussion of the boundary issue.

Stoics.[12] The Greek debate concerned whether it was appropriate to think of the gods in human form and whether the earth was made for the sake of human beings. At the end of the third century AD, Celsus uses the arguments of the Greek Academic philosophers to attack Christianity for its naïve belief that human beings are the aim and centre of creation; in Origen's *Against Celsus* in the third century, he uses Stoic arguments to reject Celsus's critique and justify an anthropocentric view of the world.[13] In English, the term 'anthropo-centrism' only dates from the late nineteenth century. One of the earliest uses of the word was in an 1883 English translation of a book by Ernst Haeckel, the atheist German biologist who was a major influence in the continental reception of Charles Darwin's ideas. Haeckel identifies two great errors in the Mosaic creation narrative: the geocentric error of thinking the earth to be the centre of the universe, and 'the anthropocentric error that man is the premeditated aim of the creation of the earth, for whose service alone all the rest of nature is said to have been created'.[14] Debate concerning whether or not the universe is teleologically anthropocentric in this sense has been somewhat confused, however, by different interpretations of the term, including an *episte-mological* sense where human knowledge about God's purposes is restricted to the human,[15] a *perspectival* sense where the term names the inevitable position from which we view the world,[16] a *metaethical* sense in which humans are the

---

[12] Henry Chadwick treats this issue in his discussion of Origen's dispute with Celsus about the rationality of animals: Henry Chadwick, 'Origen, Celsus and the Stoa', *Journal of Theological Studies* 48 (1947), 36–7.

[13] Origen, *Origen: Contra Celsum*, trans. Henry Chadwick (Cambridge: Cambridge University Press, 1965), 4.74–99. (See Chapter 1 for a discussion of this text).

[14] Ernst Haeckel, *The History of Creation, or the Development of the Earth and its Inhabitants by the Action of Natural Causes*, trans. E. Ray Lankester (London: Kegan Paul, Trench, 1883), 38–9.

[15] For example, in defending natural law V. A. Demant argues 'To confine theological seriousness to God's redemptive work in man, and to refuse to recognize some knowledge of His creative and preservative work by which man can say something about the orders themselves (not merely about man's conduct within them at each moment) is a disguised form of the very anthropocentrism which this doctrine intends to oppose' (V. A. Demant, *Christian Polity* (London: Faber & Faber, 1936), 102–3).

[16] For example, Francis Watson argues that anthropocentrism is inevitable for humans 'since our primary perspective on the world is a human one' (Francis Watson, 'In the Beginning: Irenaeus, Creation, and the Environment', in *Ecological Hermeneutics: Biblical, Historical and Theological Perspectives*, eds. David Horrell, Cherryl Hunt, Christopher Southgate and Francesca Stavrakopoulou (London; New York: T & T Clark International, 2008), 129. Tim Hayward describes this as an inevitable aspect of anthropocentrism (Tim Hayward, 'Anthropocentrism: A Misunderstood Problem', *Environmental Values* 6 (1997), 51).

only source of moral value[17] and an *ethical* sense in which human interests are the only ones that matter.[18]

The question of whether the world is anthropocentric in a *teleological* sense – created for the sake of human beings – is a substantive theological debate discussed at length in Chapter 1. The *epistemological* sense, that we only have theological knowledge in relation to God's dealings with ourselves, may cause us to be appropriately cautious before presuming too much knowledge of God's relationship to other creatures, but should not prevent us from seeking the knowledge concerning our place before God in relation to other creatures that we need to guide our actions towards them. The *perspectival* sense should be rejected as unhelpful and misleading: to say that we see through our own eyes is both platitudinous and irrelevant to the teleological, metaethical or ethical questions. This can be seen by comparison with the problem of egocentrism: the fact that I look at the world from my position in it does not prevent me from trying to resist the egocentric views that the universe was created for me, that moral value only relates to my view of the world or that my interests are the only ones that count. The *metaethical* sense of anthropocentrism, that humans are the sole source of value, represents the philosophy of atheistic humanism, and should be rejected by Christian theology on the basis of its affirmation that God is the source of all value. Finally, in a theological context the *ethical* sense that human interests are the only ones that count is dependent on the teleological question: if God made the world for the sake of humanity, presumably human interests should predominate, but, if this is not the case, then ethical anthropocentrism seems hard to justify.[19]

---

[17] This seems to be Hayward's point in his observation that 'so long as the class of valuers includes human beings, human values are ineliminable' (Hayward, 'Anthropocentrism', 57).

[18] This is Bryan Norton's interpretation of anthropocentrism in Bryan G. Norton, 'Environmental Ethics and Weak Anthropocentrism', *Environmental Ethics* 6 (1984). In this article he distinguishes between 'felt preferences', i.e. what people want, and 'considered preferences', i.e. what people want after having adopted a rational world view. Value theories that are concerned only for the satisfaction of felt human preferences are 'strongly anthropocentric' on his terms; value theories that treat considered preferences are 'weakly anthropocentric' (134). Both have in common that they attribute no intrinsic value to any aspect of the world beyond the human, which, on the basis of my argument against teleological anthropocentrism in Chapter 1, is a significant error.

[19] The theological delimitation of this point is crucial. In an atheistic context it is hard to see what could constitute an adequate basis for the teleological anthropocentrism I am arguing is the most significant issue, which leaves only the perspectival, metaethical and ethical aspects. In this case, Hayward's claim that the concerns of those who object to anthropocentrism would be better characterized as speciesism or human chauvinism are valid (Hayward, 'Anthropocentrism', 57–8). It therefore seems

There have been some recent theological attempts to distinguish between an anthropocentrism that is unavoidably part of Christianity and an 'anthropomonism' that should be rejected. Anthropocentrism here is the view that human beings are central to God's creative and redemptive project but other parts of creation are not excluded as a more peripheral concern. Anthropomonism, in contrast, is the view that humanity is God's sole and exclusive concern in creation.[20] This suggests in relation to the categories identified above that we should distinguish an *inclusive* teleological anthropocentrism that allows that other creatures have a peripheral place in God's purposes from an *exclusive* teleological anthropocentrism (labelled 'anthropomonism' by these authors) that denies that non-human creation is of any interest at all.[21] Obviously the

that anthropocentrism is an appropriate concern only in a theological context, where it represents what I argue in Chapter 1 to be an inappropriately narrow interpretation of God's purposes in creation. Hayward believes that the cause of those opposed to anthropocentrism would be advanced by dropping the term because it wrongly suggests that the problem is giving too much regard to human beings, whereas the real problem is giving too little regard to other creatures. I am sympathetic to the point that human and other-than-human interests are usually not in competition, but in a theological context consider that the term anthropocentrism used in its teleological and ethical senses usefully names a position that can be recognized to be inadequate in comparison to a theocentric one.

[20] See, for example, Patriarch Bartholemew's definition of anthropomonism as 'the exclusive emphasis on and isolation of humanity at the expense and detriment of the natural environment' (Bartholomew I, *Cosmic Grace, Humble Prayer: The Ecological Vision of the Green Patriarch Bartholomew I*, ed. John Chryssavgis (Grand Rapids, MI: Eerdmans, 2003), 19); Lukas Vischer, 'Listening to Creation Groaning: A Survey of Main Themes of Creation Theology', in Lukas Vischer ed. *Listening to Creation Groaning: Report and Papers From a Consultation on Creation Theology Organised by the European Christian Environmental Network at the John Knox International Reformed Center from March 28 to April 1 2004* (Geneva: Centre International Reforme John Knox, 2004), 21–2, and Watson, 'In the Beginning'. Vischer's definition is cited and discussed in Cherryl Hunt, David Horrell and Christopher Southgate, 'An Environmental Mantra? Ecological Interest in Romans 8:19–23 and a Modest Proposal for its Narrative Interpretation', *Journal of Theological Studies* 59 (2008), 574–5.

[21] In a careful reading of Romans 8.19–21 in the context of ecological questions Cherryl Hunt, David Horrell and Christopher Southgate suggest that Christianity is anthropocentric – believing humans to be 'of central importance in the divine economy of salvation' – but not anthropomonist – believing that non-human creation exists only to serve human interests. They argue that in this passage human redemption stands at the centre of the story of creation and that a 'chastened and humble anthropocentrism' can remain key to an ecological theology (Hunt et al., 'An Environmental Mantra?', 574–5). While there is no doubt that Paul's cosmic vision of redemption pictures human redemption as a key stage in the process, it would be dangerous to move from this recognition to embracing teleological anthropocentrism (and it

inclusive version of teleological anthropocentrism is to be preferred to the exclusive kind: indeed, as we shall see in later chapters, the exclusive kind is unsustainable on any adequate reading of relevant biblical texts. The position I wish to defend, however, is that we should resist construing the Bible and theology as teleologically anthropocentric at all, even in the inclusive sense. Clearly the Bible and the theological tradition are inevitably perspectivally anthropocentric, in that they look at God and the world from a human point of view and take an understandable interest in how God and the world relate to the human situation. Teleological anthropocentrism goes further in asserting that this human view of things is also the viewpoint of God: not only are we central in our own view of God and the world, but this human perspective is also an accurate representation of our centrality in God's acts of creation and redemption. Throughout this book I will argue that taking this step of maintaining the centrality of humanity to God's purposes is biblically and theologically both unnecessary and undesirable, and therefore that Christianity should be distinguished by its theocentrism, rather than anthropocentrism.

Pausing with Animals

To focus on animals in this work is clearly to undertake something that is partial: there is no reliable boundary between animals and other forms of life and I have no interest in restricting the subjects of moral regard to the boundaries of 'the animal'. The reflections offered here will therefore have to take their place in a broader vision of theology and ethics, in due course, just as I argue in this work that our reflections on the human must take their place in broader thinking about our common animality with other creatures. For some

is not clear that this is the kind of anthropocentrism the authors would endorse). In particular, we need to enquire exactly what it means that humans are 'of central importance'. If this means that humanity is God's chief concern in creation and redemption, this is the teleological anthropocentrism I have described above. This is not demonstrated by the Romans passage, however, which states that the revealing of the children of God is awaited with eager longing by creation. This is the way salvation will come, Paul tells the Roman church: he is not making a claim about the relative importance of different parts of creation. What happens to the humans is therefore 'of central importance' to creation, here but as a means to the freedom of bondage of all creation: this might be termed an instrumental anthropocentrism. Romans 8 should, therefore, not be interpreted as giving support for the view that Christianity is teleologically anthropocentric. See also Christopher Southgate, *The Groaning of Creation: God, Evolution, and the Problem of Evil* (Louisville, KY; London: Westminster John Knox, 2008), Chapter 6, where Southgate discusses forms of anthropocentrism and explicitly rejects its teleological forms.

ecologists and eco-theologians, taking animals as subjects in this way will be seen as improper in failing to appreciate that animals exist only as parts of much larger ecosystems, which can only be seen adequately as a whole. Here we reach a difference of approach between those who begin with concern for animals and those who begin with a concern for ecological systems, which occasionally results in ethical disagreement about what should be done when hedgehogs eat the eggs of seabirds on the islands of the Outer Hebrides, for example.[22] To recognize that animals exist in a wider environmental context is not an argument, however, against the theological discussion of animals in favour of some broader ecological awareness. We cannot rush from the acknowledged narrowness of an anthropocentric perspective to the broadest possible vision encompassing all creation, because that would cause us to miss the theological and moral significance of those particular living things that are most like us. It was a vital theological and moral task to appreciate the particularity of human beings, their commonality with one another and their difference, and recognize the most significant features of what this meant for how human beings should treat one another. It is an additional vital theological task to recognize the particularity of the wider category of animal, encompassing the human and all other creatures with the breath of life, in their commonality and difference. To fail to pause to attend to this part of God's creation would be to judge that, unlike human beings, animals have significance only as part of the ecosystems to which they belong, rather than being worthy of attention as individuals, communities and species.

One way of capturing the position argued for in this book is with reference to the famous early modern scientist and philosopher Francis Bacon, who was demonized among ecologists for the understandable reason that he gave fulsome endorsement to the ambition of advancing human mastery over nature. On the way to this affirmation, however, Francis Bacon dismisses two less worthy ambitions: trying to increase one's personal power within the nation is 'common and base' and trying to extend the power of their country among human beings has 'more dignity, but no less greed'.[23] Even in this extreme

---

[22] See Paul Kelbie, 'Campaign Wins Reprieve for Uist Hedgehogs', *The Independent*, 20 February, 2007. The disagreement is discussed in Andrew Linzey, 'So Near and Yet So Far: Animal Theology and Ecological Theology', in Roger S. Gottlieb ed. *The Oxford Handbook of Religion and Ecology* (Oxford: Oxford University Press, 2007). T. C. Boyle presents a fictional account of the issues surrounding killing non-human animals to preserve ecosystems in the interesting, if one-sided, recent novel, T. C. Boyle, *When the Killing's Done* (London: Bloomsbury, 2011).

[23] Francis Bacon, *The New Organon*, Cambridge Texts in the History of Philosophy, Lisa Jardine and Michael Silverthorne (eds), (Cambridge: Cambridge University Press, 2000), bk. 1, aph. 129, p. 100.

of anthropocentric enthusiasm we must recognize in Bacon's statement an admirable recognition of the dangers of human egoism. We can picture his moral analysis as a series of three concentric circles of increasing radii, pushing out the boundaries of self-interest from the smallest perimeter of the individual, to the larger ring of national common interest, and on to the largest compass of the whole human race. One kind of response to this Baconian project simply rejects such a geometry: it desires that the board be swept clean of the limitations represented by these circles, so that we can replace anthropocentrism with an ecocentrism that has an absolute regard for ecosystems and the multitudinous species of life they support with no attention to the locus of the human – or the animal – within them.[24] My position is a different one: it seems to me to be at odds with theological trajectories of thought to set aside doctrinal and moral categories that represent significant wisdom in the overcoming of human egoism. I propose that Bacon's figure needs not rejection but supplement. We are now in a position to see beyond the outer circumference of Bacon's scheme and to become aware that our endemic human self-preoccupation is evident even in his widest circle of advancing the interests of humanity. At least in relation to our own planet, Bacon's project of trying to extend the power of the human race over the rest of the universe has met with untrammelled success: few ecosystems are sufficiently isolated from human activity to remain unchanged by human efforts to make earth a more comfortable environment, and human-induced climate change promises to extend this reach still further with disastrous effects for humans and other creatures. We can therefore appreciate the need for a supplement to Bacon's circles of interest: to add a ring for advancing the interests of all animals, human and other-than-human. The problem with his approbation of the mastery of nature is analogous to his disapprobation of the mastery of other nations by one's own. Mastery of other nations can be recognized as greedy when seen in the context of the wider circle of the interests of all human beings; mastery of other animals can be recognized as greedy when seen in the wider circle of the interests of all animal life.

To accept Bacon's circles of interest with this supplement is not to endorse a necessary hierarchy of moral value between human and non-human interests, any more than Bacon's placing of self-interest at the centre represented

---

[24] Among those taking this view might be those inspired by Aldo Leopold's 'Land Ethic' and impressed by the irreducible value inherent in the complex interrelated webs of life he so lyrically describes. See Aldo Leopold, *A Sand County Almanac and Sketches Here and There* (Oxford: Oxford University Press, 1949) and the commentary in J. Baird Callicott ed. *Companion to a Sand County Almanac* (Madison, WI: University of Wisconsin, 1987), together with the Deep Ecology of Arne Naess, originating in Arne Naess, 'The Shallow and the Deep, Long-Range Ecology Movement', *Inquiry* 16 (1973), 95–100.

approval of egoism above the wider circles. In fact, the moral logic of the image is quite the reverse – not centripetal but centrifugal – spinning our concern away from the centre where our self-preoccupation tends to rest towards the perimeter where our moral capacity is at fullest stretch. To accept this model is also therefore not to accept any kind of anthropocentrism: the concentric rings represent the moral task we face, being the kind of creatures we are, not a normative grounding for the appropriateness of these limitations on our moral awareness. We must see this supplemented image as a practical guide to ethics: being the kind of creatures we are, we need to take the steps of first appreciating that our neighbours have interests like ours that we should attend to, then that those far away as well as those nearby also merit such consideration, and then that species-membership is an inadequate basis for failing to notice the needs of other creatures.

There are two key advantages to construing the task of attending to the place of animals in this way. First, it does not dismiss the moral importance of becoming aware of the needs first of neighbours and then of fellow human beings: developing such a concern – in theory though too rarely in practice – is a proper and deep-rooted theological concern. Adding a concentric circle representing all animals does not contradict, or necessarily compete with, such moral concern for human beings, but simply situates our awareness of the importance of caring for other human beings in a wider context in which it is seen to be inappropriate to care only for them. It can therefore be seen that the many theological voices proclaiming God's grace to humanity do not need to be contradicted: God is indeed gracious to human beings and so should we be. What is required is merely an appreciation that this is an important part of a more general whole, that God's graciousness does not end with this grace towards us. The second advantage of seeing the theological task with the help of this figure is that it makes clear why attending to animals in particular is a legitimate and important task. To pause at this ring of moral concern for creatures with the breath of life is not to deny it will later itself require encircling by one containing all creaturely life including vegetation, and then by a circle that includes the ecosystems and geological structures that enable life on the planet earth, and so on in relation to solar system, galaxy and universe. For the same reason that it was appropriate in theological and moral traditions to pause at the circles of neighbour and human being, it is also appropriate to stop and pay attention to what may be required of us in relation to this next circle of moral concern, the other animals who live alongside us. This book is therefore in one sense an argument for the theological necessity of adding this fourth ring to the three that Bacon recognized.

Synopsis

The following chapters undertake the task of examining the appropriate doctrinal place of animals under three main headings: creation, reconciliation and redemption.

Part I, 'Creation', begins in Chapter 1, 'The End of Creation', with consideration of the question of teleological anthropocentrism raised above, arguing that there are important theological reasons for judging it to be a theological mistake to consider human beings to be God's aim in creation. Chapter 2, 'The Place of Animals', sets out the particular place and vocation of animals in creation, in distinction both from their creator and the other parts of creation. Chapter 3, 'Creaturely Difference', treats the ways in which distinctions are made between animals, discussing the problems evident in the ways human beings have distinguished themselves from other animals and the limitations of the classificatory schemes we have used to set out relationships between animals.

Part II, 'Reconciliation', discusses where animals belong in God's act of becoming incarnate in Jesus Christ and overcoming the separation caused by a creation gone astray. Chapter 4, 'Incarnation', argues that this doctrine is best understood as God becoming creature, rather than God becoming human, showing that this is far from innovative in relation to the theological tradition. Chapter 5, 'Atonement', considers this closely related doctrine and argues that the whole of creation, rather than just human beings, stands in need of the overcoming of sin by the life, death and resurrection of Christ.

Part III, 'Redemption', traces the place of animals in God's redemptive purposes, arguing in Chapter 6, 'The Scope of Redemption', that there are strong scriptural and theological grounds to affirm God's redemption of human and other-than-human animal life. Chapter 7, 'The Shape of Redeemed Living', considers the biblical vision of peace between all God's creatures and explores the limits of what we can conceive of the implications of this for lions and lambs.

The final concluding chapter traces the significance of the doctrinal location of animals argued for under these three headings and considers the implications of accepting this account of the theological place of animals.

Part I

CREATION

Chapter 1

THE END OF CREATION

What is the point of creation? If God's purpose in creating the universe was to establish a relationship with human beings[1] and all other-than-human parts of creation are intended by God to prepare and provide for the human,[2] then everything else is scenery.[3] This scenery may be crucial to the staging of the drama – we could not have human beings in a universe like this without elementary forces and particles, stars, planets, oceans, water, carbon, hundreds of other elements and compounds, plate tectonics, vegetation, and myriad forms of non-human animal life, as necessary elements in sustaining human living and as evolutionary precursors[4] – but, finally, all this is the backdrop to the real action of humanity and its relationship with God. The ethical

---

[1] For example, the twentieth-century theologian Karl Barth: 'the purpose and therefore the meaning of creation is to make possible the history of God's covenant with man' (Karl Barth, *Church Dogmatics*, vol. III/1, eds G. W. Bromiley and T. F. Torrance, trans. J. W. Edwards, O. Bussey and Harold Knight (Edinburgh: T. & T. Clark, 1958), 42), although later in this chapter I argue that this is not an adequate understanding of the breadth of Barth's view of the issue.

[2] The late eighteenth-century atheistic geologist, George Hoggart Toulmin complained that 'the whole magnificent scene of things is daily and confidently asserted to be ultimately intended for the peculiar convenience of mankind' (George Hoggart Toulmin, *The Antiquity and Duration of the World* (Boston: J. P. Mendum, 1854), 73, cited in Keith Thomas, *Man and the Natural World: Changing Attitudes in England 1500–1800* (London; New York: Penguin, 1984), 17). As Thomas demonstrates, Toulmin's concern was not without foundation.

[3] An unfriendly characterization of this way of construing God's purposes is given by Feuerbach's famous contention that 'Nature, the world, has no value, no interest for Christians. The Christian thinks only of himself and the salvation of his soul ... The practical end and object of Christians is solely heaven' (Ludwig Feuerbach, *The Essence of Christianity*, trans. George Eliot (New York: Prometheus Books, 1989), 287–8).

[4] I consider that the description modern biology provides of the evolution of organisms from one another is the most plausible scientific account of the development of life on earth, and that this account is compatible with Christian affirmations of the universe as a creation of God.

implications of this position, which we could label 'It's all about us', means the stakes are high: it provides a divine mandate for humans to satisfy their needs and desires through the use of all other creatures in the confidence that this was the relationship God intended. Perhaps human beings should not be unnecessarily cruel to other living things, but given the respective places accorded them in the ordering of creation, such responsibilities will be derivative and secondary, reflecting the derivative and secondary place of creatures other than the human in God's purposes.[5]

As a ground-clearing exercise at the outset of any consideration of the place of animals in Christian doctrine, the question of the purpose of creation must be addressed. The central argument of this chapter is that for key theological reasons and in contrast to influential philosophical world-views, Christian theologians have strong reasons to reject the 'It's all about us' position and recognize the theological dangers in asserting that God's purposes in creation can be exclusively identified with human beings. While, as we shall see, not all theologians have agreed on this point, the chapter argues that the arguments theologians have made demonstrating the mistake inherent in specifying humanity as the end of creation, are both decisive and largely uncontroversial.

Not Answering the Question

Biblical texts are reticent about the purpose of creation. God creates; creation comes into being – the texts are more concerned to establish and celebrate this than to assert God's end in this activity. The creation narrative of Genesis 1 records phases of God's creative action, the fruits of which are declared 'good' or 'very good' unconditionally, without reference to humanity.[6] Genesis 2 gives human beings the task of caring for the world into which they are placed, but does not provide an explanation for its existence. The celebrations of God's creative power in psalms such as Psalms 104 and 148 extol God's ability to rule

---

[5] The Jewish theologian Elijah Schochet provides an uncompromising statement of this view: the world of non-human animals is 'far removed from its Maker's hand or concern' and while humans should not abuse or mistreat other animals, these obligations are more 'the relationship of a master toward his servant, or even an artisan toward his tool, than that of a living being toward his fellow living being, also fashioned by the hand of God' (Elijah Judah Schochet, *Animal Life in Jewish Tradition: Attitudes and Relationships* (New York: KTAV, 1984), 4).

[6] Von Rad comments that the ascription of goodness to the parts of creation is 'less an aesthetic judgment than the designation of purpose and correspondence', telling of the 'marvellous purpose and order of creation' (Gerhard von Rad, *Genesis* (London: SCM, 1972), 52).

over the parts of creation, to provide and sustain God's creatures, and call all creatures to praise, but make no claims concerning why God chose to create. Some celebrated texts stress the relative importance of human beings among the creatures, such as the unique identification of humans as made in God's image (Gen. 1.26–7), the opening of Psalm 8 picturing humanity as 'a little lower than God' and Jesus' reassurance that 'you are of more value than many sparrows' (Lk. 12.7), but these do not concern the aim of the project of creation.[7] God's speech to Job from the whirlwind (Job 38–41) reminds Job of the magnitude and diversity of creation and of his small place in it, but gives no account of motive for the decision to initiate it. New Testament passages link the act of creation decisively with Jesus Christ, through whom all things were made (Jn 1.3; Heb. 1.2; Col. 1.16; 1 Cor. 8.6), but give no more indication of its purpose.

We may see this biblical reticence as theological reserve. In order for creator and creation to be recognized as distinct and for creation to be recognized as an act of God's gracious love, it must not be the case that it is necessary for God to create. Instead, creation must be contingent: wholly dependent on God for its origin, including being dependent on God's free choice to create.[8] But if God's decision to create is to be free and unconstrained, it might seem that the decision must in some regard be inexplicable to God's creatures, as to be able to give an explanation of it would suggest that God was bound to create by some reason external to Godself. Perhaps, then, the biblical authors considered it would be inappropriate to trespass on this divine prerogative. It is notable that the ecumenical creeds follow this lead in affirming God's motivation for the incarnation – the Nicene 'for us and for our salvation'[9] – but not God's motivation for creation. This would point to a case for espousing a negative theology of the purpose of creation: a theologically motivated refusal to speculate on God's aim in creating.

It is instructive, however, to note that rejecting the question of the purpose of creation has not been the course that Christian theologians have taken. This may be in part because it threatens to make creation seem an arbitrary act by God with ambiguous consequences for God's creatures, but is better understood as an irresistible overflow of the belief that God acted in Christ as the redeemer of God's creation. If it is 'for us and for our salvation' that a loving God came in Christ, then it is hard to avoid understanding creation, too, as an

---

[7] See Chapter 3 for a discussion of the differences between human beings and other creatures identified in these texts and elsewhere.

[8] For discussion of this point, see, for example, Barth, *CD* III/1, 15 or Colin E. Gunton, *The Triune Creator: A Historical and Systematic Study* (Edinburgh: Edinburgh University Press, 1998), 113 ff.

[9] G. Alberigo and Norman P. Tanner (eds), *Decrees of the Ecumenical Councils Vol.1: Nicaea I to Lateran V* (London: Sheed & Ward, 1990), 5.

act of love of creator to creatures, with these acts of creation and reconciliation awaiting completion in redemption as the fulfilment of God's creative purposes. If the incarnation of God in Jesus Christ has the cosmic significance attributed to it in the New Testament texts (see Chapter 4), then the purpose of creation must be related to this event. While there can be no objection to affirming that God creates in love, has acted in Christ to bring reconciliation to creation and is working through the Spirit to bring its redemption, this affirmation does suggest a potential tension between affirming creation as good in itself – as we have noted that God seems to be on record as doing in the Genesis creation narrative – and viewing creation as a means of achieving God's project of redemption. There need not be an antagonistic relationship between these two emphases: if God's project is the fulfilment of the good creation, then creation can be understood both as good in itself and as instrumental to the redemption God intends for it. If emphasis is given only to the second of these elements, however, where creation is merely a means to an end, the way is opened to the 'It's all about us' theologies referred to at the beginning of this chapter, where creation is a disposable stage for the project of saving (some) human souls.

In the remainder of this chapter, I survey and critique key focal answers to the question of the purpose of creation, treating in turn answers that identify God's creative purposes with humanity, with Godself and with creation as an end in itself. My proposal is that 'It's all about us' theologies are at least insufficient, if not plain heretical, and we need to reject these in favour of an account that sees the end of creation as its participation in the triune life of God.

Creation: All About Us?

Philo

Philo of Alexandria (*c.* 15 BC–AD 50) was a Jewish philosopher and theologian, one of the earliest commentators on the Genesis creation narrative and perhaps the most theologically influential advocate of the 'It's all about us' position concerning the purpose of creation. He was strongly influenced by Platonism, and sought to interpret the Mosaic Pentateuch as a philosophical book. Philo's commentary on Genesis clearly has Plato's *Timaeus* in mind as a point of comparison.[10] In the *Timaeus*, creation takes place in two stages: first the

---

[10] On Philo's intellectual background, see Samuel Sandmel, *Philo of Alexandria: An Introduction* (Oxford: Oxford University Press, 1979), Dorothy I. Sly, *Philo's Alexandria* (London; New York: Routledge, 1996) and David Runia's introduction in Philo of Alexandria, *On the Creation of the Cosmos According to Moses*, ed. David

eternal world and world soul are made by the deity, then demiurges are charged with the task of making human beings within a second creation that exists in time. Beginning with immortal souls, they create different bodily parts to encase it, but then find that placing it in the hostile environment of the fire and air, their creature quickly perishes. The demiurges therefore make 'another nature' to grow: trees, plants and seeds, to create an environment more congenial to the new mortal creature. In Plato's account, women, birds, animals and fish then descend from mortal creatures that are deficient in some respect: unjust or cowardly, simple-minded, wild or stupid, respectively.[11] Here is a universe with the immortal soul of man – used in the gender-exclusive sense – placed clearly at the centre.[12] His mortal body, the physical environment and all vegetation are built around the soul in order to protect it from its harsh environment, and women and other living creatures exist only as some falling away from the ideal human male state.

Philo is frequently troubled by discrepancies between this Platonic account and the Genesis narrative, and one of his first questions is why in Genesis human beings were created last of all the creatures, suggesting their inferiority, in contrast with the Platonic account. He provides four reasons to explain this oddity. First, he pictures God as the host at a banquet who does not summon his guests until the feast his prepared, or the organizer of a gymnastic contest who does not gather spectators until the performers are ready. Similarly, Philo states, God ordered things 'so that, when the human being entered into the cosmos, he would immediately encounter both a festive meal and a most sacred theatre'. The second reason Philo gives for the late human appearance is that for the first human being to find everything required for living was a lesson to succeeding generations that if they follow the example of their original ancestor they will live without toil or trouble amidst a lavish supply of what they need. Third, to indicate the harmony of creation, God began by making heaven, the most perfect of the immortal beings, and ended with human beings, the best of the mortal creatures. The fourth reason Philo provides for why the human being had to be created last is so that the other creatures will be amazed by the sudden human appearance and worship the human being as their natural master. After announcing and listing these reasons, Philo throws in one more: just as charioteers come after their team of horses and pilots take their place at

T. Runia (Leiden: Brill, 2001). Colin Gunton briefly surveys the significance of his doctrine of creation for Christian theology in Gunton, *Triune Creator*, 44–7.

[11] Plato, *Timaeus*, trans. Donald J. Zeyl (Indianapolis, IN: Hackett, 2000), 69c–92b.

[12] On the contrast between Platonic and Aristotelian philosophy on the centrality of the immortal male soul, see Catherine Osborne, *Dumb Beasts and Dead Philosophers: Humanity and the Humane in Ancient Philosophy and Literature* (Oxford: Clarendon, 2007), 114.

the stern of the ship, so God made human beings last so they 'could guide and steer earthly affairs, taking on the care of animals and plants like a governor acting on behalf of the first and great King.'[13]

Philo's interpretation of this point in Genesis, his question and his answer, have had a significant influence on the commentators on Genesis who followed him. Later Jewish sources echo Philo's conclusion that the world came into being only to serve the needs of humanity despite being last in creation, although interpretations are also preserved that see the creation of gnats before humans as a prompt to humility.[14] Lactantius follows Philo's reasoning, stating that human beings were brought into the world 'as if into a house ready prepared' where everything had been made for their sake,[15] as well as elsewhere stating that 'The world was made in order for us to be born' to worship God and be made immortal.[16] Gregory of Nyssa repeats Philo's question exactly, and offers very similar explanations: rulers should be manifested when their subjects have been assembled; the palace of the future king needed assembly before the king arrived; confrontation with these riches allows human beings to see the power of their maker, and a host only invites his guests once all things are ready for their refreshment.[17] John Chrysostom also feels the need to provide an explanation of this anomaly, asking in his homilies on Genesis why, if human beings are more important than the other creatures, they were created after the others. His comparison is with a king's bodyguard sent on ahead to have the palace in readiness. In the same way, God 'first erected the whole of this scenery, then brought forth the one destined to rule over it'.[18] The question reverberates through later theological commentaries on Genesis: Bonaventure suggests that humans had to be last in order shine forth as the consummation of the divine works,[19] Martin Luther repeats the point that human beings were brought into

---

[13] Philo of Alexandria, *Creation of the Cosmos*, ch. 14, §§ 77–84.

[14] *Genesis Rabba* 1:4, *Sanhedrin* 98b; *Sanhedrin* 38a, *Leviticus Rabba* 14:1 cited in Noah J Cohen, *Saʿar Baʿaley Hayim: The Prevention of Cruelty to Animals: Its Bases, Development and Legislation in Hebrew Literature* (Jerusalem: Feldheim Publishers, 1976), 32.

[15] Lactantius, *Divine Institutes*, (eds) Anthony Bowen and Peter Garnsey, trans. Anthony Bowen and Peter Garnsey (Liverpool: Liverpool University Press, 2003), bk. 2, ch. 8.

[16] Lactantius, *Divine Institutes*, (eds) and trans. Anthony Bowen and Peter Garnsey (Liverpool: Liverpool University Press), bk 7, ch. 6.

[17] Gregory of Nyssa, 'On the Making of Man', in *A Select Library of Nicene and Post-Nicene Fathers of the Christian Church. Second Series*, vol. 5, ed. Philip Schaff (Edinburgh: T & T Clark, 1997), II.

[18] John Chrysostom, Saint, *Homilies on Genesis*, Fathers of the Christian Church, trans. Robert C. Hill (Washington, DC: Catholic University of America, 1986), Homily 8, §5.

[19] See Alexander O. F. M. Schäfer, 'The Position and Function of Man in the Created World, Part I', *Franciscan Studies* 20 (1960), 316.

a furnished home for them to enjoy[20] and John Calvin repeats Philo's motif of creation as a spectacle: humanity was placed in creation 'as in a theatre' of God's works, where everything is ordained for human use.[21] In his contribution to *the Bridgewater Treatises* in 1835, William Kirkby similarly feels the need to speculate about the rationale for the order of God's creation, noting that it is not revealed in scripture and 'we can only conjecture' that 'the most perfect animal' was created last so that there was progress from the lowest to highest animals.[22]

In reflecting on the import of this tradition of reflection on why human beings were created last by God, we need to note that the endurance of this as a hermeneutical issue in reading the Genesis creation narrative is a *prima facie* indication of the difficulty of reconciling it with the anthropocentrism of the *Timaeus*. For Plato's *Timaeus*, human beings are the centre of the second creation, the world created in time. This world is constructed as a place to house immortal human souls, just as Philo pictures God creating in order a feast or spectacle for human honoured guests. The first chapter of Genesis, on which Philo and the theologians who follow him are commenting, does not accord the same priority and centrality to the human. Human beings are distinguished from other creatures as bearing the image of God (Gen. 1.26) – as will be discussed in Chapters 3 and 4 – but the world is not declared to be a place to give them a home, as in Philo's influential Platonic interpretation. In the first chapter of Genesis, human beings are given their own place and role in a diverse creation declared good in every respect by its maker, the purpose of which is not reduced to the human. Philo's question of why human beings are created last is motivated by his prior commitment to an interpretation of the *Timaeus;* his answer that they were created last in order to demonstrate that everything else was made for their sake is without basis in the text, as Kirkby explicitly notes. In short, the doctrine that human beings are the aim, centre and goal of creation is being read into the Genesis text in order to make it congruent with a view of the place of the human in creation derived from other sources.

---

[20] Martin Luther, *Luther's Works*, (eds) Helmut T. Lehmann and Jaroslav Pelikan (Philadelphia, PA: Muhlenberg Press, 1958), I.39. For a detailed discussion of Luther's thought in relation to animals, see David Clough, 'The Anxiety of the Human Animal: Martin Luther on Non-Human Animals and Human Animality', in *Creaturely Theology: On God, Humans and Other Animals,* (eds) Celia Deane-Drummond and David Clough (London: SCM, 2009).

[21] John Calvin, *Genesis*, ed. and trans. John King, (Edinburgh: Banner of Truth Trust, 1965), 64.

[22] William Kirby, *On the Power, Wisdom and Goodness of God as Manifested in the Creation of Animals and in Their History, Habits and Instincts*, Bridgewater Treatises, vol. VII (London: W. Pickering, 1835), 4.

Origen

The Genesis narrative is not the only locus of theological arguments suggesting human beings as the purpose of creation. One of the most thoroughgoing statements of this view is found in Origen's disputation with Celsus. Origen cites Celsus's argument that, contrary to the Christian view 'that God made all things for man', 'everything was made just as much for the irrational animals as for men'.[23] The context of Stoic philosophy is immediately apparent, as Origen begins by replying that Celsus fails to see that he is here criticizing the Stoics, who were right to 'put man and the rational nature in general above all irrational beings, and say that providence has made everything primarily for the sake of the rational nature', recognizing that rational beings have the value of children born, 'whereas irrational and inanimate things have that of the after-birth which is created with the child'.[24] Origen adds another image:

> just as in cities those who are in charge of the stalls and the market-place are concerned only with men, though dogs and other irrational animals share the surplus food; so providence primarily cares for the rational beings, while the fact that the irrational animals also share in what is made for men has been a subsidiary result. And just as a man is wrong who says that the market authorities are no more concerned for men than for dogs since dogs also share the surplus food on the market stalls, so also Celsus and those who agree with him act far more impiously against the God who cares for the rational beings when they say: *Why were these things made for men's nourishment any more than for plants, trees, grass, and thorns?*[25]

---

[23] Origen, *Contra Celsum*, bk 4, §74.

[24] Origen, *Contra Celsum*, bk 4, §74. For example, Cicero, the first-century BC Roman Stoic proclaims: 'In the first place the world itself was created for the sake of gods and men, and the things that it contains were provided and contrived for the enjoyment of men' (Marcus Tullius Cicero, *De Natura Deorum; Academica*, Loeb Classical Library, trans. H. Rackham (London: William Heinemann, 1933), bk 2, ch. 62). Gary Steiner observes that in contrast to Aristotle, the Stoics elevate the dividing line between human beings and other animals 'to the status of a cosmic principle' (Gary Steiner, *Anthropocentrism and Its Discontents: The Moral Status of Animals in the History of Western Philosophy* (Pittsburgh, PA: University of Pittsburg Press, 2005), 77). On Stoic anthropocentrism, see also Keimpe Algra, 'Stoic Theology', in Brad Inwood ed. *The Cambridge Companion to the Stoics* (Cambridge: Cambridge University Press, 2003) and Richard Sorabji, *Animal Minds and Human Morals: The Origins of the Western Debate* (Ithaca, NY: Cornell University Press, 1993).

[25] Origen, *Contra Celsum*, bk 4, §74 (italics in original).

Origen's argument with Celsus on this point continues from §73–§99. Much of the discussion consists in Origen citing a supposed example of the superiority of animals, and then refuting it on the basis that the behaviour of animals is based on instinct, whereas what is truly valuable is rationality, reason being a common possession of human beings, divine and heavenly beings, and probably also God. As Henry Chadwick notes, however, this is not primarily a debate between Christianity and a Platonic opponent, but is a rehearsal of a well-established argument between Stoic and Academic philosophers: the latter regularly attacked Stoic anthropocentrism on the basis of arguments similar to those used by Celsus, and most of what Origen says in reply are standard Stoic responses.[26] Chadwick also suggests that Origen's opposition to Celsus is frequently formulaic at some points, including this one: 'If Celsus takes one side in the debate, Origen will usually take the other.'[27] The best that can be said of Origen's position here, therefore, is that he recognized and took advantage of common ground between Stoicism and Christianity on the centrality of human beings to God's purposes in creation. Given his strong dependence on the Stoic view of rationality as a division between human beings and all other animals, and the lack of any theological appeals in his argument, it seems more likely that he is over-influenced here by traditional Stoic positions, which are convenient in his overall aim of opposing Celsus at every possible point.[28]

---

[26] See Chadwick's introduction to Origen, *Contra Celsum*, x–xi, and his article: Henry Chadwick, 'Origen, Celsus and the Stoa'. Origen's points also overlap significantly with Philo's affirmation of rationality as a uniquely human attribute in his dialogue *On Animals* (Philo of Alexandria, *Philonis Alexandrini de Animalibus*, Studies in Hellenistic Judaism, ed. and trans. Abraham Terian (Chico, CA: Scholars Press, 1981)), §§77–100. See also, Silke-Petra Bergjan, 'Celsus the Epicurean? The Interpretation of an Argument in Origen, Contra Celsum', *Harvard Theological Review* 94 (2001).

[27] Chadwick, 'Origen, Celsus and the Stoa', x.

[28] It seems that the degree to which Origen embraced Platonic thought has been exaggerated: Mark Edwards makes a persuasive case, for example, that Origen rejects the possibility of a creation populated by incorporeal entities, denies Platonic forms and does not believe that the material world is the result of the fall of souls from heaven (Mark Julian Edwards, *Origen Against Plato* (Aldershot: Ashgate, 2002), 160). Paul Santmire's critique of Origen relies on a strongly Platonic interpretation of his thought (H. Paul Santmire, *The Travail of Nature: The Ambiguous Ecological Promise of Christian Theology* (Minneapolis, MN: Fortress Press, 1985), 45–52, 72). Despite these divergences from Plato, however, Origen accepts uncritically from Platonism and especially Stoicism the radical divide between rational and irrational elements of creation, and derives from this the judgement that only the rational part of creation is immortal and fitted for participation in and union with God (see Hans Urs von Balthasar, *Origen: Spirit and Fire: A Thematic Anthology of His Writings*, trans. Robert J. Daly (Edinburgh: T & T Clark, 1984), 56–9), which means that for him the purpose of creation must be closely tied to God's relationship with rational

While other Patristic theologians share Origen's view that the universe was created for the sake of human beings, this is most commonly stated formulaically rather than argued for and often seems influenced by contemporary philosophies. Justin Martyr was first taught philosophy by a Stoic teacher[29] and his writings regularly debate with philosophy.[30] While he has no hesitation in opposing Stoic ideas where he sees them to be in conflict with Christian teaching, he seems to concur with Stoic views on human beings as God's purpose in creation, with a specific reference to human salvation.[31] Irenaeus of Lyons similarly states that God creates for the sake of humanity – 'creation is suited to man; for man was not made for its sake, but creation for the sake of man'.[32] The lack of argument supplied by these authors, and the lack of biblical or theological support for them, suggests this affirmation of the centrality of the human was common ground between themselves and their Stoic and Platonic interlocutors.

Gnostic authors were radically opposed to the Stoics and Platonists on many points of doctrine, in particular taking an opposite view of what observation of the created order means for discerning the intentions of its creator towards humanity.[33] Where the Stoics saw evidence for the gods' particular providential

creatures. Gerhard May notes the anthropocentric influence of Stoicism on Christian theologians in Gerhard May, *Creatio Ex Nihilo: The Doctrine of 'Creation Out of Nothing' in Early Christian Thought*, trans. A. S. Worrall (Edinburgh: T & T Clark, 1994), 3, as does Marcia Colish in more detail in Marcia L. Colish, *Stoicism in Christian Latin Thought Through the Sixth Century*, The Stoic Tradition From Antiquity to the Early Middle Ages (Leiden: E. J. Brill, 1985).

[29] St Justin Martyr, *Dialogue With Trypho*, ed. Michael Slusser, trans. Thomas B. Falls and Thomas P. Halton (Washington, DC: Catholic University of America Press, 2003), ch. 2, §2.

[30] See, for example, Justin Martyr, 'First Apology', in *The Ante-Nicene Fathers: Translations of the Writings of the Fathers Down to AD 325*, 1, vol. 1, (eds) A. Cleveland Coxe, James Donaldson and Alexander Roberts (Edinburgh: T & T Clark, 1997), ch. 20.

[31] See May, *Creatio Ex Nihilo*, 128.

[32] Irenaeus, 'Against Heresies', in *The Ante-Nicene Fathers: Translations of the Writings of the Fathers Down to AD 325*, vol. 1, (eds) A. Cleveland Coxe, James Donaldson and Alexander Roberts (Edinburgh: T & T Clark, 1997), bk 5, ch. 29, §1. Wingren comments that while Irenaeus speaks at great length about humanity, he does so 'not in opposition to the theocentricity of early Christianity, which, in fact, he himself represents, but in opposition to the Gnostics' false idolisation of man or contempt for man' (Gustaf Wingren, *Man and the Incarnation: A Study in the Biblical Theology of Irenaeus* (Edinburgh and London: Oliver and Boyd, 1959), xii). Canlis agrees that Irenaeus abandons gnostic anthropocentrism in favour of a theocentrism that safeguards humanity as well as God (J. Canlis, 'Being Made Human: The Significance of Creation for Irenaeus' Doctrine of Participation', *Scottish Journal of Theology* 58 (2005), 438).

[33] Michael Williams notes several problems with the term 'gnostic', drawing attention

care for human beings, gnostic thinkers considered the world to be such an evil place that any god worth worshipping could not be associated with it.[34] While this is a wholesale rejection of an anthropocentric interpretation of the purpose of creation, gnostics such as Marcion also believed in a redeemer god who acted to save human souls from their dire plight of being trapped in the material world. Humanity remains at the centre of this redeemer god's purposes, therefore, making anthropocentrism a common attribute of gnostic, Stoic and Platonic world views, for all their other differences.[35] These three major components of the intellectual thought world of Patristic Christianity each espoused the centrality of the human to the creation of the universe or, in the gnostic case, to the project of salvation from it. Given the concern of Christian theologians to preach the good news of God's grace towards human beings, it is perhaps unsurprising that they sought alliance with aspects of philosophies that went one step further in identifying humanity as God's primary or sole end in creation and salvation. As we shall see below, this foundation based on strategic alliances with classical philosophies was strongly influential on subsequent Christian thinking.

Later Authors

John Calvin's concern to affirm God's special providence in relation to human beings, while far removed in time from the Patristic context, seems close in motivation. In the *Divine Institutes*, after outlining his uncompromising view

to the need to be cautious in collecting disparate groups and doctrines under it, but it is not clear that his suggestion of 'biblical demiurge traditions' as an alternative collective description is preferable (Michael Allen Williams, *Rethinking 'Gnosticism': An Argument for Dismantling a Dubious Category* (Princeton, NJ: Princeton University Press, 1999)). See reviews of Williams' book by Robert Grant (Robert M. Grant, 'Review of Rethinking "Gnosticism": An Argument for Dismantling a Dubious Category', *The Journal of Religion* 81 (2001), 645–7) and David Brakke (David Brakke, 'Review of Rethinking "Gnosticism": An Argument for Dismantling a Dubious Category', *Church History* 67 (1998), 119–21).

[34] See May, *Creatio Ex Nihilo*, 55–7, where he cites Spanneut's judgement that Marcion in particular should be seen as an anti-Stoic.

[35] Canlis notes that Clement of Alexandria recognized the gnostic preoccupation with the human, citing the gnostic Theodotus's questions: 'Who were we? What have we become? Where were we? Into what have we been cast? Towards what do we hasten? From what have we been set free?' and von Balthasar's conclusion that 'Never have man, his structure, his sufferings and his tragedy, been more plainly projected on to the screen of heaven in order to fascinate him and, professedly, to redeem him by the contemplation of this magnified image of himself' (Canlis, 'Being Made Human', 437).

of general providence, he states that, within these wider providential purposes, God is especially concerned with human beings, although at this point he states only 'we know' that the world was made chiefly for the sake of human beings.[36] Elsewhere the clearest argument he makes for this position is in his commentary on Genesis, where he suggests that the dominion granted to human beings in Genesis 1.28 allows us to infer that the end for which all things were created was that 'none of the conveniences and necessaries of life might be wanting' to human beings.[37] Calvin's inference here is by no means a necessary one – humans could be given the task of governing the rest of creation for its own benefit as well as their own on an analogy with theological accounts of political authority – and one is struck by the difficulty of establishing the centrality of human beings to God's purposes on biblical grounds.[38]

Where Patristic Christianity was surrounded by the anthropocentric philosophies of Platonism, Stoicism and gnostic thinkers, early modern theologians wrote in a context of boundless optimism concerning human capacities to discover new lands, gain new knowledge of the natural world and thereby exercise mastery over their environment.[39] Francis Bacon wrote of the attempt 'to renew and extend the power and empire of the human race itself over the universe of things' as the most majestic of ambitions, which could only be achieved by advances in the arts and sciences[40] and interpreted the Prometheus myth as indicating that humanity is the centre of a world that works together to serve humanity.[41] There was no shortage of other theologians keen to identify

---

[36] John Calvin, *Institutes of the Christian Religion*, trans. Henry Beveridge (Grand Rapids, MI: Eerdmans, 1989), 1.16.6.

[37] Calvin, *Genesis*, 96.

[38] Calvin's thought in relation to nature is discussed in Santmire, *Travail of Nature*, 121–43 and his thought in relation specifically to animals is treated in Peter A. Huff, 'Calvin and the Beasts: Animals in John Calvin's Theological Discourse', *Journal of the Evangelical Theology Society* 42 (1999). Colin Gunton criticizes the anthropocentric narrowing of Calvin's thought, alongside Luther's, in Colin E. Gunton, 'The End of Causality? The Reformers and Their Predecessors', in Colin E. Gunton ed. *The Doctrine of Creation: Essays in Dogmatics, History and Philosophy* (London: T & T Clark, 2004).

[39] For an overview of changing attitudes, see Clarence J. Glacken, *Traces on the Rhodian Shore: Nature and Culture in Western Thought From Ancient Times to the End of the Eighteenth Century* (Berkeley, CA: University of California Press, 1967), pt 3 and Thomas, *Man and the Natural World*.

[40] Francis Bacon, *The New Organon*, Cambridge Texts in the History of Philosophy, eds Lisa Jardine and Michael Silverthorne (Cambridge: Cambridge University Press, 2000), bk 1, aph. 129, p. 100.

[41] Francis Bacon, *The Essays*, ed. John Pitcher (London: Penguin, 1985), 270. It is notable, however, that Bacon protests against philosophical views that 'impress the stamp of our own image on the creatures and works of God, instead of carefully

this new-found power with God's purpose. Of the many examples cited by Keith Thomas in *Man and the Natural World,* we note the Irish bishop Williā Cowper's statement early in the seventeenth century that, 'The creatures were not made for themselves, but for the use and service of man', Henry More's striking view in 1653 that cattle and sheep were only given life to keep their meat fresh until we need to eat them, Jeremy Burroughs' 1657 affirmation that God 'made others for man, and man for himself' and Richard Bentley's statement that all things were created 'principally for the benefit and pleasure of man' in 1692. A century later the atheist geologist George Hoggart Toulmin complained that 'the whole magnificent scene of things is daily and confidently asserted to be ultimately intended for the peculiar convenience of mankind'.[42]

It is clear from this brief survey that it is not difficult to find Christian theologians stating that human beings are God's sole or primary purpose in creation. It is harder, however, to find good theological argument in defence of this proposition. Philo's interpretation of the Genesis creation narrative seems driven more by the need to show its congruity with the anthropocentrism of the *Timaeus* rather than by any more adequate theological argumentation. Origen's extensive argument that all things were made for human use turns out to be a Stoic one taken off the peg to refute Celsus's equally rote-learned critique of anthropocentrism. Calvin's view that God's aim in creation can be inferred from the granting of dominion in Genesis 1.26–8 seems stretched and unpersuasive. Finally, it is hard to resist the impression that the early modern emphatic assertion of the divine right of humanity to use all other parts of creation for their own benefit is a weak and formal baptism of a new technological order promising many benefits to the powerful nations in a position to take advantage of it. At every point, the central Christian concern to preach the good news of God's love for human beings seems to be unnecessarily allied with contemporary philosophical and social pressures, emphasizing anthropocentric views of the universe. The weight of theological opinion that human beings are God's aim in creation, therefore, is not matched by a similar weight of theological argument.[43]

---

examining and recognising in them the stamp of the Creator himself', lead to human dominion being forfeited a second time (Francis Bacon, 'The Natural and Experimental History for the Foundation of Philosophy: Or Phenomena of the Universe: Which is the Third Part of the Instauratio Magna', in *The Works of Francis Bacon,* vol. 5, eds. James Spedding, Robert Leslie Ellis and Douglas Denon Heath (London: Longman & Co., 1858), cited in Glacken, *Traces on the Rhodian Shore,* 471–2).

[42] All cited in Thomas, *Man and the Natural World,* 17–20.
[43] René Descartes, infamous for denying souls to non-human animals (see Chapter 6), nonetheless rejected the view that the earth was made for the benefit of humankind:

Creation: All About God?

At the beginning of this chapter I cited Karl Barth as an example of resolute anthropocentrism, and it is not hard to find him averring the centrality of human beings to God's purposes in terms no less strong than the authors surveyed in the previous section. Here we find no reticence about the purpose of creation: 'The reason why God created this world of heaven and earth, and why the future world will be a new heaven and a new earth, is that God's eternal Son and Logos did not will to be an angel or animal but a man, and that this and this alone was the content of the eternal divine election of grace'.[44] God's faithful covenant with the creature is one of the focal themes of Barth's theology. The covenant precedes creation so that creation can be seen as 'the external basis of the covenant'[45] and the purpose and meaning of creation can therefore be summarized as making possible God's covenant with humanity 'which has its beginning, its centre and its culmination in Jesus Christ'.[46] Barth repeats Calvin's theatrical image of creation, calling it 'the stage for the story of the covenant of grace'.[47] Yet Barth is also aware of the danger of interpreting God's purposes as the creation of ideal humanity and its deification. On this basis he criticizes a range of positions: the Jewish formulation 'The meaning of creation is to prepare a place in which the will of God will be done'; Lactantius's statement that the world was created in order that we might be born; Kant's view that the purpose of the world is the existence of rational beings living under the moral law; Ritschl's view that the purpose of the world was that spirits might exist in fellowship with God, and Troeltsch's statement that God's purpose is 'the training of divinely filled personality', among others.[48] Barth argues that the better declarations of the theological tradition do not put humanity 'into the centre of the quest for the meaning of creation'. In support of this interpretative line he cites the Didache 'Thou didst create all things for Thy name's sake', Irenaeus's view that God created Adam to have someone on whom to bestow benevolence, Tertullian's statement that God created for an ornament of His majesty and Calvin's assertion that the world was created to display God's glory.[49] Barth judges that these latter authors avoid the error of 'surrendering ... the purpose of creation' into the doubtful hands

---

see Rod Preece, *Animals and Nature: Cultural Myths, Cultural Realities* (Vancouver: UBC Press, 1999), 120.

[44] Barth, *CD* III/1, 18.

[45] Barth, *CD* III/1, 94.

[46] Barth, *CD* III/1, 42.

[47] Barth, *CD* III/1, 44.

[48] Barth, *CD* III/1, 46–7.

[49] Barth, *CD* III/1, 47.

of humanity, and argues that God's goal in creation is best understood as the Word of God.[50] Elsewhere, Barth protests at the dangerous anthropocentrism of the doctrine of supralapsarianism, which claims that 'It is to serve this one end, the bringing of individual x to heaven and individual y to hell, that there is brought into being the monstrous apparatus of the creation of heaven and earth' making humanity 'and indeed the individuals x and y the measure and centre of all things to a degree which could hardly be surpassed' and running the risk of replacing theology with anthropology.[51]

Properly understood, therefore, and despite some appearances, Barth cannot be grouped consistently with those theologians identifying the purpose of creation with humanity. He recognizes the theological dangers of making human beings the goal of the divine project: such a move suggests that the aim of creation could be achieved merely by the arrival and 'spiritualization' of human beings, with little if any reference to God's covenant of grace, and threatens to turn our attention away from theology and towards anthropological navel-gazing. God's project, for Barth, is to be gracious to the creature and thus the purpose of creation can only be rightly characterized by the fulfilment of this covenant of grace in Jesus Christ. Now given the emphasis Barth places on the humanity of Christ, and therefore on humanity as God's covenant partners, the point he makes here against Lactantius, Kant, Ritschl, Troeltsch *et al.* may seem a narrow one: we seem to be merely replacing humanity as the goal of creation with God's covenant with humanity.[52] If, however, we see God's covenant as having significance for the whole of creation, rather than merely for the species *Homo sapiens* (as I argue in Chapter 2), and if we see similarly that the incarnation of God in Christ must also be understood to have a wider significance (as I argue in Chapter 4), then Barth's strong theological arguments for construing God's covenant in Christ, rather than humanity, as the aim of creation become decisive.[53]

Another suggestion that such an extension of Barth's thinking should not be

---

[50] Barth, *CD* III/1, 48.

[51] Barth, *CD* II/2, 136–7 (italics in original).

[52] Wolfhart Pannenberg suggests that the strongest argument for thinking human beings to be the purpose of creation is the fact that God became incarnate in the human being Jesus Christ (Wolfhart Pannenberg, *Systematic Theology*, trans. Geoffrey W. Bromiley (Edinburgh: T & T Clark, 1994), 72). Whether the incarnation can be used to privilege the human in this way is discussed in detail in Chapter 4.

[53] Kathryn Tanner notes that Barth's treatment of the world seems to have 'an anthropocentric cast' because of his focus on the humanity of Christ (Kathryn Tanner, 'Creation and Providence', in John Webster (ed.), *The Cambridge Companion to Karl Barth* (Cambridge: Cambridge University Press, 2000), 125). My argument in Chapter 4 is that even within the structure of Barth's theology it is unnecessary to construe the incarnation in this way.

considered unsympathetic to his own project is that Barth himself recognized the limited evidence in biblical creation narratives for declarations about the centrality of humanity. After declaring human beings the unity of heaven and earth he notes with characteristic honesty:

> It is surprising that man is not seen more frequently and emphatically in this context, although it is undoubtedly as the climax and goal of the divine work that he appears in the two creation narratives in Gen. 1 and 2. In the great creation Psalm 104 he is mentioned only incidentally: 'When the sun ariseth,' and the young lions return to their dens, 'man goeth forth unto his work and to his labour until the evening' (v. 23). In the rest of the Psalm he is then completely lost in a host of other creatures. Similarly, in the great speech of God 'out of the whirlwind' in Job 38 f., there is no mention of him among the other wonderful created figures. Unforgettable things are said about the earth, the sea and the stars, the foolish ostrich and the spirited horse, and finally the hippopotamus and the crocodile; but man seems to be ignored, except that it is he, in the person of the murmuring Job, who must constantly allow himself to be led *ad absurdum* by the question whether he had conceived, elected, determined and posited all these things.[54]

Barth is disconcerted by the lack of fit between the anthropocentric view he has just set out and the accounts of creation present in Psalm 104 and the closing chapters of Job. This is a moment of disruption in an anthropocentric interpretation of a biblical doctrine of creation that we should not quickly pass over. If we take the Psalms and Job alongside Genesis 1 and 2, Barth sees here, the view of humanity as central to the project of creation is not a sufficient account of what the Bible has to say about creation: Psalm 104 and the end of the book of Job indicate that a wider vision of God's purposes is necessary.[55]

In his consideration of the purpose of creation Thomas Aquinas cites

---

[54] Barth, *CD* III/1, 20.

[55] Sang Hyun Lee notes that Jonathan Edwards, another representative of the Reformed tradition, sees clearly the need to relate God's end in creation to God rather than humanity: 'God's end in creation … is to communicate or repeat God's internal dynamic fullness now in time and space', which means that that 'the physical universe is also created for the same end and thus has the same destiny as humanity – namely to repeat God's internal glory in time and space' (Sang Hyun Lee, 'Edwards on God and Nature: Resources for Contemporary Theology', in *Edwards in Our Time: Jonathan Edwards and the Shaping of American Religion*, (eds) Sang Hyan Lee and Allen C. Guelzo (Grand Rapids, MI: Eerdmans, 1999), 20. I am grateful to KC Choi for this reference.

Proverbs 16.4a, which the Vulgate rendered as 'The Lord has made all things for himself'.[56] Aquinas considers that the end of the universe must be understood in four stages: each creature exists for its own perfection, lesser creatures exist for the nobler, each creature exists for the perfection of the entire universe, 'and, finally, the whole universe and all its parts have God as their goal, in so far as the divine goodness is reflected through them and thus his glory manifested'.[57] In an earlier discussion of whether God is the final cause of all things, Aquinas argues that God acts for the end of communicating God's perfection, which is God's goodness: since '[e]ach and every creature stretches out to its own completion, which is a resemblance of the divine fulness and excellence … divine goodness is the final cause of all things'.[58] Bonaventure cites the same verse from Proverbs in affirming that the final end of creation cannot be anything outside God.[59] The accounts Aquinas and Bonaventure give of creation have an affinity for a Neo-Platonic pattern of creation as emanation from God and redemption as return to God, so their opposition to construing the aim of creation as humanity is rather different from Barth's. In this context to think of human beings as the goal of creation would be radically to miss the overarching structure and meaning of the creation of the universe. Yet the force and import of the objection is the same: to construe God's purposes in creation as merely human and therefore make human beings the centre and measure of all things is an absurd misconstrual of God's works, mistaking a part for the whole.

Alongside the lack of convincing theological argument in favour of humanity as the purpose of creation, therefore, we see strong theological objections to construing God's purposes in this way. It is for this reason that, despite the anthropocentric exuberance noted in the previous section arising from perceived common ground between Christianity and Greek philosophy in the Patristic period, or from new visions of human technological power in the early modern period, the better of the theological argument has always been on the side of those recognizing the importance of affirming the purpose of creation in a theocentric context.[60]

---

[56] See the beginning of the following section for Wolfhart Pannenberg's critique of the use of this verse.

[57] Thomas Aquinas, *Summa Theologica*, trans. Fathers of the English Dominican Province (London: Blackfriars, 1963), 1.65.2. See John Berkman, 'Towards a Thomistic Theology of Animality', in *Creaturely Theology: On God, Humans and Other Animals*, (eds) Celia Deane-Drummond and David Clough (London: SCM, 2009), 24 and Pannenberg, *Systematic Theology*, 53 n.

[58] Aquinas, *Summa Theologica*, 1.44.4.

[59] See Schäfer, 'Position and Function of Man', 271.

[60] Christoph Schwöbel observes that this recognition that 'The end of God's creating

Creation: All About Itself?

The theocentric position on the purpose of creation that God creates for God's own glory is not without its difficulties. Wolfhart Pannenberg argues in critique of Aquinas that 'the idea that God, not creatures, is the final end of his world government has a harsh sound and leaves the impression that his rule is one of oppression'.[61] Pannenberg notes that Aquinas was working with a mistaken Vulgate translation of Proverbs 16.4: where the version he cites says that God made everything for himself, the correct translation has the very different emphasis that God creates each creature for its own sake.[62] To picture God's aim in creation as self-glorification is inadequate, Pannenberg argues: 'the creature was not created in order that God should receive glory from it' and God has no need of glorification by creatures.[63] He prefers to see God's goal in creation as God's creatures: 'As the activation and expression of his free love, God's creative action is oriented wholly to creatures. They are both the object and goal of creation. Herein is his glory as Creator, the glory of the Father, who is glorified by the Son and by the Spirit in creatures.'[64] This line of argument is supported by a long tradition affirming the goodness of God in creation, originating in the Psalms. Psalm 104 represents an astonishing catalogue of God's oversight and care for all of God's creatures, providing water for the wild animals, homes for the birds, making grass grow for the cattle and plants for people, watering the cedars of Lebanon so that birds may nest in them, providing high mountains for wild goat and rocks for rabbits, even making the darkness so that the wild animals of the forest may seek their prey from God (Ps. 104.10–22). All creatures are created through the sending of God's spirit, have their food from the open hand of God and return to dust when God takes their breath away (Ps. 104.27–30).[65] This grand vision of God's project

is God's own glory' became a theological commonplace from Aquinas to the Lutheran and Reformed divines of the seventeenth century (Christoph Schwöbel, 'God, Creation and the Christian Community', in *The Doctrine of Creation: Essays in Dogmatics, History and Philosophy*, ed. Colin E. Gunton (London: T & T Clark, 2004), 168).

[61] Pannenberg, *Systematic Theology*, 53 n., citing Karl Barth, *Church Dogmatics*, vol. III/3, (Edinburgh: T. & T. Clark, 1960), 171.

[62] Pannenberg, *Systematic Theology*, 55 in critique of Aquinas, *Summa Theologica*, 1.65.2. The Vulgate text of Prov. 16.4a is *universa propter semet ipsum operatus est Dominus* (The Lord has made all things for himself). Modern translations translate the original very differently, e.g. 'The Lord has made everything for its purpose' (New Revised Standard Vesion [NRSV]).

[63] Pannenberg, *Systematic Theology*, 56.

[64] Pannenberg, *Systematic Theology*, 56.

[65] In his commentary on Psalm 104, John Goldingay contrasts its stance with Genesis:

of creation is echoed in many places; for example, in his *Hexaemeron,* Basil of Caesarea tells his congregation that 'the world was not devised at random or to no purpose, but to contribute to some useful end and to the great advantage of all beings'.[66]

Alongside the question of whether creation as a whole should be considered God's aim in creation, there is the question of the place of each of God's creatures. Pannenberg cites Barth's objections to totalitarian accounts of God's governance of creation in this context. Barth wrote that the subordination of creatures to God is a coordination of creatures with one another. Such a coordination means creatures are not abandoned to individualism in relation to one another, but Barth emphasizes that 'the fact of this relationship does not encroach upon the individual meaning and right of even the most lowly of creatures'.[67] Barth notes the question of Lutheran theologians as to whether God is really concerned 'with the growth of caterpillars in the grass sprouting in the province of Saxony in a given year' and judges that they were right to answer in the affirmative, citing Augustine's commentary on Matthew's gospel that if God despised little things, God would not have created them.[68] Pannenberg therefore affirms not only that creation as a whole is an end in itself, but that for God 'no creature is merely a means'. Rather, the existence of every creature is ordered to 'the *kairos* of the manifestation of the Son' so that 'each creature has a part in the saving purpose of the Father'.[69]

Christoph Schwöbel recognizes the problems Pannenberg identifies in characterizing a theocentric view of the purpose of creation, but insists that we should not rush to dismiss such a position in favour of affirming creatures as God's end in creation. He maintains that creation cannot be said to be an end in itself, and that the tradition of identifying God's end in creation as the glorification of God cannot be interpreted as merely divine self love:

'Whereas Genesis gives humanity authority over creation, commissions it to fill the world, and thus emphasizes the sexual difference between man and woman, the psalm makes humanity one more part of creation; there is no hint of human dominion of creation.' (John Goldingay, *Psalms,* Baker Commentary on the Old Testament, vol. 3 (Grand Rapids, MI: Baker Academic, 2008), 196–7.

[66] Saint Basil, 'On the Hexaemeron', in *Exegetic Homilies,* trans. Sister Agnes Clare Way, C.D.P. (Washington, DC: Catholic University of America, 1963), 1.6. Alvyn Pettersen argues that a corollary of Athanasius's view that all things were brought into being through God's goodness is 'that the creative act was for the creatures' and not the Creator's benefit' (Alvyn Pettersen, *Athanasius* (London: Geoffrey Chapman, 1995), 25. (For further discussion of this text, see the beginning of Chapter 3).

[67] Barth, *CD* III/3, 169.

[68] Barth, *CD* III/3, 169.

[69] Pannenberg, *Systematic Theology,* 7.

on the basis of a trinitarian understanding of God, glory is not a self-directed attitude, but the mutuality of glorifying the other and receiving glory from the other which constitutes the communion of the divine life … Including creation into the mutuality of communicating and communicated glory is the end of God's creating, which in this way defines the destiny of creation to join with the Spirit in the glorification of the Father through the Son.[70]

Schwöbel notes that in a seventeenth century dogmatic context identifying the objective of creation as the glory of God 'had a regulative function for the human relationship to the world: its use for the human is at best an intermediate end of creation, it is never its ultimate end' and argues that a theocentric view excludes 'the self-glorification of the human creature' and prevents 'the kind of anthropocentric attitude where the greater glory of the human creatures has to be achieved at the expense of the rest of creation'.[71]

God's Fellowship with Creatures

We have seen the arguments in favour of an anthropocentric view of the purpose of creation are frail and easily defeated by the range of theological arguments against such a position. The theocentric view that God aims in creation to glorify God is an aid in avoiding human self-glorification, but without further explanation risks portraying God as self-concerned and ungracious. The view that God's purpose in creating is to do good to creatures is an important and longstanding theological insight, but in isolation risks the same dangers of creaturely self-preoccupation as the human version of the claim. The obvious remedy suggested by this analysis, already evident in some of the theological accounts cited, is that the purpose of creation can only be rendered adequately as a balance between these two latter perspectives. From one side, this appears as Schwöbel's affirmation that the glorification of God could only be seen in a trinitarian context as the inclusion of creation into the mutual communion of the divine life of Father, Son and Spirit.[72] From the other side, it is represented as Pannenberg's affirmation of the action of God as wholly directed towards the creature as its object and goal, but through this action 'glorified by the Son and by the Spirit in creatures'.[73] In Aquinas, this balance is present in his formulation

---

[70] Schwöbel, 'God, Creation and the Christian Community', 169.
[71] Schwöbel, 'God, Creation and the Christian Community', 169–70.
[72] Schwöbel, 'God, Creation and the Christian Community', 169.
[73] Pannenberg, *Systematic Theology*, 56.

that creation glorifies God by demonstrating God's goodness.[74] In Barth, it is recognized in the specification of the goal of creation as the realization of the covenant between creator and creature.[75] An apt summary of this consensual view is Pannenberg's statement that the goal of creation is 'the participation of creatures in the trinitarian fellowship'.[76] Alongside this affirmation of the place of creation in God's purposes, we should also not omit the recognition of Barth and Pannenberg that not only creation but every creature has a part in God's creative and salvific purposes.[77]

If this is the best theological construal of the purpose of creation, what are we to make in retrospect of the impressive body of theological opinion surveyed earlier in this chapter that judged the goal of creation as humanity? Alongside the arguments I have developed showing the inadequacy of this view, it is important to note that the theological move necessary from this anthro-pocentric position to the one I am commending is not merely rejection, but the preparedness to see the truth expressed in the anthropocentric formulations in a larger context. For example, in Martin Luther's 'Large Catechism', he interprets the first line of the creed 'I believe in God, the Father almighty, maker of heaven and earth' as follows:

> I hold and believe that I am a creature of God; that is, that he has given and constantly sustains my body, soul, and life, my members great and small, all the faculties of my mind, my reason and understanding, and so forth; my food and drink, clothing, means of support, wife and child, servants, house and home, etc. Besides, he makes all creation help provide the comforts and necessities of life – sun, moon, and stars in the heavens, day and night, air, fire, water, the earth and all that it brings forth, birds and fish, beasts, grain and all kinds of produce.[78]

It is easy to see the inadequacy of interpreting the doctrine of creation in such an

---

[74] Aquinas, *Summa Theologica*, 1.65.2.
[75] Barth, *CD* III/1, 42.
[76] Pannenberg, *Systematic Theology*, 71. Robert Jenson agrees: 'for God to create is for him to open a place in his triune life for others than the three whose mutual life he is' (Robert W. Jenson, 'Aspects of a Doctrine of Creation', in Colin E. Gunton ed. *The Doctrine of Creation: Essays in Dogmatics, History and Philosophy* (London: T & T Clark, 2004), 24). Mike Higton's rendering of a similar position is that the purpose of creation is 'the extension of God's life for the inclusion of creation' (Mike Higton, *Christian Doctrine*, SCM Core Texts (London: SCM, 2008), 185).
[77] Barth, *CD* III/3, 169; Pannenberg, *Systematic Theology*, 7.
[78] Theodore G. Tappert ed. *The Book of Concord: The Confessions of the Evangelical Lutheran Church* (Philadelphia, PA: Fortress Press, 1959), 2.13–14.

individualistic, instrumental and gendered sense,[79] but presumably Luther's aim in rendering the work of the creator in such an outrageously personal fashion was to convince male catechists repeating these words that God in creation was gracious to them. To move towards a more adequate interpretation of the doctrine of creation does not require the rejection of the proclamation of God's graciousness towards this one believer, but the enlarging of this intense vision of God's grace to include all humanity and all God's creatures. Luther was not wrong to preach God's grace to the sinner, but we can see that our account of God's grace must be on a bigger canvas.[80]

Another way of seeing the relationship between an anthropocentric view of the purpose of creation and a broader vision is to consider a parable the medieval Jewish thinker Moses Maimonides uses to illustrate his critique of anthropocentrism in *The Guide of the Perplexed*:

> Thus an individual from among the people of a city might think that the final end of the ruler consists in safeguarding his house at night against robbers. And this is true from a certain point of view. For since his house is safe-guarded and this benefit comes to him because of the ruler, the matter looks as if the final end of the ruler were the safeguarding of the house of that individual.[81]

If the individual came to realize that the ruler also safeguards the houses of others in the city, it would not require him to give up his belief that the ruler safeguards his house: the transformation in his understanding is the setting of his true prior belief in the wider context of the ruler's activity in relation to others. Similarly, appreciating that the purpose of creation is for God to include creatures into the trinitarian fellowship does not deny the particular place of human beings in this fellowship, but simply expands our idea of the fellowship in which we will participate.

To recognize that God's purposes in creation are more than human is a significant initial step. It rules out the doctrinal position cited at the beginning of the chapter that the remainder of creation is scenery for the drama of human redemption, and therefore undermines the related ethical position that sees the

---

[79] See Colin Gunton's critique in Gunton, 'End of Causality', 72 and Paul Santmire's discussion in Santmire, *Travail of Nature*, 124.

[80] Tom Greggs makes an analogous argument in developing a case for universal salvation from Christian particularist premises in Tom Greggs, *Barth, Origen, and Universal Salvation: Restoring Particularity* (Oxford: Oxford University Press, 2009), especially 171–205.

[81] Moses Maimonides, *The Guide of the Perplexed*, trans. Shlomo Pines (Chicago, IL: University of Chicago Press, 1963), 3.13.

use of all other creatures for human ends as theologically authorized. It means that all creaturely life, and each creature, has a part in God's purposes. In terms of developing a systematic theology of animals, it is clearly, however, only a prolegomena, opening a space for a range of questions concerning the place of animals in God's work of creation, reconciliation and redemption. The two following chapters begin this task by asking what animals have in common in relation to God's act of creation and in what respects they differ.

Chapter 2

THE PLACE OF ANIMALS

If, as the previous chapter argued, the meaning of non-human animal creatures before God is not exhausted in their relationship to human beings, and, as proposed in the Introduction, the category of animals is worthy of theological attention, we are faced with the fundamental question of how to think theologically about animals. This question will be explored in different ways in each of the remaining chapters of this book, but it seems a reasonable starting point in this chapter to ask what animal creatures have in common in a theological perspective, before turning in the next chapter to ask how differences between them should be rendered theologically. This chapter, therefore, explores doctrinally and biblically the novel question of what it means to be an animal creature.

The Commonality of Creatures

The Christian confession that God created all things from nothing (*creatio ex nihilo*) establishes a fundamental and categorical distinction between God as the creator of everything and the creatures of God. In the face of many philosophical and religious views that posited various forms of continuity between God and creation, Christian theologians have insisted on the importance of a clear boundary between the two.[1] Colin Gunton finds the definitive expression of this in Basil of Caesarea's rejection of the eternity of the heavenly bodies and Neoplatonic orders of creation in favour of the affirmation of ontological homogeneity:

---

[1] For an overview of early Christian thinking on the topic, see Gerhard May, *Creatio Ex Nihilo*; David A. S. Fergusson, *The Cosmos and the Creator: An Introduction to the Theology of Creation* (London: SPCK, 1998), 23–36. Colin Gunton notes that Augustine's reason for affirming creation rather than emanation was Christological: the only alternative to *creatio ex nihilo* is for creation to be made of God's substance and therefore equal to Christ (Colin E. Gunton, *The Triune Creator: A Historical and Systematic Study* (Edinburgh: Edinburgh University Press, 1998), 77.

What is meant by homogenous here is that, by virtue of his belief that God is the creator of everything, Basil comes to the conclusion, against the assumptions of almost the whole of the ancient world, that there are no degrees of being: that is to say, that everything created has the same ontological status. Neoplatonism in particular held that reality formed a hierarchy or ladder, by climbing which it was possible to ascend to divinity. Thus one ascends through matter via higher forms of being like mind to the divine. This doctrine presupposed a fundamental dualism between the material or sensible and the spiritual or intellectual. It also presupposed the inferiority of matter to mind. Christianity's teaching of the incarnation of the Son of God in material reality was fundamentally opposed to this notion, although, as we shall see, it continued to die hard, and, indeed, still does. Basil's attack on the idea of the eternity or superiority of the heavenly bodies had the effect of subverting the dualism in favour of a very different duality. The fundamental division in being is now between creator and created: God and the world he has made, continues to uphold and promises to redeem. The creation is homogenous in the sense that everything has the same ontological status before God, as the object of his creating will and love. All is 'very good' because he created it, mind and matter alike.[2]

Here is a radical and distinctively Christian insight that the affirmation of God as creator of all things means the subversion of all human attempts to create hierarchy among creatures.[3] As Gunton notes, this recognition was both novel and imperfectly received by the later tradition and many of the attempts to distinguish between creatures treated in the next chapter are rejections of Basil's position. If we confess God as creator *ex nihilo* we must recognize that our basic relationship to creation is to recognize that we are part of it. Like all other creatures, we owe our existence, our sustaining from moment to moment and our future life to God. Like other creatures we are frail and finite, in contrast to the power and eternity of God. Like other creatures we are made of the dust of the earth and will return to it. Therefore, we exist in solidarity with all other creatures, sisters and brothers of a single parent.

This basic creaturely solidarity is between all things made by God: stars and

---

[2] Gunton, *Triune Creator*, 71–2. In the next sentence Gunton refers forward to his later discussion of the particularity of human beings, but this later discussion does not take away from the basic affirmation expressed here. Gunton quotes Robert Jenson's view that the same rejection of the orders of creation can be found in Gregory of Nyssa.

[3] As Gunton notes, Basil's formulation has obvious precedents in Irenaeus and Athanasius. Irenaeus states that 'in this respect God differs from man, that God indeed makes, but man is made' (Irenaeus, 'Against Heresies',bk 4, ch. 11, §2).

galaxies, rocks and seas, as well as other living things. In relation to the latter, however, we share still more. In commentary on Genesis 1. 11, Karl Barth observes that with the creation of plants there is a new beginning:

> According to the explanation now given, a creature is alive when through its seed it can continue in the existence of similar creatures, and in addition can bear fruit. This could not be said of light (with darkness), of day (with night), of the firmament (with the waters above and below), of land (with sea). These all have a distinctive glory, but they are not alive. Life commences after these works of separation, and on the basis of the final work. Hence there is an end which belongs to this new beginning. The vegetable kingdom which grows out of the dry land in obedience to the Word of God will not be the only living creature. But it is the first, and the presupposition of all the rest. Every living creature is alive because of that which it has in common with the vegetable kingdom.[4]

Barth adds later that the creation of plants is 'a precursory type and also a substratum of the history of the covenant of grace'.[5] Wolfhart Pannenberg sees a similar significance in the origin of creatures with life:

> the development of living creatures, and especially animals, notwith-standing the frailty and vulnerability of their existence, carries with it a higher degree of independence that we find in atoms, molecules, stars, rivers, seas, or mountains. We do not refer to greater duration, in terms of which other forms of creation are far superior to living creatures. Nevertheless, independent existence reaches a higher stage with living creatures, i.e., independence as self-organization of the forms of existence. With living creatures we have for the first time self-directed activity that is not merely an effect of external causes.[6]

An immediate question arises here, however, in relation to Pannenberg's characterization of living things as more independent than other creatures. There are strong reasons to suggest the opposite is true, and that living things are in fact *more* dependent on other creatures than simpler forms of life. Basic school science projects demonstrate the dependence of plants on light, water and nutrients from the soil. Dependence, rather than independence, is therefore a crucial characteristic of all living creatures, as hinted at in Pannenberg's

---

[4] Barth, *CD* III/1, 143.
[5] Barth, *CD* III/1, 154.
[6] Pannenberg, *Systematic Theology*, 133–4.

reference to their frailty and vulnerability. Certainly, living things are striking in their self-organizing abilities, giving rise to the attribution of souls to plants as well as animals in Greek thought.[7] We are very likely to be misled, however, if we construe such a capacity in comparison to simpler creatures as increased independence without qualification.[8]

The recent analysis of the human genome alongside the genome of other creatures is a striking genetic test of relationships between living creatures, and a striking parallel to this theological recognition of what living creatures have in common. We now know that we share 21 per cent of our genes with all other cellular life forms. This means all things we consider to be living, with the possible exception of viruses, the status of which is hard to determine.[9] A fifth of our genetic make-up, therefore, is common between us and bacteria, seaweed, cabbages and oak trees. Over half of our genes are shared with genes in all eukaryotes; that is, all cellular life apart from bacteria and archaea,[10] including protozoa, algae, fungi as well as all plants and animals. Three-quarters of our genes are shared with all other animals, 97 per cent with orangutans, 98.5 per cent with gorillas and 98.9 per cent with chimpanzees.[11] This discovery of shared genetic inheritance finds an echo in recent

[7] For an account of Aristotle's view of the soul, see Richard Sorabji, 'Body and Soul in Aristotle', in Michael Durrant (ed.), *Aristotle's de Anima in Focus* (London; New York: Routledge, 1993).

[8] This recognition of the dependence of more complex organisms on simpler ones relates to Catherine Osborne's argument that the value Aristotle placed on simplicity as an ideal property means it is very difficult to see more complex organisms at the top of any hierarchy in the context of his thought (see Osborne, *Dumb Beasts*, 98–132).

[9] Mark Ridley, *Evolution*, 3rd edn (Malden, MA; Oxford: Blackwell, 2004), 558. For discussion of whether viruses are alive, see Luis P. Villarreal, *Viruses and the Evolution of Life* (Washington, DC: ASM Press, 2005), ix–xii.

[10] Archaea share with bacteria the characteristics of having prokaryotic cells and being mostly unicellular and microscopic, but their differences from bacteria are now generally recognized by biologists to justify identifying them with an entire domain of life alongside those of bacteria and Eukarya (see Neil A. Campbell and Jane B. Reece, *Biology*, 7th edn (San Francisco, CA: Benjamin Cummings, 2005), 13.

[11] Ridley, *Evolution*, 558; Morris Goodman, Lawrence I. Grossman and Derek E. Wildman, 'Moving Primate Genomics Beyond the Chimpanzee Genome', *Trends in Genetics* 21 (2005), 511. In *Not a Chimp*, Jeremy Taylor argues that the observation that we share around 99 per cent of our genes with chimpanzees should not be misinterpreted as showing that we are 99 per cent chimpanzee or that chimpanzees are 99 per cent human (Jeremy Taylor, *Not a Chimp: The Hunt to Find the Genes That Make Us Human* (Oxford: Oxford University Press, 2009)). He explores disputes between primatologists concerning how experiments testing the cognitive abilities of chimpanzees should be interpreted and sets out the case that cognitive differences between humans and chimpanzees amount to a qualitative, rather than merely quantitative, difference in brain functions. He supports this case against the over-interpretation of genetic similarity with surveys of experiments on crows that show they exceed the cognitive capacities of chimpanzees

studies revealing the sophistication of the life of other animals and therefore the capacities they share with human beings. On a broad front, in relation to all kinds of animals, what we now know about non-human capacities makes clear that we have much more in common with other animals than we previously thought. We now have reason to believe that sheep are capable of recognizing hundreds of faces;[12] crows are able to fashion tools in order to solve problems;[13] chimpanzees exhibit empathy, morality and politics,[14] and can outdo human subjects in numerically based memory tests;[15] dolphins are capable of processing grammar;[16] parrots can differentiate between objects in relation to abstract concepts such as colour and shape;[17] and sperm whales have developed culturally specific modes of life and communication.[18] We cannot read a theological account of our relatedness to other living creatures from our genome or a comparison of capacities, but these two new areas of knowledge constitute a remarkable scientific illustration of the theological affirmation of the commonality of living things.

in some tasks, despite their much greater genetic difference from human beings. He also argues that the evolution of the human genome has accelerated in the past 10,000 years so that our divergence from chimpanzees is increasing. He is concerned that some primatologists have exploited insatiable human anthropomorphism and created a 'chimps are us' industry (287). Taylor is right that we cannot move quickly from observations of genetic similarities to judgements of similarities between creatures: small genetic differences may give rise to very large effects in how genes are expressed in the development of organisms. His argument does not detract, however, from the shock of discovering how much of our genes are shared with the other creatures we find around us.

[12] Keith M. Kendrick, 'Sheep Don't Forget a Face', *Nature* 414: 4860 (2001).

[13] Alex A. S. Weir, Jackie Chappell and Alex Kacelnik, 'Shaping of Hooks in New Caledonian Crows', *Science* 297: 5583 (2002).

[14] Frans de Waal, *Good Natured: The Origins of Right and Wrong in Humans and Other Animals* (Cambridge, MA: Harvard University Press, 1996); Frans de Waal, *Chimpanzee Politics: Power and Sex Among Apes* (Baltimore, NJ: Johns Hopkins University Press, 1998).

[15] Sana Inoue and Tetsuro Matsuzawa, 'Working Memory of Numerals in Chimpanzees', *Current Biology* 17: 23 (2007). The remarkable videos of the experiment are available as supplemental data to the paper from the *Current Biology* website (URL: <http://www.cell.com/current-biology/supplemental/S0960-9822(07)02088-X>). It is striking to compare the poor adult human performance (Movie S5) with the nonchalance of the chimpanzee (Movie S6).

[16] Louis M. Herman, Stan A. Kuczaj and Mark D. Holder, 'Responses to Anomalous Gestural Sequences by a Language-Trained Dolphin: Evidence for Processing of Semantic Relations and Syntactic Information', *Journal of Experimental Psychology: General* 122: 2 (1993).

[17] Irene M. Pepperberg, *The Alex Studies: Cognitive and Communicative Abilities of Grey Parrots* (Cambridge, MA: Harvard University, 2000).

[18] Hal Whitehead, *Sperm Whales: Social Evolution in the Ocean* (Chicago, IL: University of Chicago, 2003).

The Life of Animals

When we come to consider what we have in common not only with other living creatures but with animals in particular, the Genesis creation narratives provide an obvious starting point. On the fifth day of creation, God did a new thing. Already in place are day and night, sky, sea and land bringing forth vegetation, and sun and moon, but now living creatures (*nephesh hayyah*) are created. God called on the waters to bring forth 'swarms of living creatures' and for birds to fly across the sky, creating great sea monsters 'and every living thing that moves, of every kind, with which the waters swarm' and 'every winged bird of every kind' (Gen. 1.20–1). God saw that these new creatures were good, and blessed them in the commandment to 'be fruitful and multiply' in their realms of sea and air (Gen. 1.22). On the sixth day it was the turn of the creatures of the land. God called on the earth to bring forth living creatures of every kind: cattle and creeping things and wild beasts of the earth of every kind, before turning to creating human beings as well. God saw these too as good, although this time there is no blessing (Gen. 1.24–8). God provided the creatures of the earth and sky with food: to humankind was given 'every plant yielding seed' and 'every tree with seed in its fruit', and to the beasts of the earth and the birds of the air God gave 'every green plant' (Gen. 1.29–30). Then God looked at all creation and saw that it was very good (Gen. 1.31).

The second chapter of Genesis pictures the order of creation differently: the human is made first from the dust of the ground, and into the nostrils of the human God breathes the breath of life so that the human becomes the first living creature (*nephesh hayyah*, Gen. 2.7), although other creatures also have the breath of life (Gen. 2.19). God forms from the earth the beasts of the field and the birds of the air and brings them before the human to be named and as possible companions. Theodore Hiebert notes that the commonality between humans and other animals in Genesis 2 has been obscured by English translators:

> The common lot of humans and animals is a conspicuous feature of the Yahwist's creation narrative. A clear line distinguishing the essential nature of one from the other is difficult to detect. Human and animal alike are called *nepeš ḥayyâ*, 'animate creature' (2.7, 19). As with the breath of life, *nepeš ḥayyâ* is used by J for both, and this term also attributes to neither a soul or spiritual being separate from their physical life. This point has been muddled for centuries in English translations by a succession of translators determined to draw a distinction between human beings and animals where none exists in the Hebrew text. In the King James Version

(1611), *nepeš ḥayyâ* was rendered 'living creature' when used of the animals (2.19), but 'living soul' when used of the human being.[19]

Hiebert notes that even in the New Revised Standard Version the distinction is maintained, albeit more subtlely, translating *nephesh hayyah* as 'living creature' when used to describe the animals in v. 19 and 'living being' when used of humans in v. 9.[20] He also observes that in the Yahwist's account, humans are not unique in possessing wisdom or language: the snake is the wisest of the beasts (Gen. 3.1) and Balaam's donkey has better judgement than her owner (Num. 22.23–35).[21]

Basil of Caesarea also remarks on the new beginning God makes on the fifth day: 'Now, for the first time an animal was created which possessed life and sensation. Plants and trees, even if they are said to live because they share the power of nourishing themselves and of growing, yet are not animals nor are they animate.'[22] Martin Luther notes the new mode of procreation beginning on the fifth day of creation in his commentary on Genesis and its association with God's blessing of these first animals.[23] Throughout his commentary he notes the commonality between human beings and other animals. Human beings share the life of the other land animals: they are created on the same day and have a 'common table' in the herbs and fruit of trees.[24] God meant Adam's physical life to be similar to that of other animals, like them in need of food, drink and rest to refresh himself.[25] Human beings increase, multiply and gestate their young in the same way as other animals.[26] He notes that there is no difference between human beings and donkeys in relation to their shared animal life:

Animal life has need of food and drink; it has need of sleep and rest; their bodies are fed in like manner by food and drink, and they grow; and through hunger they become faint and perish. The stomach receives the food, and when the food has been digested, passes it on to the liver, which

[19] Theodore Hiebert, *The Yahwist's Landscape: Nature and Religion in Early Israel* (New York: Oxford University Press, 1996), 63.
[20] Hiebert, *Yahwist's Landscape*, 63.
[21] Hiebert, *Yahwist's Landscape*, 63.
[22] Basil, 'On the Hexaemeron', Homily 7, §1. While this passage restricts the meaning of 'animate' to animals, examples of its usage in the Oxford English Dictionary include both references to animals (including human beings) and to all living things, including plants.
[23] Luther, *Luther's Works*, I.53.
[24] Luther, *Luther's Works*, I.36.
[25] Luther, *Luther's Works*, I.57.
[26] Luther, *Luther's Works*, I.83.

produces blood, by which all the limbs are given fresh strength. In this regard there is no difference between man and beast.[27]

Karl Barth is also struck by the fifth day as another new beginning: what God creates on the fifth day of creation: 'in contrast not only to light, heaven, earth and the luminaries, but also to the vegetable kingdom, consists of creatures which live in autonomous motion, abounding and flying'. God's fiat 'sets them in independent motion in their own elements', the first inhabitants of these spheres of life, new races of self-propelled beings, the first creatures with independent life.[28] In blessing the fish and birds (Gen. 1.22) God begins dealing with creation and we see 'the beginning of its history, or at least an introductory prologue which announces the theme of this history, i.e., the establishment of a covenant between God and His creation which moves independently like Himself and renews itself by procreation after its kind'.[29] Wolfhart Pannenberg similarly sees a particular significance to animal creation: whereas plants are spatially fixed, animals can move about freely and therefore relate not only to their environment, but also 'to themselves, to the future of their own lives, as we see very clearly in their search for food'.[30]

The references of both Barth and Pannenberg to the independence of animal life return us to the consideration of the dependence of animals discussed above in relation to all living creatures. In this context it is notable that one of the central biological characteristics of members of the kingdom *Animalia* alongside locomotion and different lifecycle stages is their dependence on other organisms.[31] Like fungi, but unlike plants, animals are unable to produce all the organic molecules they need and so must ingest other organisms to survive.[32] All that we noted above in relation to the dependence of living things, therefore, is especially true of the life of animals. In animals this dependence is raised to a second order for those that consume plants, and to third and higher orders

[27] Luther, *Luther's Works*, I.85. For further examples of Luther's view of the life that humans and other animals share, and discussion of the wider context of these observations, see Clough, 'Anxiety of the Human Animal', 49–50.

[28] Barth, *CD* III/1, 168–9.

[29] Barth, *CD* III/1, 170.

[30] Pannenberg, *Systematic Theology*, 134.

[31] Aquinas distinguishes between immovable animals, such as shellfish, which lack the locomotive power of the soul and perfect animals that are able to move (Aquinas, *Summa Theologica*, 1.78.1).

[32] See, for example, Campbell and Reece, *Biology*, 626. Catherine Osborne argues that in an Aristotelian scheme the complexity of human beings and dependence on other forms of life means 'not that humans are at the top of some scale of being, but that they are far down the ladder and struggling with a whole lot of relatively ineffective tasks' (Osborne, *Dumb Beasts*, 122).

for those dependent on consuming other animals. This gives us an interesting perspective on the late arrival of animals on the fifth day of creation in the narrative of Genesis 1: animals are more needy than other creatures, and can only survive in an environment in which the other organisms they need to consume are already thriving.[33] A key part of understanding our common-ality with other animals is therefore a humbling recognition of our shared dependence on the availability of other living organisms to provide us with what we need to survive.

To name this commonality between animals is not to pretend that the category is clearly defined at its boundaries. When discussing sea squirts and sponges, Aristotle commented that 'Nature passes in a continuous gradation from lifeless things to animals, and on the way there are living things which are not actually animals, with the result that one class is so close to the next that the difference seems infinitesimal'.[34] Biologists are able to give reasons for attributing particular species to the kingdom *Animalia* rather than a different one, but not all the members of this kingdom are obviously contained within the term 'animal' in common usage: sponges are a good example here. There is no reason why the biological definition should trump all others: the biologist and philosopher John Dupré has argued that there is an important sense in which whales are 'fish', contrary to a recently established orthodoxy based on a particular system of scientific classification.[35] While sponges belong to the kingdom *Animalia*, therefore, it may be that they are not animals in non-biological contexts. I am using 'animals' to mean human beings and the creatures most like us: those that are alive, able to sense the world, capable of voluntary movement and dependent on other kinds of creatures for their suste-nance. To work with such a broad definition of this category of creatures means that it will be a category with fuzzy edges, and sponges are a good example of creatures that seem to be more like animals in some respects and more like plants in others. Such blurred edges would only be problematic if it were necessary to be able to give an exhaustive account of precisely which creatures were animals and which were not. To consider the theological place of animals such as I am attempting here gives rise to no such necessity: some kinds of creatures are clearly animals, such as cows, wrens, human beings and salmon; some kinds are clearly not, such as quartz, beech trees and the streptococcus bacterium; and about some kinds it is hard to say, such as sponges. To admit

---

[33] This is in striking contrast to Philo's explanation of the late creation of human beings at the beginning of Chapter 1.

[34] Aristotle, *Parts of Animals*, Loeb Classical Library, trans. A. L. Peck (London; Cambridge, MA: William Heinemann; Harvard University Press, 1937), 681 a.

[35] John Dupré, 'Are Whales Fish?'.

that there are fuzzy edges to the category of animals does not mean it is foolish to consider the category, any more than the difficulty of deciding whether a day in May in the northern hemisphere is late spring or early summer renders the concept of seasons obsolete.

The depiction of life shared by humans and other animals is by no means restricted to the first two chapters of Genesis: the Bible pictures them together in its narratives, law, wisdom teaching, psalmody, prophecy, in the teaching of Jesus and in apocalyptic vision. The biblical similes and metaphors that use other animals to describe human beings also speak of this commonality. Clearly such comparisons cannot be taken as necessarily affirming similarity beyond the immediate rhetorical context: Jesus' reference to Peter as a rock (Mt. 16.18) is presumably intended to convey his reliability rather than his capacity for action. The comparisons of Israel to sheep under threat from predators, birds or fish caught by nets, or beasts appointed for slaughter, however, function only insofar as they engage in an empathetic identification with the plight of other creatures whose lives are fragile like ours.[36] Similarly, the Psalmist comparing himself to a deer longing for flowing streams, a lonely owl in the wilderness and a worm indicates his appreciation of a common creatureliness.[37]

In Old Testament narratives beyond those of creation, God decides to bring a flood because *the earth* is corrupt and *all flesh* (*basar*) has corrupted its ways, filled the earth with violence and must be destroyed (Gen. 6.11–13).[38] Noah is

---

[36] For comparisons to sheep, see 1 Kgs 22.17; Ps. 44.11, 22; 49.12–14, 20; 68.10; 78.52; 79.13; 80.1; Isa. 40.11; 53.7–8; 63.11; Jer. 10.21; 31.10, 12; Ezek. 34; 36.37–8; Mic. 2.12; for comparisons to birds and fish threatened by nets, see Ps. 91.3–4; 124.7; 141.9–10; Prov. 6.5; 7.22–3; Eccl. 11.12; Jer. 5.26–7; for comparisons to beasts sent for slaughter see Ps. 44.11, 22; 49.12–14, 20. The comparison with animals destined for slaughter recalls the Talmudic story of the calf who was about to be slaughtered and ran to Rabbi Judah Ha-Nasi, nestling in his robes and whimpering. The Rabbi told the calf to go because it was created to be slaughtered, and the Talmud records that heaven decreed suffering for him because he had no mercy (B. *Bava Metzia* 85a: see Norman Solomon, 'Judaism and the Environment', in *Judaism and Ecology*, World Religions and Ecology, ed. Aubrey Rose (London: Cassell, 1992), 48 and Y. Michael Barilan, 'The Vision of Vegetarianism and Peace: Rabbi Kook on the Ethical Treatment of Animals', *History of the Human Sciences* 17: 4 (2004), 84).

[37] Ps. 42.1; 102.6–7; 22.6.

[38] Elsewhere the narrative specifies only human sinfulness as provoking God's anger (Gen. 6.5). Luther notes Nicolas of Lyra's view that the birds and other animals had departed from their nature before the flood as well as the humans, drawing on Rabbinic traditions. Luther rejects this view on the basis that the other animals did not sin, were created only for this physical life and therefore do not hear the Word (Luther, *Luther's Works*, 2.58). This verse raises the question of whether human disobedience in Genesis 3 has implications for the whole of creation, which is a key doctrinal issue I discuss in the context of atonement in Chapter 5.

to save representatives of every kind of flesh on the ark (Gen. 6.11–13, 18–19) and when the waters come the ark is born up, but all flesh on the earth – birds, cattle, wild beasts, all swarming creatures that swarm on the earth, and all human beings – all things on land 'in whose nostrils was the breath of life' died (Gen. 7.21–2). After the flood God remembers both Noah and every living thing and the cattle that were with him, and makes the waters recede, so that the human beings together with all the birds and beasts and creeping things on the earth can abound on the earth and be fruitful and multiply (Gen. 8.6–17) and God makes a covenant with Noah, his sons, and every living creature of all flesh with them, that all flesh will never be cut off again (Gen. 9.1–17).

The people of Israel are always to be found in the company of domestic animals: when God chooses Abram and sends him to Egypt he is given sheep, oxen, donkeys and camels by Pharaoh along with human slaves (Gen. 12). Oxen, sheep, goats and birds continue to be used for sacrifice as well as for food and clothing (e.g. Gen. 15.7–11). The stories of Isaac, Rebekah, Jacob, Esau and Joseph are full of animals.[39] Many of the Egyptian plagues affect humans and animals alike.[40] On Passover night even the dogs cooperate by not barking at the Israelites and their domestic animals (Exod. 11.7) and great numbers of livestock accompany the Israelites from Egypt (Exod. 12.37–8). The law of Israel applies to both humans and other animals. The first born males of both Israelite children and livestock are to be set apart for God (Exod. 13.11–16, 22.29b–30). Livestock are protected alongside humans by the Sabbath legislation (Exod. 20.8–11, 23.12, Deut. 5.14) and even the wild beasts benefit from it by being able to feed on the produce of the land in Sabbath years (Lev. 25.6–7). Oxen that kill humans are to be put to death just as humans are (Exod. 21.12; 28–32). If a man or woman has sexual intercourse with a beast both must be killed (Lev. 20.15–6) and hostility to the Lord will result in the destruction of both children and livestock (Lev. 26.21–2). In the holy wars of Israel the inhabitants of towns are to be destroyed together with their livestock.[41]

Job's woes include the death of his livestock and children (Job 1.13–19) and he recommends turning to the beasts, birds, plants and fish for wisdom concerning the ways of the God in whose hand 'is the life of every living thing and the breath of every human being'.[42] God's speech out of the whirlwind reminds Job that he is but one of the many creatures made by God 'just as I made you' and for which God provides (Job 38–41).[43] Psalm 104 similarly

---

[39] Gen. 22.1–14; 24.19–20; 30.25–43; 36.6–7; 37; 41.

[40] Exod. 7.11–21; 8.16–19; 9.8–12; 9.22–26; 12.1–29.

[41] For example, Deut. 13.12–16; 20.16; Josh. 10.40; 1 Sam. 15.

[42] Job 12.7–10, cf. Ps. 104; 136.25; 145.16; 147.9.

[43] Susannah Ticciati sees in the whirlwind speeches 'a great eruption or huge explosion' forcing Job beyond the point in which he has 'contracted creation to the zero point

declares the breadth of God's creative purposes and God's provision for wild and domestic animals and birds. 'All flesh' shall come to God in praise (Ps. 65) and 'all the earth' is called to offer praise to God and is said to sing praises to God.[44] Psalm 36 praises God on the basis that 'you save humans and animals alike, O Lord' (Ps. 36.6). Ants, bees, oxen, donkeys, storks, turtledoves, swallows, cranes, jackals birds and lilies are cited as examples to emulate[45] and the lovers in the Song of Songs praise each other using a wealth of imagery from other animals.[46]

The prophets frequently make clear that God's judgement falls both on human beings and other animals. Jeremiah declares that the anger of the Lord will be poured out on human beings and beasts, the trees of the field and the fruit of the ground, and observes that the birds and beasts are being swept away for the wickedness of those who live in the land (Jer. 7.20; 21.6; 12.4). All are affected by the drought in Judah: the doe in the field forsakes her newborn fawn because there is no grass, the wild asses pant for air like jackals and their eyes fail because there is no herbage (Jer. 14.1–6). Jeremiah warns of the consequences of God's wrath for the enemies of Israel together with their domestic animals.[47] In Ezekiel, Mortal is told that when the people acts faithlessly the hand of the Lord is stretched out against it, both human beings and beasts suffer and wild beasts make the land desolate so that no one may pass through it (Ezek. 14.13–21). When the Lord comes, the fish of the sea, the birds of the air, the beasts of the field, all creeping things and human beings will quake at the Lord's presence (Ezek. 38.19–20). Joel recalls the plague of locusts that has devastated the fields so that the ground mourns, the beasts groan, the cattle

of extinction' so that the other elements of creation 'become masses that must be considered for their own sake' (Susannah Ticciati, *Job and the Disruption of Identity: Reading Beyond Barth* (London; New York: T & T Clark, 2005), 110.

[44] Ps. 66.1–4; 98.7–8; 145.9–16; 148.7, 10; Isa. 42.10–12; 43.20. On this theme, see Richard Bauckham, 'Joining Creation's Praise of God', *Ecotheology* 7 (2002) and David Horrell and Dominic Coad, 'The Stones Would Cry Out' (Luke 19.40): A Lukan Contribution to a Hermeneutics of Creation's Praise', *Scottish Journal of Theology* 64 (2010).

[45] Prov. 6.6–8; 30.24–8; Isa. 1.3; Jer. 8.7; Lam. 4.3; Job 12.7–11. Hatton notes that the Greek translation of Proverbs adds a parallel set of verses concerning the industry of bees, apparently influenced by Aristotle's *Historia Animalium* (Peter T. H. Hatton, *Contradiction in the Book of Proverbs: The Deep Waters of Counsel*, Society for Old Testament Study Series (Aldershot: Ashgate, 2008), 123–6). Ellen Davis calls for a rediscovery of such 'nature wisdom' and cites contemporary biologists who draw similar morals from observation of ants (Ellen Davis, *Proverbs, Ecclesiastes, and the Song of Songs* (Louisville, KY: Westminster John Knox, 2000), 57.

[46] Song 1.7–9, 15; 2.14–16; 4.1, 5; 5.2, 11–12; 6.2, 6, 9; 7.3.

[47] Jer. 49.28–9, 32, 33; 50.3; 51.37.

On Animals I: Systematic Theology

wander about with no pasture, the flocks of sheep are dazed and even the wild beasts cry to God because the watercourses have dried up and fire has devoured the wilderness pastures (Joel 1.4, 10, 18, 20; 2.4–5, 7). The judgement that Zephaniah pronounces on Judah will sweep away everything from the face of the earth: humans and beasts, birds of the air and fish of the sea (Zeph. 1.2–3). Haggai announces the drought the Lord has called for on human beings and beasts, and all their labours (Hag. 1.11).

Humans do not merely share with other animals the consequences of God's judgement: they also share in responding to prophecy and enjoying God's blessing. In Jonah, on hearing Jonah's word, the whole of Nineveh repents, all humans and beasts stop eating and drinking and are covered with sackcloth (Jon. 3.7–8). When Jonah protests at God's forgiveness of Nineveh, God explains the decision not to destroy it on the basis that it contains more than 120,000 people and also many beasts (Jon. 4.11). Ezekiel declares that, under God's blessing, human beings and beasts will increase and be fruitful in Israel (Ezek. 36.11). Hosea speaks God's promise to make a covenant for Israel on that day with the wild beasts, the birds of the air and the creeping things on the ground, and to abolish the bow, sword and war from the land (Hos. 2.18). Isaiah proclaims that hope will come from the shoot growing from the stump of Jesse: on him the spirit of the Lord will rest, and he will bring righteousness, equity, faithfulness and peacefulness between wolves, lambs, leopards, kids, calves, fatlings, children and lions (Isa. 11.6–9; 65.25–6). The most striking affirmation of commonality between human beings and other animals in the biblical canon comes from Ecclesiastes:

> I said in my heart with regard to human beings that God is testing them to show that they are but animals. For the fate of human beings and the fate of animals is the same; as one dies, so dies the other. They all have the same breath, and humans have no advantage over the animals; for all is vanity. All go to one place; all are from the dust, and all turn to dust again. Who knows whether the human spirit goes upward and the spirit of animals goes downward to the earth? (Eccl. 3.18–21)[48]

---

[48] Eric Christianson collects an interesting range of responses to this text (Eric S. Christianson, *Ecclesiastes Through the Centuries* (Oxford: Blackwell, (2007)), 177–9. Augustine considers the text several times. In *On the Soul and its Origin* and in *City of God* he cites Eccl. 3.21 as evidence that non-human animals have souls just as human beings do, though he is clear in both texts that the souls of other animals do not have understanding (Augustine, 'A Treatise on the Soul and its Origin', in Philip Schaff (ed.), *A Select Library of Nicene and Post-Nicene Fathers of the Christian Church. First Series*, vol. 5, ed. Philip Schaff (Edinburgh: T & T Clark, 1994), 4.37; Augustine, *The City of God Against the Pagans*, trans. R. W. Dyson (Cambridge:

The affirmation of a life shared between humans and other animals is also present in New Testament texts. Jesus calls Peter, Andrew, James and John away from their fishing boats to fish for people (Mt. 4.18–21 ‖ Mk. 1.16–20). In the Sermon on the Mount he commends as examples of care-free recipients of God's providence the birds of the air and lilies of the field (Mt. 6.25–30 ‖ Lk. 12.24–28). Later he tells his disciples that even though two sparrows are sold for a penny, not one falls to the ground apart from their Father (Mt. 10.31 ‖ Lk. 12.6–7). In response to a disciple's commitment to follow him, Jesus replies that foxes have holes and birds have nests, but the Son of Man has nowhere to lay his head (Mt. 8.20 ‖ Lk. 9.58). Jesus has compassion on the people who are harassed and helpless like sheep without a shepherd (Mt. 9.36 ‖ Mk. 6.34), sends out the twelve as sheep among wolves (Mt. 10.16 ‖ Lk. 10.3) and tells them to be wise as serpents and innocent as doves (Mt. 10.16). Jesus calls all who have heavy burdens to accept instead his yoke, which is light (Mt. 11.28–30). In debating with the Pharisees about sabbath law, Jesus reminds them that they would save a lamb that had fallen into a pit on the sabbath (Mt. 12.11–12). In his encounter with the Canaanite woman, Jesus tells her he was sent to the lost sheep of Israel and that it is not fair to give the children's food to the dogs; she responds that even dogs eat the crumbs under their master's table (Mt. 15.24–7 ‖ Mk. 7.27–8). In the parable of the lost sheep, Jesus counts on his hearers knowing that a shepherd would leave 99 sheep to search for the lost one, and rejoicing over it more than all the others that did not go astray (Mt. 18.12–14 ‖ Lk. 15.4–7). He mourns over the city of Jerusalem, saying that he longed to gather her children together as a hen gathers her brood under her wings (Mt. 23.37). After Jesus has shared bread and wine at the Passover meal, he recalls the prophecy of Zechariah that the shepherd will be struck and the sheep scattered (Mt. 26.31 ‖ Mk. 14.27; Zech. 13.7). Mark's gospel pictures kingdom of God as a mustard seed that grows into a shrub with large branches so that the birds of the air can make nests in its shade (Mk. 4.31–2 ‖ Lk. 13.19). In Luke's gospel Joseph and Mary and their new baby share the place of animals for the nativity, the Christ child is laid in a feeding trough for cattle and the shepherds are keeping watch over their flock when told by the angels of the Christ child (Lk. 2.8–12). After the teaching about not worrying about food or clothing, Jesus says 'Do not be afraid, little flock' (Lk. 12.32). Luke records a debate with the leader of the

Cambridge University Press, 1998), 13.24). Gregory the Great interprets the text as a voicing of an opinion based on suspicion, corrected by the conclusion based in reason of Eccl. 6.8, 'What has the wise man more that the fool', which Gregory interprets as showing that the wise man has an advantage over the fool and the beast (Gregory the Great, *Saint Gregory the Great: Dialogues*, Fathers of the Church, vol. 39, trans. O. J. Zimmerman (Washington, DC: Catholic University of America, 1959), 195).

synagogue objecting to a healing on the Sabbath: Jesus tells him that everyone unties an ox or donkey from the manger on the Sabbath to lead it to water (Lk. 13.15). He also includes the debate with the lawyers and Pharisees, and where Matthew's account pictured a sheep in a pit, Luke's features a child or an ox fallen in a well (Lk. 14.5). Finally, in the book of Revelation, the four creatures that lead the praises of God are likened to a lion, an ox, a human being and an eagle, echoing Ezekiel's vision (Rev. 4.6–11; 5.11–14; Ezek. 1.5–10), and surround 'a lamb standing as if it had been slaughtered' (Rev. 5.6).

This brief biblical survey makes clear the extent to which human beings and other animals are thought of together in Christian scripture. Together they are given life by their creator as fleshly creatures made of dust and inspired by the breath of life, together they are given a common table in Eden and beyond, together they experience the fragility of mortal life, together they are the objects of God's providential care, together they are given consideration under the law of Israel and its Rabbinic interpreters, together they are subject to God's judgement and blessing, together they are called to praise their maker and together they gather around God's throne in the new creation. Obviously there are great differences between the animals God has made, and the question of the adequate rendering of this difference is discussed in the next chapter, but before taking the familiar step in the philosophical and theological tradition to examine these differences, it is important to pause on this less familiar step of appreciating the common life of animals of all kinds before God. To fail to do so would be to underestimate the importance of our determination as one among God's many animal creatures, who live and move and have their being in God.[49]

The Vocation of Animals

In commentary on God's blessing of the fish and birds (Gen. 1.22), Calvin comments that it seems futile for God to speak to these creatures. He answers that 'this mode of speaking was no other than that which might be understood' and that the experiment of God addressing the creatures in this way shows that 'the force of the word which was addressed to the fishes was not transient, but rather, being infused into their nature, has taken root, and constantly bears fruit'.[50] Barth considers the address indirect, in contrast to the direct address to

[49] The words, familiar from Paul's address to the Athenians in Acts 17.28, clearly have the potential to name a distinctive mode of live that animals in particular share before God.
[50] John Calvin, *Genesis*, 90.

human beings, but recognizes that other animals are the objects of direct address when God condemns the serpent to crawl on its belly (Gen. 3.14), when the ravens are commanded to provide food for Elijah (1 Kgs 17.4), when the fish is commanded to spew out Jonah (Jon. 2.11), when the angel in Revelation calls the birds to feast on the flesh of the defeated armies (Rev. 19.17) and when the beasts, cattle, creeping things and birds are summoned to praise God in Psalm 148 (Ps. 148.10).[51] To this list of texts we could add the Psalmist's request to God to rebuke the wild beasts that live in the reeds (Ps. 68.30), the word Mortal is given in Ezekiel to call the birds of every kind and the wild beasts to feast, taken up in Revelation 19 (Ezek. 39.17–20; Rev. 19.17), and the words of Joel reassuring the beasts of the field that they need not be afraid (Joel 2.22). Alongside the call to praise of Psalm 148, we should note the prophecy of Psalm 145 that all the Lord's works will give thanks and the calls of Psalms 66 and 98 for 'all the earth' to praise the Lord (Ps. 66.1–4; 98.4–8). When Israel is restored by God, Isaiah prophesies that the jackals and ostriches will honour the Lord for providing waters in the wilderness and rivers in the desert (Isa. 43.20). In the vision of the heavenly praise of God in Revelation, the elders are called to worship by the four living creatures of Ezekiel's vision: one like a lion, the second like an ox, the third with a face like a human face and the fourth like a flying eagle (Ezek. 1.5–10; Rev. 4.6–11; 5.11–14), suggesting that the praise of all animals continues in the new creation. Even more striking in this context are God's words to Noah after the flood: a reckoning will be demanded for the lifeblood of Noah and his descendants from non-human and human animals (Gen. 9.5) and the eternal covenant God establishes never again to destroy all flesh is emphatically and repeatedly not only with Noah but with every living creature of all flesh (Gen. 9.9–17). It is clear from these texts that it is not only human animals that are addressed by God and called to live lives in response to God.

There are also many other places where animals play a role in fulfilling God's purposes without the need for direct address. The raven and dove let the

[51] Barth, *CD* III/1, 174. Later in this volume, Barth warns that 'we must not maintain that we … know a universal, all-inclusive command addressed to all creatures and therefore valid for us' because it would involve 'an encroachment of naturalism and evolutionism which we have no reason to support' (Barth, *CD* III/4, 333; see also Andrew Linzey's critique of this Barthian position in Andrew Linzey. 'The Neglected Creature: The Doctrine of the Non-Human Creation and its Relationship with the Human Creation in the Thought of Karl Barth', PhD thesis. University of London, 1986, 308). My argument in this chapter is that there are biblical grounds for considering seriously God's commands to other animals and their vocation before God. This does not mean that he is wrong that there is 'universal, all-inclusive command addressed to all creatures and therefore valid for us', but it does mean that other animals are addressed by God as well as human ones.

inhabitants of the ark know when the waters have receded (Gen. 8.6–12). A ram caught in a thicket is God's means of saving Isaac (Gen. 22.13) and the huge apparatus of animal sacrifice within Israelite ritual is similarly a contribution made by non-human animals towards the religious life of Israel.[52] Many kinds of animals are God's instruments in plaguing Egypt (Exod. 7–9); Balaam's donkey sees the angel long before Balaam does and warns him, despite being beaten for its trouble (Num. 22.20–33); she-bears punish the boys taunting Elisha (2 Kgs 2.23–4); the Lord sends lions among those sent to replace the Israelites taken from Samaria (2 Kgs 17.25–6); Jeremiah is told to assemble all the wild animals to devour Israel (Jer. 12.8–9; cf. 15.3); the lions to which Daniel and his fellow Israelites are thrown have their mouths shut by angels. In the New Testament Jesus lives 'with the wild beasts' when in the wilderness (Mk 1.13);[53] pigs are his means of exorcising demoniacs (Mt. 8.28–32 and par.); he uses fish to feed the crowds (Mt. 14.19–21; 16.34–7 and par.) and pay his temple tax (Mt. 17.24–7); he rides on a colt into Jerusalem (Mt. 21.1–7 and par.); the crow of a cock is the sign he has been betrayed by Peter (Mt. 26.74–5 and par.); he guides fishermen to shoals of fish and cooks them for breakfast (Jn 21.1–13).

The occasions animals are held up as examples for the people of God to emulate are further evidence of the biblical recognition of commonality between humans and other animals in how creaturely life is to be lived. In commentary on Jesus' teaching about emulating the birds of the field and the lilies of the field in the Sermon on the Mount, Richard Bauckham observes that his argument only makes sense insofar as we recognize ourselves to be fellow creatures, dependent on the same creator.[54] This theme of other animals as positive exemplars is not unique to Jesus' teaching: Job tells his tormentors to turn to the beasts, birds, plants and fish for wisdom concerning the ways of the God in whose hand 'is the life of every living thing and the breath of every

---

[52] Among the many places regulations are set out for sacrificing non-human animals are Lev. 1, 3–5, 6–9, 14–16, 22–3; Num. 6–8, 15, 18–19, 28–9. Andrew Linzey argues that the sacrificial system affirmed the value of animal creation (Linzey, 'Neglected Creature', 44–5). On this question see also J. W. Rogerson, 'What Was the Meaning of Animal Sacrifice?', in Andrew Linzey and Dorothy Yamamoto (eds), *Animals on the Agenda: Questions About Animals for Theology and Ethics* (London: SCM, 1998) and Kimberley C. Patton, 'Animal Sacrifice: Metaphysics of the Sublimated Victim', in Paul Waldau and Kimberley C. Patton (eds), *A Communion of Subjects: Animals in Religion, Science, and Ethics* (New York: Columbia University Press, 2006).

[53] This text is discussed in Richard Bauckham, 'Jesus and the Wild Animals (Mark 1:13): A Christological Image for an Ecological Age', in Joel B. Green and Max Turner (eds), *Jesus of Nazareth: Lord and Christ (Essays on the Historical Jesus and New Testament Christology)* (Grand Rapids, MI: Eerdmans, 1994).

[54] Richard Bauckham, 'Reading the Sermon on the Mount in an Age of Ecological Catastrophe', *Studies in Christian Ethics* 22: 1 (2009), 83.

human being' (Job 12.7–10), the Proverbs praise ants, hyraxes, locusts, lizards, lions, cockerels and billy goats (Prov. 6.6–8; 30.24–31), Isaiah praises oxen and donkeys (Isa. 1.3),[55] Jeremiah is impressed by storks, turtledoves, swallows and cranes (Jer. 8.7) and Lamentations approves of the maternal care of jackals (Lam. 4.3). In common with other animals, therefore, humans share not only particular characteristics, but a vocation to live as creatures in a particular animal way.

The Place of Animal Creatures before God

The aim of this chapter has been to make a biblical and theological case that animals have a particular place before God – in relationship to one another and in relationship to other creatures – that merits attention. To be a creature of God is one thing. To be a living creature of God is another. And to be the kind of living creature of God that is an animal is still another, and means that animals have much in common. Animals find themselves located in a particular place within the created order, are subject to the same dependency on other living organisms making their lives vulnerable in particular ways, are capable of kinds of independent action that distinguishes them from other creatures and are therefore able to live in response to their creator in ways not open to other creatures. To be an animal creature of God, therefore, is to be in a particular place before God and the theological characteristics of this place deserve investigation.

This animal place before God needs securing on two sides. On one side it is vulnerable to humans seeking to absent themselves from it, denying that they belong with other fleshy creatures with the breath of life. This has resulted in a radical impoverishment of our vision of the place of animals before God, because what is animal has come to be understood as the opposite to all that is characteristically human: animals on this account are irrational, driven by instinct, unintelligent, amoral, unsophisticated, uncreative, poor in relationality and lacking in the ability to transform their environment. To rehearse this list in the context of the biblical, theological and scientific accounts of animals presented in this chapter is hopefully already to make clear the wild inaccuracy and injustice of such views. As I will argue in more detail in the next chapter, such characterizations of animals result not from carefully attending to their particularity, but from using them collectively as a rhetorical trope in order to

---

[55] For a survey of Patristic interpreters on this text, see Steven A. McKinion and Thomas C. Oden (eds), *Isaiah 1–39*, Ancient Christian Commentary on Scripture, vol. X (Downers Grove, IL: IVP, 2004), 1–2.

prop up particular understandings of human nature. If instead we are prepared to acknowledge what humans have in common with other animal creatures, we are freed to see other animals for what they are, in all their particularity and diversity. To recognize that humans are animals too is not to deny the characteristics that make us a particular animal: humans possess – like all other animals – a unique and distinctive combination of capacities and attributes that make us what we are. To conceive of our place as separate to that of all other animals, however, risks ignoring key aspects of what it means to be human that intersect with what it means to be animal. It is therefore important to recognize that humans dwell in the place of animals before God, though they occupy a distinctive territory within it.

On the other side, the place of animals needs securing against the rush to the totality of living things or creatures. As I noted in the Introduction, recognizing the particularity of what it means to be animal means resisting shifting directly from an anthropocentric perspective to one that values creatures only insofar as they are part of ecosystems. This chapter suggests a biblical and theological grounding for the view that it makes sense to pause with animals, human and non-human, and recognize what distinguishes them from other creatures in terms of their modes of life, dependence on other creatures, capacity for action and vocation before God. If there are good theological reasons for recognizing the ways in which humans and other animals stand in the same place before God, these are also good reasons to make animal life the object of theological attention, rather than merely part of a wider environment.

With the place of animals identified and secured theologically in this way, the next task is a theological investigation of the diversity of the creatures that occupy this space. It is with this task that the next chapter is concerned.

Chapter 3

CREATURELY DIFFERENCE

The recognition that all animals are creatures of one creator with particular shared vulnerabilities and capabilities enables an appreciation of their commonality. This was the task of the previous chapter. With this recognition in place, we have a context in which we may attend to the myriad kinds of such creatures and reflect on the significance of their differences. How these differences are rendered theologically is crucial for how we think about animals. Most fundamentally, as we shall see, the question of how humans differ from other animals has been the subject of extended and diverse philosophical and theological speculation, although this speculation has often been inattentive to the characteristics of other animals and more interested in anthropology than zoology. Of course, to critique ways in which the boundary between human and non-human animals has been construed is not to deny that it is only meaningful to speak of human beings at all because of the differences between ourselves and other animals. This chapter argues, however, that we need to speak of human uniqueness with considerably more care and sophistication than has commonly been the case. Beyond this human/non-human boundary, however, the way humans have chosen to put other animals in their place, through ordering and classification, needs to be subjected to theological examination. There seems to be a powerful residual influence of schema such as the Great Chain of Being, where all creatures are lined up in an order representing some criterion of value. Theologians have particular reason to be sceptical of such attempts to determine the value of creatures to their creator and to concern themselves with what can be said appropriately in theological terms regarding creaturely difference.

Revelling in Diversity

At the beginning of the previous chapter, I noted Colin Gunton's view that Basil of Caesarea was one of the first theologians to affirm the ontological homogeneity of creation – that all creatures have the same basic status as creatures of God. In Basil's *Hexaemeron*, we also find one of the most striking theological affirmations of the variety among creatures. In response to Aristotle's account of animals, and informed by his own experience, Basil's enthusiasm concerning the wondrous diversity of the animal creation is apparent through many of the sermons and the pains he took to expound God's work in creating other-than-human animals seems to have left little time for the human kind.[1] Following the days of creation, Basil devotes his seventh homily to the creatures of the sea:

> Of one kind are those which are called testaceans, such as mussels, scallops, sea snails, conchs, and numberless varieties of bivalves. Again, another kind besides these are the fish named crustaceans: crayfish, crabs, and all similar to them. Still another kind are the so-called soft fish, whose flesh is tender and loose: polyps, cuttlefish, and those like them. And among these, again, there are innumerable varieties. In fact, there are weevers, and lampreys, and eels, which are produced in the muddy rivers and swamps, and which resemble in their nature venomous animals more than fish. Another class is that of ovipara, and another, that of vivipara. The sharks and the dogfish and, in general, the cartilaginous fish are vivipara. And of the cetaceans the majority are vivipara, as dolphins and seals; these are said to readmit and hide in their belly the cubs, while still young, whenever they have for some reason or other been startled.[2]

Basil 'passes over the deceitfulness and trickery of the octopus'[3] but is impressed by the way nature allots to each creature its own habitat suited to its needs[4] and by the wonders of the great migrations of fish, which he has witnessed himself.[5] He concludes the homily on grounds of the weakness of his body and the lateness of the hour, but regrets the many wonders he is thereby forced to leave out.[6]

In his eighth homily, Basil begins to consider the creation of land animals, before realizing that he has left out the winged creatures. He is again impressed by their variety:

---

[1] On Basil's sources for the *Hexaemeron*, see Robert McQueen Grant, *Early Christians and Animals* (London: Routledge, 1999), 77 and David Runia, *Philo in Early Christian Literature* (Assen, the Netherlands; Minneapolis, MN: Van Gorcum; Fortress, 1993), 237. Basil's brother, Gregory of Nyssa, opens his treatise 'On the Making of Man' with the observation that it aims to supplement what is lacking in Basil's *Hexaemeron* (Gregory of Nyssa, 'On the Making of Man'.

[2] Basil, 'Hexaemeron', Homily 7, §2.

[3] Basil, 'Hexaemeron', Homily 7, §3.

[4] Basil, 'Hexaemeron', Homily 7, §4.

[5] Basil, 'Hexaemeron', Homily 7, §5.

[6] Basil, 'Hexaemeron', Homily 7, §6.

There are also numberless varieties of species among the birds, and if one will go through these varieties in the same manner as we applied ourselves in part to the examination of the fish, he will find one name for the winged creatures but numberless variations among them in size and form and color; also an indescribably great difference among them in regard to their lives, their actions, and their customs. In fact, some have already tried to use coined names, so that the characteristic of each kind might be known through the unaccustomed and strange name as if through a certain brand. Some they called Schizoptera, as the eagles; others, Dermoptera, as the bats; others, Ptilota, as the wasps; and others, Coleoptera, as the beetles and the insects which, generated in certain chests and clothes, split their shell and free themselves for flight.[7]

Basil discusses their behaviour, and is again impressed by the differences in their actions and their lives, attending to the ingenuity and wisdom of the honey bee, the way cranes take turns as night sentries, the defensive alliance between storks and crows which is 'not far from reasoning intelligence' the inventiveness of swallows building nests, among many others.[8] Again, he stops because he perceives that his speech 'is going beyond due limits' but he observes 'when I take into consideration the variety of the wisdom manifested in the works of creation, I acknowledge that I have not even begun my explanation'.[9] In the ninth homily, he takes up the land animals again. He considers that brute beasts share in a single irrational soul, but are distinguished by their characteristics:

The ox is steadfast, the ass sluggish; the horse burns with desire for the mare; the wolf is untamable and the fox crafty; the deer is timid, the ant industrious; the dog is grateful and constant in friendship. As each animal was created he brought with him a distinctive characteristic of nature. Courage was brought forth with the lion, also the tendency to a solitary life and an unsocial attitude toward those of his kind … The leopard is violent and impetuous in attack. He has a body fitted for agility and lightness in accord with the movements of his spirit. The bear is sluggish and his ways peculiar to himself, treacherous and deeply secretive.[10]

We need not accept the accuracy of Basil's attribution of moral characteristics to particular animals in order to appreciate the passage as further evidence

[7] Basil, 'Hexaemeron', Homily 8, §3.
[8] Basil, 'Hexaemeron', Homily 8, §§4–8.
[9] Basil, 'Hexaemeron', Homily 8, §8.
[10] Basil, 'Hexaemeron', Homily 9, §3.

of a vivid appreciation of the diversity among the creatures of the land. His attribution of moral characteristics to particular animals has antecedents in Aesop's Fables and the second century *Physiologus*, and anticipates the later development of the bestiary tradition.[11] Basil calls on his congregation to learn that the solicitude of the creator extends to all things and that if even brute beasts can take care of their lives through rational prudence, so should human beings have forethought for the salvation of their souls.[12] Basil wonders at the cleverness and gratitude of dogs, the match between how prolific animals are in reproduction and how easily they are caught, the sharp teeth of carnivorous animals and the many stomachs of herbivores, the length of the camel's neck to allow it to reach down to the ground and the shortness of the necks of lions and tigers who do not have to bend down, and the way the elephant's trunk allows it to reach the ground without the need for a neck to support its huge head. Even the mouse and scorpion show the craft of their creator.[13] After these reflections, Basil seems to recollect himself again, and observes 'I have long been asked explanations about the creation of men'. Accordingly, he discusses the creation of human beings in the image of God briefly in the last few pages of the ninth and final homily.[14]

Basil's homilies convey an awestruck awareness of the astonishing diversity among the creatures of God whose ways he describes. The works of God, he suggests, are more various and more strange than we generally realize. Alongside the ontological homogeneity of God's creatures, we also learn from Basil therefore, of their magnificent variety. God has made an abundance of creatures that are unlike us and unlike each other. Recognizing what animals, human and other-than-human, have in common is not an obstacle to a vivid appreciation of their difference.

Thomas Aquinas cites Basil's *Hexaemeron* appreciatively as making clear the different gradations of perfection of land and sea creatures, although he is critical of Basil's view that fish do not have memory. Aquinas considers the question of the cause of the distinctions between creatures in both the *Summa theologica* and the *Summa contra gentiles*. In the *Summa theologica* he considers arguments that the distinction of things must have some cause apart from God: since God is one and naturally therefore creates unity, since God's

---

[11] On the *Physiologus*, see Grant, *Early Christians and Animals*, 52–72. Grant finds no evidence of the *Physiologus* in Basil's homilies, which he attributes to Basil's dislike of allegory (p. 77). On the development of the bestiary tradition, see the Introduction in Colin Clair, *Unnatural History: An Illustrated Bestiary* (London; New York; Toronto: Abelard-Schuman, 1967).

[12] Basil, 'Hexaemeron', Homily 9, §3.

[13] Basil, 'Hexaemeron', Homily 9, §§4–5.

[14] Basil, 'Hexaemeron', Homily 9, §6.

intention in creation was unitary and since the end of creation is the unitary one of the divine goodness. In response, Aquinas cites God's division of light from darkness and God's division of the waters in Genesis 1, and dismisses arguments that distinction in creation originates either in matter itself or the actions of agents other than God. As a result of the inadequacies of such arguments, he reasons that 'we must say that the distinction and multitude of things come from the intention of the first agent, who is God'.[15] Aquinas goes further, however, than merely attributing the creation of distinction to God by a process of elimination: he also sees particular value in a diverse creation:

> For He brought things into being so that His goodness might be communicated to creatures and be represented by them, and because His goodness could not be adequately represented by one creature alone, He produced many and diverse creatures, that what was wanting to one in the representation of the divine goodness might be supplied by another. For goodness, which in God is simple and uniform, in creatures is manifold and divided; and hence the whole universe together participates in the divine goodness more perfectly, and represents it better than any single creature whatever.[16]

In the following article on whether the inequality of things is from God, Aquinas considers the view of Origen that originally God created only equal rational agents, and that inequality between them arose from their free decisions to turn towards or away from God. He refutes this position on the grounds that it would mean that all bodily creatures are the effects of the punishment of sin rather than the communication of the goodness of God.[17] In the *Summa contra gentiles*, Aquinas considers and rejects a wider range of possible causes of distinction: chance, matter, multiple or opposing secondary agents, the order of secondary agents, a secondary agent introducing forms into matter and the merits or demerits of rational agents.[18] The last of these addresses Origen's argument and, again, here Aquinas shows an appreciation of a diverse creation:

> For among effects, the better a thing is, the more does it obtain precedence in the intention of the agent. Now the greatest good in things created is the perfection of the universe, consisting in the order of distinct

[15] Aquinas, *Summa Theologica*, 1.47.1.
[16] Aquinas, *Summa Theologica*, 1.47.1.
[17] Aquinas, *Summa Theologica*, 1.47.2.
[18] Saint Thomas Aquinas, *Summa Contra Gentiles*, trans. English Dominican Fathers (London: Burns Oates & Washbourne, 1923), 2.39–44.

things: because in all things the perfection of the whole takes precedence
of the perfection of each part. Wherefore the diversity of things results
from the principal intention of the first agent, and not from a diversity
of merits.[19]

For Aquinas, therefore, the Genesis 1 creation narrative can only be read as
affirming that the diversity of creatures is a deliberate choice by God in order
to make creation more perfect than it would be if it only contained one kind of
creature or fewer kinds of creatures.

These theological appreciations of the diversity of creation have clear
antecedents in biblical creation narratives (e.g. Gen. 1; Job 38–41; Ps. 104).
In Genesis 1, the emphasis on the various kinds of life is remarkable: with
every recorded act of creation of life, 'every kind' is repeated, celebrating the
astonishing breadth of God's creative act. Of the many examples taking up the
theme later in the Christian tradition, we may note Saint Francis's 'The Song
of Brother Sun' and the nineteenth-century natural theology of William Paley
and William Kirby.[20] Kirby begins his 1830 contribution to the Bridgewater
Treatises with the words: 'In no part of creation are the POWER, WISDOM and
GOODNESS, of its beneficent and almighty Author more signally conspicuous
than in the various animals that inhabit and enliven our globe.'[21] He comments
on the 'infinite diversity of their forms and organs' and observes that if God
had created only a pair of creatures 'a void would soon be felt, something
more would seem wanting to animate the otherwise lovely scene'.[22] There is
something theologically striking about the sheer abundance of differentiation
between creatures.

[19] Aquinas, *Summa Contra Gentiles*, 2.44.
[20] St Francis of Assisi, *The Little Flowers of Saint Francis*, trans. L. Sherley-Price
(Harmondsworth, Middlesex: Penguin, 1959), 199–200; William Paley, *Natural
Theology, or, Evidences of the Existence and Attributes of the Deity: Collected
From the Appearances of Nature* (London: C. J. G. and F. Rivington, 1830); William
Kirby, *On the History, Habits and Instincts of Animals*, The Bridgewater Treatises
on the Power and Wisdom of God as Manifested in the Creation, vol. VII (London:
Pickering, 1835).
[21] Kirby, *History, Habits and Instincts*, 1.
[22] Kirby, *History, Habits and Instincts*, 1, 3.

Classifying Creatures

In Genesis 2.19–20 the beasts and the birds God has formed from the earth are brought before Adam 'to see what he would call them' and Adam names the cattle, birds and beasts. Adam's action has often been interpreted as an indication of power over other creatures, but the giving of a name to each animal rather suggests attention to its particularity.[23] Adam's attempt to comprehend the fellow creatures he found about him has been echoed throughout human history by attempts to order creaturely diversity. Jorge Luis Borges quotes a wonderful – if historically dubious – system of classification from an ancient Chinese encyclopaedia:

> On those remote pages it is written that animals are divided into (a) those that belong to the Emperor, (b) embalmed ones, (c) those that are trained, (d) suckling pigs, (e) mermaids, (f) fabulous ones, (g) stray dogs, (h) those that are included in this classification, (i) those that tremble as if they were

[23] In his early nineteenth-century commentary, Matthew Henry described the naming as a proof of Adam's knowledge and power (Matthew Henry, *An Exposition of the Old and New Testament* (London: Samuel Bagster, 1811), Gen. 1:18–20, §2, II) and Gerhard von Rad also reminds his readers that 'name-giving in the ancient Orient was primarily an exercise of sovereignty, of command' (von Rad, *Genesis*, 83). Older commentaries emphasize Adam's knowledge rather than his power, however: although it is striking that both Luther and Calvin stress Adam's giving of names that suited the animals. Luther writes that Adam 'arrives at such a knowledge of their nature that he can give each one a suitable name that harmonizes with its nature' (Luther, *Luther's Works*, I.119) and Calvin says that God endued the animals with obedience 'so that they would voluntarily offer themselves to the man, in order that he, having closely inspected them, might distinguish them by appropriate names, agreeing with the nature of each' (Calvin, *Genesis*, 132). Claus Westermann states explicitly that 'The meaning is not, as most interpreters think, that the man acquires power over the animals by naming them' and interprets the meaning instead as 'the man gives the animals their names and thereby puts them into a place in his world' (Claus Westermann, *Genesis 1–11: A Commentary*, trans. John J. Scullion, SJ (London: SPCK, 1974), 228). Paul Santmire notes that this naming has often been characterized as an act of dominance, but this interpretation is not required by the context (H. Paul Santmire, 'Partnership With Nature According to the Scriptures: Beyond the Theology of Stewardship', in *Environmental Stewardship: Critical Perspectives, Past and Present*, ed. R. J. Berry (London; New York: T & T Clark, 2006), 263). Erica Fudge notes the link between Adam's naming of animals and dominance over them, though is also aware of reinterpretations of the text that suggest stewardship (Erica Fudge, *Animal* (London: Reaktion, 2002), 13–15). One particular problem is the connection between this naming of the animals and Adam's naming of Eve in verse 23: unless some plausible case can be made for separating the two acts, the establishment of power in relation to animals would also seem to apply to male power over women.

mad, (j) innumerable ones, (k) those drawn with very fine camel's hair brush, (l) others, (m) those that have just broken a flower vase, (n) those that resemble flies from a distance.[24]

Basil's more linear categorization, discussed in the previous section, is clearly indebted to Aristotle's *Historia animalium* and other zoological works, as indeed is almost every biological account since the fourth century BC.[25] Aristotle was aware that the process of classifying animals was not straightforward, however. The *Historia animalium* begins with a list of the various ways animals could be differentiated: by the colour or shape of the parts of their bodies, by their manner of life, their dispositions or their activities. His first example of differentiation by mode of life is to consider water-animals and land-animals. Even in this exemplary introduction, the scale of the task is clear:

> There are two ways of being water-animals. Some both live and feed in the water, take in water and emit it, and are unable to live if deprived of it: this is the case with many of the fishes. Others feed and live in the water; but what they take in is air, not water; and they breed away from the water. Many of these animals are footed: e.g., the otter, the beaver, the crocodile; many are winged, e.g., the shearwater and the plunger; many are footless, e.g., the water-snake. Some animals, although they get their food in the water and cannot live away from it, still take in neither water nor air: examples are the sea-anemones and shellfish. Again, some water-animals live in the sea, some in rivers, some in lakes, some in marshes (e.g., the frog and the newt).[26]

Aristotle proceeds to distinguish kinds of land-animals and animals that live half their lives in the water and half on the land. He then notes that some animals

[24] Jorge Luis Borges, 'The Analytical Language of John Wilkins', in *Other Inquisitions, 1937–52*, trans. Ruth L. C. Simms (Austin, TX: University of Texas Press, 1964), 103. Borges attributes the quotation to the (real) translator Franz Kuhn, but provides no reference to the source, himself raises the possibility that the entry is apocryphal, and is known to make up such references. Michel Foucault discusses the categorization at the beginning of the Preface to Michel Foucault, *The Order of Things: An Archaeology of the Human Sciences* (London; New York: Routledge, 2002), xvi–xvii.
[25] Aristotle, *Historia Animalium*; Aristotle, *Parts of Animals*; Aristotle, *Generation of Animals*, Loeb Classical Library, trans. A. L. Peck (London; Cambridge, MA: William Heinemann; Harvard University Press, 1943). For an account of the significance of Aristotle's work for biology, see Marjorie Glicksman Grene and David J. Depew, *The Philosophy of Biology* (Cambridge: Cambridge University Press, 2004), 1–34.
[26] Aristotle, *Historia Animalium*, 487 a 14–28.

are stationary while others move about; some are gregarious (e.g. human beings, bees, wasps, ants and cranes) while others are solitary; some are carnivorous, some frugivorous, others omnivorous; some build homes, others do not; some are nocturnal, others live by daylight; some are tame, others always wild, others tameable; some make noise, some are mute; some especially prone to copulation, others less prone. As regards disposition, some animals are gentle, others ferocious; some intelligent and timid (e.g. the deer and hare), others mean and scheming (e.g. snakes). Only one sense is common to all animals, according to Aristotle: that of touch. Other differences between animals are those that are blooded and bloodless and those that are two-footed or four-footed. Mode of reproduction is a further distinguishing feature: whether animals are viviparous – giving birth to live young; oviparous – producing eggs hatched outside the body; or larviparous – giving birth to larvae. Some animals are swimmers, others fliers. At the end of this passage Aristotle identifies seven main groups of animals: (1) birds; (2) fishes; (3) cetacea (whales, dolphins, etc.); (4) shellfish; (5) soft-shelled animals such as crayfish, crabs and lobsters; (6) 'softies' such as calamari and cuttlefish; and (7) insects. Of the remaining animals (including human beings), Aristotle comments that there are no large groups.[27]

In his work the *Generation of Animals*, Aristotle adopts the mode of reproduction as his primary classificatory tool, because he considers it to represent a scale of perfection, with viviparous animals the most perfect and larviparous the least.[28] He notes, however, that these categories overlap a good deal with others:

> Bipeds are not all viviparous (birds are oviparous) nor all oviparous (man is viviparous); quadrupeds are not all oviparous (the horse and ox and heaps of others are viviparous), nor all viviparous (lizards and crocodiles and many others are oviparous). Nor does the difference lie even in having or not having feet: some footless animals are viviparous (as vipers, and the Selachia [sharks, etc.]), some are oviparous (as the class of fishes, and the rest of the serpents); and of the footed animals many are oviparous, many viviparous (e.g., the quadrupeds already mentioned). There are footed animals which are internally viviparous (as man), and footless ones also (as the whale and the dolphin). So we find no means here for making a division: the cause of this difference does not lie in any of the organs of locomotion.[29]

---

[27] Aristotle, *Historia Animalium*, 487 a–490 b.
[28] Aristotle, *Generation of Animals*, 733 b.
[29] Aristotle, *Generation of Animals*, 732 b 19–28.

In short, the various classes of differentiation Aristotle identifies are no better than Borges's Chinese ones cited above for reliably identifying divisions between animals. Most modern taxonomists who have reviewed Aristotle's work have pronounced themselves similarly dissatisfied with his classificatory schemes, although others have argued that Aristotle was more interested than compilation than classification, at least in *Historia animalium*.[30]

The Levitical categorization of non-human animals as clean or unclean are another obvious biblical reference point for reflecting on the categorization of animals. In Leviticus 11, the Lord tells Moses and Aaron:

> Any animal that has divided hoofs and is cleft-footed and chews the cud – such you may eat. But among those that chew the cud or have divided hoofs, you shall not eat the following: the camel, for even though it chews the cud, it does not have divided hoofs; it is unclean for you. The rock badger, for even though it chews the cud, it does not have divided hoofs; it is unclean for you. The hare, for even though it chews the cud, it does not have divided hoofs; it is unclean for you. The pig, for even though it has divided hoofs and is cleft-footed, it does not chew the cud; it is unclean for you. (vv. 3–8)

The rules go on to specify that everything in the water with fins and scales may be eaten, but not water creatures without fins and scales. There then follows a list of unclean birds: the eagle, the vulture, the osprey, the buzzard, all kites, all ravens, the ostrich, the nighthawk, the seagull, all hawks, the little owl, the cormorant, the great owl, the water hen, the desert owl, the carrion vulture, the stork, all herons, the hoopoe and the bat (vv. 13–19). Insects with jointed legs above their feet may be eaten (v. 21), but 'all other winged insects that have four feet' are unclean (v. 23), a rule that does not seem very restrictive. Also unclean are animals that walk on their paws (v. 27) and those creatures that swarm upon the earth, such as the weasel, the mouse, the great lizard, the gecko, the land crocodile, the sand lizard and the chameleon (vv. 29–30).

David Grumett and Rachel Muers discuss the wide range of explanations that have been given for these food laws in their monograph *Eating and*

---

[30] See Pierre Pellegrin, *Aristotle's Classification of Animals: Biology and the Conceptual Unity of the Aristotelian Corpus*, trans. Anthony Preus (Berkeley, CA: University of California Press, 1986), 144; A. L. Peck, 'Introduction', in *Historia Animalium*, Loeb Classical Library, trans. A. L. Peck (London; Cambridge, MA: William Heinemann; Harvard University Press, 1965), vi. We should recognize the distance between Aristotle's way of thinking and modern scientific approaches: Pellegrin characterizes his approach as 'etiological moriology' (155) – a concern to discover the causes of the differentiation between parts of animals.

Believing. They note that some scholars provide cosmological and cultural-historical explanations, such as Mary Douglas's argument that the pig was considered abominable because it failed to fit into clear categories. Others consider the food laws arose to establish Israel's national and religious self-definition: pigs were widely offered to pagan gods, or were considered demonic and offered to infernal deities. Grumett and Muers note that the biological explanation that pig carried the disease trichinosis is implausible, on the basis that the disease is not mentioned in the Hebrew Bible and other animals were also sources of the disease. They also note that Douglas revised her earlier position to suggest that the regulation of Israel's use of non-human animals was not a concern for category confusion on a structuralist analysis, but a mark of respect for them.[31] Grumett and Muers note the basic categorization of the Hebrew Bible is on the basis of the spacial location of animals: creatures of the air, the land and the water. Christian traditions extend this to consider land animals, and quadrupeds in particular, as the closest human neighbours and therefore most likely to be avoided in dietary regulation. Among these, a concern for consuming the blood of other animals, grounded in Genesis 9.4, and the original vegetarian diet for all animals specified in Genesis 1.29–30, may have led to the judgement that the animals most obviously unclean are those with characteristics of predation, such as those with paws, and the list of predatory birds.[32] Other Christian traditions discriminate between non-human animals on the basis of various spiritual or moral characteristics attributed to them.[33] If it is the case that other-than-human animals are unclean on the basis of their consumption of other animals, or on the basis of their perceived moral standing, there are clear implications for the question of whether they stand in need of reconciliation and redemption, as discussed in Chapters 5 and 6.

Thomas Aquinas faces difficulties similar to those of Aristotle in discussing the classification of animals in the account of creation in Genesis 1. He reasons that land animals are more perfect than birds and fishes because their limbs are more distinct and their 'higher manner of breeding'.[34] In this emphasis on

---

[31] David Grumett and Rachel Muers, *Theology on the Menu: Asceticism, Meat and Christian Diet* (Abingdon: Routledge, 2010), 73.

[32] Grumett and Muers, *Theology on the Menu*, 77–8.

[33] Grumett and Muers, *Theology on the Menu*, 81–6.

[34] Aquinas, *Summa Theologica*, I.72 *ad*. 1. In reaching this judgement, Aquinas rejects using the supposed lack of memory of fish as a basis for their inferiority, taking Augustine's side against Basil of Caesarea. In his *Hexaemeron* Basil wrote of fish: 'Their sense of hearing is slow and, since they look through the water, they see but dimly; moreover, they have no memory, no imagination, no recognition of the familiar' (Basil, 'Hexaemeron', Homily 8, §1), although in his previous homily Basil had commented on 'a certain wisdom among them' in knowing the place allotted to

mode of reproduction, Aquinas is clearly following Aristotle. Aquinas concedes, however, that this scale of perfection does not reflect intelligence, because some 'imperfect' animals, such as ants and bees, are more intelligent in certain ways. Responding to an objection, Aquinas argues that Genesis 1.24 appropriately describes the earth bringing forth 'living souls' (*animam viventem*), excluding the fish called 'creeping creatures having life' (*reptile animæ viventis*), because fish are 'bodies having some kind of soul in them' (*corpora habentia aliquid animæ*) while land animals have a higher perfection and are 'living souls' (*animam viventem*).[35] Next Aquinas feels obliged to respond to the objection that the same verse makes a category mistake in listing 'cattle', 'beasts' and 'quadrupeds'. He explains, that 'cattle' means domestic animals, i.e. those which are of service to human beings in any way, 'beasts' means 'wild animals, e.g. bears and lions' and 'creeping things' means those animals who have no feet or whose feet are too short to lift them far from the ground, such as lizards and turtles. It is then necessary, Aquinas reasons, to add 'quadrupeds' because of animals such as deer and goats that fall into none of these classes, or perhaps 'quadruped' is used first as the genus followed by the others as species.[36] It seems that classifying animals on the basis of biblical principles is no easier than attempting it in Aristotelian terms.[37]

What is impressive about Aristotle's account is that he is sufficiently committed to giving an account of the many differences between those creatures he is aware of to avoid over-simplistic classificatory schemes that neglect this diversity and complexity. Contrast his account with that of Plato, for example, who explains in the *Timaeus* how male human beings were created, before adding a brief

---

them by their creator (Basil, 'Hexaemeron', Homily 7, §3). Augustine rejected Basil's view of fish memory on the basis of his direct observation: 'the fact that fish have a memory is beyond question). I myself have observed this fact, and anyone who has the occasion and the desire may do likewise. There is at Bulla Regia a large fountain abundantly stocked with fish. Whenever an object is thrown into the pond by a person above, the fish carry it off as they swim by or tear it apart in their struggle to possess it. Having become used to being fed in this way, whenever people walk by the edge of the fountain, the fish will swim in schools back and forth alongside of them, waiting for a morsel from those whose presence they perceive' (Augustine, *The Literal Meaning of Genesis*, Ancient Christian Writers, trans. John Hammond Taylor, SJ (New York: Mahwah, NJ: Paulist Press, 1982), bk 3 ch. 8).

[35] Aquinas, *Summa Theologica*, 172.1 *ad.* 1.

[36] Aquinas, *Summa Theologica*, 1.72.1 *ad.* 2.

[37] A more simple and successful categorization of animals on the basis of Genesis 1:20–24 is provided by John McKeown, who suggests 'swimmers, flyers, walkers and crawlers' (John McKeown. 'An Ecologically Motivated Critique of Modern Natalist and Cornucopian Reception of Genesis 1:28a, "Be Fruitful and Multiply", and Other Biblical "Fertility" Texts, as a Mandate for Unlimited Reproduction and Population Growth'. PhD thesis. University of Chester, 2011).

footnote concerning how other living things came to be from this first generation of men. Those who lived lives of cowardice or injustice were reborn as
women, Plato reports; those who were innocent but simple-minded and thought
that sight provided the best guide to truth gave rise to birds; those who had no
philosophy and therefore did not look up to the heavens became four-footed
land animals bowed down to the earth or, in the case of the most foolish, lost
their legs entirely and crawled on the earth; and those who were most senseless
and ignorant were made aquatic creatures not worthy of breathing the pure
medium of air.[38] In one of Augustine's responses to the Manichees, he seems to
be responding to a still simpler classification of animals as 'useful to us, or pernicious or superfluous'. In response to Manichean questions about why God made
the latter two categories, Augustine responds that the pernicious ones are 'either
to punish us or to put us through our paces or to frighten us, so that instead of
loving and desiring this life, subject to so many dangers and trials, we should
set our hearts on another better one' and of the superfluous ones we should be
thankful they do no harm rather than complaining that they are no use.[39]

One influential attempt to provide a more systematic account of the differences between animals and all other beings was the Neo-Platonic idea of a
chain of being stretching from God at the height to the most insignificant
aspects of material reality. In his influential study, Arthur Lovejoy characterizes
two guiding principles of this view of the world.[40] The principle of plenitude
requires that every possible configuration of being exists in the universe, since
otherwise a perfect God would have created a less than perfect universe. The
principle of continuity, which can be deduced from it, requires that every
possible gradation of being exists in the universe, because if there were some
theoretically possible intermediate type between two species, there would be a
gap in the universe and the universe would not be 'full'.[41] These principles of
plenitude and continuity are supplemented by what Lovejoy terms the principle
of 'unilinear gradation', which supposes that all things may be ordered in a line
with God at one end and nothingness at the other.[42] While Plato's thought was

---

[38] Plato, *Timaeus*, 90 e–92 b.

[39] Augustine, *On Genesis: On Genesis: A Refutation of the Manichees, Unfinished
Literal Commentary on Genesis, the Literal Meaning of Genesis*, The Works of Saint
Augustine, ed. John E. Rotelle, trans. Edmund Hill, OP (New York: New City Press,
2002), bk 1, ch. 16, §26.

[40] Arthur O. Lovejoy, *The Great Chain of Being: A Study of the History of an Idea*
(Cambridge, MA: Harvard University Press, 1942). For a discussion of the reception
of Lovejoy's work, see Daniel J. Wilson, 'Lovejoy's the Great Chain of Being After
Fifty Years', *Journal of the History of Ideas* 41: 2 (1980).

[41] Lovejoy, *Great Chain of Being*, 58.

[42] Lovejoy, *Great Chain of Being*, 59.

the dominant root for this way of seeing reality, Aristotle also proposed that all things could be graded in order of their being infected with potentiality.[43] Lovejoy argues that the scheme was only fully organized in Neoplatonism.[44] The framework was remarkably resilient: Lovejoy cites lines from the sixteenth-century poet George Herbert, showing embracing the Chain of Being ideas, and these famous lines from Pope in the seventeenth century:

> Vast chain of being! which from God began,
> Natures aethereal, human, angel, man,
> Beast, bird, fish, insect, what no eye can see,
> No glass can reach; from Infinite to thee,
> From thee to nothing. – On superior pow'rs
> Were we to press, inferior might on ours;
> Or in the full creation might leave a void,
> Where, one step broken, the great scale's destroyed;
> From Nature's chain whatever link you strike,
> Tenth, or ten thousandth, breaks the chain alike.[45]

There are attractive features of the world-view of the Great Chain of Being from the point of view of seeking a theological account of animals. Theologians have been drawn to it as an expression of God's harmonious and providential ordering of creation. The unsubstitutability of every created being is striking: each particular creature exists because the universe would be incomplete without it and because if it were absent, there would be a break in the chain. The Great Chain also emphasizes the continuity and proximity between different creatures: every creature must be next to another like to it in almost every respect, including human beings.[46] This world-view is also unattractive in significant respects, however. Positing a hierarchical structure of creation provided the perfect rationale for a hierarchy within human society, so that not only non-human animals but women, slaves and foreigners were kept in their place.[47] In addition, the Jewish and Christian creation narrative does not

---

[43] Lovejoy, *Great Chain of Being*, 59, citing David Ross, *Aristotle*, 6th edn (London: Routledge, 1995), 183.

[44] Lovejoy, *Great Chain of Being*, 61.

[45] Alexander Pope, 'Essay on Man', VIII, cited in Lovejoy, *Great Chain of Being*, 60.

[46] Rod Preece and David Fraser note that it is wrong to think of the Great Chain of Being primarily as a tool of oppression, since many writers used it to emphasize the proximity between humans and other animals (Rod Preece and David Fraser, 'The Status of Animals in Biblical and Christian Thought: A Study in Colliding Values', *Society and Animals* 8: 1 (2000), 251–2).

[47] On the early development of these trends in Greek thought, see Page duBois, *Centaurs*

allow for some creatures being more distant from God than others: all were spoken into being, and, as Chapter 2 argued, all animals have in common that they are inspired by the God's breath and intimately and directly cared for by their creator. Such weighing of the attractiveness of the thought world of the Great Chain of Being is beside the point, however, given the weighty theological reasons for rejecting it. Primary among these is that the principle of plenitude threatens to make both God's work of creation and the detail of what is created a necessity rather than the free act of God. If a perfect God must give rise to a perfect universe, it seems we are in danger of not being able to conceive of a God that did not create, so that creation is no longer a matter of God's gracious initiative. Even more strikingly, if the universe created by a perfect God must contain every possible configuration of being, then God had no freedom in determining the nature of the universe.[48] Alongside such theological blocks to adopting the Great Chain of Being, there are other issues of plausibility. Lovejoy notes that the temporal dimension of the world is fatal to Great Chain arguments:[49] any change in the universe means either that the principle of plenitude was not satisfied before the change, or was no longer following it. We could imagine a version of the principle of plenitude that dealt with this by responding that in a perfect universe every kind of being would exist at some point in time, but even this version would fail against what we know of the limited range of the space of possible creaturely life that actual creatures inhabit.[50] For all these reasons, theology must reject the principle of plenitude identified by Lovejoy and with it the principle of continuity.

and Amazons: Women and the Pre-History of the Great Chain of Being (Ann Arbor, MI: University of Michigan Press, 1982). DuBois argues that Lovejoy and others treat Plato and Aristotle as 'the absolute origin of thought on various topics', whereas in fact they come at the end of a long debate in which democracy had been rejected by conservative philosophers (11).

[48] Brian Davies argues that Aquinas made a radical break from emanationist theories for these reasons (Brian Davies, *The Thought of Thomas Aquinas* (Oxford: Oxford University Press, 1992), 144–8). Edward Mahoney notes, contra Lovejoy, that Aquinas and others set out the case for the ordering of creatures notwithstanding their infinite distance from God (Edward P. Mahoney, 'Lovejoy and the Hierarchy of Being', *Journal of the History of Ideas* 48: 2 (1987), 222–7).

[49] Lovejoy, *Great Chain of Being*, 329.

[50] There are no five-legged mammals, for example, or pigs that can fly. One might attempt to deal with this by arguing that some areas of creaturely space are non-viable, as Simon Conway Morris does in his consideration of evolutionary convergence (Simon Conway Morris, *The Crucible of Creation: The Burgess Shale and the Rise of Animals* (Oxford; New York: Oxford University Press, 1998)). Such an earthy principle as viability, however, seems ill-matched to restrict the lofty aims of the principle of plenitude, especially as viability is so frequently determined by environmental factors.

Rejecting the Great Chain of Being and its way of ordering difference between creatures on the basis of the incompatibility of the principle of plenitude with Christian theology does not mean that other hierarchical schemes can be set aside for the same reason. The reason for rejecting the principle of plenitude is its threat to divine freedom, but we could instead hold that God chose to create a particular set of creatures to inhabit the universe, but that these creatures could still be ordered hierarchically according to Lovejoy's principle of 'unilinear gradation'. If we chose the principle of ordering as the Aristotelian and Thomistic one of act and potentiality, where God is pure act and creatures more imperfect as they manifest greater degrees of potentiality, we would have a Great Chain of Being with gaps: God creates a subset of all possible creatures rather than all of them, but the creatures can nonetheless be ordered in a unilinear gradation. The difficulty with this principle of ordering, however, is that it is a mistake to think that particular creatures can be graded according to their actuality or potentiality. From one point of view, an egg may be seen as a potential chicken, or a chicken a potential flock, but in a more important sense a chicken is pure act, the realization of itself. It is the unique possessor of 'thisness' or *haecceity* in the terms of John Duns Scotus, rendered by Gerald Manley Hopkins as 'inscape' and illustrated in his well-known lines:

> Each mortal thing does one thing and the same:
> Deals out that being indoors each one dwells;
> Selves–goes itself; *myself* it speaks and spells,
> Crying *What I do is me: for that I came.*[51]

To suggest that this oak tree, or that kingfisher or this dragonfly lacks actuality because it is missing features present in supposedly higher beings, or to consider that it is a potential creature of a different kind is radically to misunderstand its integrity as a creature of God. For this reason the unilinear actuality–potentiality graded scale, either of the Great Chain of Being or of the Great Chain of Being with gaps, is not defensible.[52]

If a unilinear ordering of creatures on the basis of act versus potential is not viable, we might sustain a unilinear gradation between creatures by employing

[51] Gerard Manley Hopkins, 'As kingfishers catch fire, dragonflies draw flame', lines 5–8 in Gerald Manley Hopkins, *Poems of Gerard Manley Hopkins*, 4th edn, (eds) W. H. Gardner and N. H. Mackenzie (London: Oxford University Press, 1970), 90.

[52] For other difficulties with the Aristotelian actuality–potentiality structure, see Jonathan Barnes, 'Metaphysics', in *The Cambridge Companion to Aristotle*, ed. Jonathan Barnes (Cambridge: Cambridge University Press, 1995), 94–6. Robert Adams argues for a modified form of Scotian 'thisness' in Robert M. Adams, 'Thisness and Primitive Identity', *Journal of Philosophy* 76: 1 (1979).

other ordering factors. It is hard to find a scale of comparable universal applicability and plausibility, however. We might be tempted to think that intelligence would be an appropriate hierarchical ordering of creatures, but there are significant problems with this, such as its narrow applicability to particular kinds of animals, the difficulty in defining what intelligence might mean,[53] and our resistance to accepting intelligence as an isolated index of worth within the human species. The evolutionary complexity of an organism might be another possible ordering factor, creating a scale from the simplest to the most complex creatures,[54] except that theology has traditionally valued the opposite in the doctrine of divine simplicity and Manley Hopkins' emphasis on the inscape of each creature might well incline us to be suspicious of judging an organism to be of less value because of its simplicity.[55] Indeed, there is an argument that all organisms alive at a particular moment of time are equally evolved, since all have established a mode of life within a particular environmental niche from presumably a common origin in the first self-reproducing entities, although some organisms achieved this earlier than others. Once we have recognized that there is more than one way of ordering the differences between organisms, we encounter a plethora of possible candidates. We could order animals by size or weight – say from blue whales to nematodes – by individual longevity – giant tortoises to mayflies, perhaps – by species age – the lingula brachiopod

---

[53] For an account of the difficulty of establishing inter-species definitions of cognitive ability, see E. A. Wasserman, 'Comparative Cognition: Beginning the Second Century of the Study of Animal Intelligence', *Psychological Bulletin* 113: 2 (1993).

[54] Brian Goodwin uses organizational complexity as a way of shifting the biological focus from genes back to organisms themselves: see Brian Goodwin, *How the Leopard Changed its Spots: The Evolution of Complexity* (New York: Charles Scribner's Sons, 1994). For a discussion of the difficulty of measuring the complexity of organisms, see Christoph Adani, 'What is Complexity?', *BioEssays* 24 :12 (2002).

[55] In her chapter 'On the Disadvantages of Being a Complex Organism' Osborne criticizes the tendency to derive hierarchy from evolutionary complexity: 'There are a number of temptations to hierarchical thinking implicit in evolutionary thinking. One is the temptation to think that a more basic or simple creature is primitive or lacking in some features that others have already achieved by more successful adaptation. Another is thinking that evolution is always for the better, so that those who have survived are in some sense better equipped or more able. A third is the temptation to think that complexity is superior to simplicity, because complex organisms arrive on the scene later than simple ones. None of these are proper tenets of evolutionary theory (although they seem widespread in popular thinking about biology). On the contrary, simple organisms are often very well fitted for survival; evolution produces mutations that are less fitted for survival as well as improvements; highly evolved creatures often die out because they are specialized; there is nothing inherently valuable about complexity; and in any case there is no reason to think that survival is a measure of value' (Osborne, *Dumb Beasts*, 102 n.).

to, for example, species of the genus Cyprinodon in Lake Chichancanab[56] – by speed – peregrine falcon to sloth or snail? – by loudness – tiger pistol shrimp to (any number of silent animals) – by colour – red pandas to sparkling violet-ear hummingbirds – number of legs – millipedes to snakes – and so on, and so on. To embark on such a list of possible ways of ordering creatures in a unilinear way is already to appreciate the oddness of believing that any single principle for ordering different creatures could be thought of as definitive. We can order animals hierarchically in any number of ways, but despite our longstanding habits of thought, we need to recognize that the project of constructing one particular hierarchy as authoritative is ill-conceived.[57]

One might imagine that schemes of scientific taxonomy in biology might be one way of reestablishing a univocal and authoritative way of ordering animals. The philosopher of biology John Dupré disagrees. He suggests that it is part of the logic of Darwinism to dispose of the idea 'that an organism has an essence that determines its necessary place in a unique nested hierarchy of kinds' and this points towards the possibility of 'a variety of different classificatory schemes, suited to a variety of purposes, some scientific and some not, that may criss-cross and overlap one another in various ways'.[58] Dupré argues

[56] Ulrike Strecker, Chrisitan G. Meyer, Christian Sturmbauer and Horst Wilkens, 'Genetic Divergence and Speciation in an Extremely Young Species Flock in Mexico Formed by the Genus Cyprinodon (Cyprinodontidae, Teleostei)', *Molecular Phylogenetics and Evolution* 6: 1 (1996).

[57] Augustine provides his own list of inappropriate scales of valuing creatures in *The City of God* when discussing demons: 'Far be it, then, for the mind of the truly religious man, who is a servant of the true God, to suppose that demons are better than himself because they have better bodies. Otherwise, he will have to place above himself many beasts which surpass us in the acuteness of their senses, in the ease and rapidity of their movement, in their strength, and in the greatly prolonged vigour of their bodies. What man can equal the power of vision of the eagle and the vulture? Who can equal the dog in his sense of smell? Who can equal in speed the hare, the stag and all the birds? Who can equal the strength of the lion or elephant? Who can equal in length of life the serpent, which is said to shed old age with its skin and return again to youth? But just as we are better than all these things in our capacity to reason and understand, so ought we to show that we are better that the demons by living well and honestly' (Augustine, *City of God*, 8.15). John McKeown notes that the superiority of other animals in some respects is already present in the Old Testament: oxen are stronger (Prov. 14.4; ostriches faster (Job 39.18), eagles fly higher (Prov. 23.5) and Behemoth is the first of God's works (Job 40.19) (John McKeown, 'What Are the Main Elements in an Old Testament Anthropology?', (2006) unpublished paper. In Luther's earliest extant sermon he compares human care for their neighbours unfavourably with that seen in other animals (H. S. Bluhm, 'The Significance of Luther's Earliest Extant Sermon', *The Harvard Theological Review* 37: 2 (1944), 179).

[58] John Dupré, *Humans and Other Animals* (Oxford: Clarendon, 2002), 4.

that even within biology, different classificatory schemes are necessary, because while the principle of classifying organisms by their evolutionary descent seems attractive in some contexts, it would make the task of classification in many areas impossible, as well as leading to implausible associations between organisms.[59] He exposes the gulf between more objective scientific taxonomy and more anthropocentric ordinary language classifications – although he notes that even scientific taxonomy fails to escape anthropocentrism in that it needs to be useful to human beings to be successful.[60] In the previous chapter I noted his rejection of the supposedly scientific orthodoxy that whales are mammals not fish: he observes that using 'mammals' to classify whales is a term of scientific taxonomy corresponding to no ordinary language equivalent; whereas 'fish' is a term of ordinary language classification corresponding to no scientific taxonomic category. Once we appreciate the existence of more than one classificatory scheme, we can recognize that whales could be *both* fish, according to ordinary language classification *and* mammals, according to scientific taxonomy.[61] His point concerning the need for different classificatory schemes for different tasks is well made in relation to onion and garlic or broccoli and cauliflower: he observes that it would be a culinary disaster if we were not able to distinguish between these pairs, but from the point of view of scientific taxonomy they are indistinguishable.[62] We need ways of identifying other creatures in this way that are inevitably anthropocentric – Augustine's classification of other creatures as 'useful', 'pernicious' and 'superfluous' noted above is the basic type here. Such anthropocentric classifications are only problematic if we fail to appreciate that they are a tactical solution to a particular human project rather than a universal and authoritative insight into the essence of things. This does not mean that classification is arbitrary or fails to correspond to reality, so that we are set adrift in a sea of postmodern uncertainty: Dupré calls his approach 'promiscuous realism', reflecting his belief that different overlapping schemes can each refer to the characteristics of things without being able to identify their place in a grand and monolithic hierarchy.[63]

We see, then, that there are different differences between animals and in different contexts different classificatory schemes will be more or less useful. Despite a long flirtation between Christian theology and Neoplatonic schemes of ordering creation, there is no theological rationale for a single and authoritative way of rendering differences between creatures. As noted above, Adam's

---

[59] Dupré, *Humans and Other Animals*, 38–9.
[60] Dupré, *Humans and Other Animals*, 32.
[61] Dupré, *Humans and Other Animals*, 27, 46.
[62] Dupré, *Humans and Other Animals*, 31, 45.
[63] Dupré, *Humans and Other Animals*, 4, 33.

naming of the animals brought before him suggests his attention to their particularity rather than a concern to order them. The great creation psalms such as 104 and 148 make a great list of God's creative works, often treating celestial and terrestrial creatures in different sections, but do not provide grounds for a hierarchical arrangement of creatures. The awe-inspiring final chapters of Job similarly emphasize the majestic breadth and complexity of God's creative endeavour but undermine the possibility of human comprehension of creation in a tidy scheme (Job 38–41). The only aspect of hierarchy amongst creatures that seems to have a biblical basis is a much simpler one than the grand scales of being we have so far surveyed: that human beings stand above the rest of the created order. It is to the theological construal of this human/non-human difference that we now turn.

The Human Difference

In Chapter 1 we saw that theologians have often asserted a fundamental teleological difference between human beings and all other creatures – that the rest of creation was brought into being for the sake of human beings – but that there are important theological arguments against identifying God's reason for creating in this way. Frequently this teleological argument has been based on an ascription of particular characteristics to human beings connoting their unique dignity among other creatures. Such a scheme does not generate the extensive hierarchy of the Great Chain of Being discussed in the previous section, but a much flatter hierarchy of God, human beings and other creatures.

The key biblical locus for the belief in this unique and particular human status is Genesis 1.26–28. Following the creation of the other land animals on the sixth day, God creates humanity:

> Then God said, 'Let us make humankind in our image, according to our likeness; and let them have dominion over the fish of the sea, and over the birds of the air, and over the cattle, and over all the wild animals of the earth, and over every creeping thing that creeps upon the earth.' So God created humankind in his image, in the image of God he created them; male and female he created them. God blessed them, and God said to them, 'Be fruitful and multiply, and fill the earth and subdue it; and have dominion over the fish of the sea and over the birds of the air and over every living thing that moves upon the earth.' (Gen. 1.26–28)

The text suggests that in some respect and uniquely among God's creatures, human beings are like God, bearing the *imago Dei*, the divine image. The image of God seems to be a clearly identified difference between human beings and all other creatures. The first question that occurs here is of what the image of God consists: in what respect human beings are uniquely akin to God. The difficulty in resolving this question is that the content of the divine image is radically underdetermined in biblical texts. Gordon Wenham notes that the term 'image' appears only 17 times in the Bible. Of these, 10 references refer to images of various physical objects and a further two in the Psalms compare human existence to an image or shadow (Ps. 39.7; 73.20). The remaining five references are all in Genesis (1.26, 27; 5.3; 9.6).[64] Genesis 5.3 refers to Adam's son Seth being in Adam's likeness and image. Only 1.26, 1.27 and 9.6 refer to the image of God and they each simply state that God made human beings in the divine image. Wenham surveys five possible interpretations of the image of God. First he notes and rejects the patristic attempt to separate the meanings of 'image' and 'likeness' on the basis that they fail to reflect the original meaning of the text. Second, he groups together attempts to identify particular mental or spiritual attributes that human beings share with God, such as rationality, intelligence, free-will, self-consciousness and so on. These he rejects because the lack of textual evidence makes one suspicious that such commentators are merely reading into the text what they consider most significant about humankind. Third, Wenham cites attempts to use Genesis 5.3 as grounds for asserting a physical resemblance between human beings and God, but rejects this on the basis that God's incorporeality and invisibility make the concept of physical resemblance theologically problematic. The fourth option that Wenham considers renders the divine image as representing God on earth, drawing on Egyptian and Assyrian texts describing the king as the image of God. This is the interpretation Wenham favours and he rejects Claus Westermann's objection that this would blur the boundary between God and humanity. The fifth and final option Wenham considers is that proposed by Karl Barth and favoured by Westermann, that the divine image is the capacity to relate to God, with the focus on the making rather than the object of the process. Wenham is unconvinced that there is textual warrant to believe that image relates to the process of divine making and considers the concept too vague to be useful in any case.[65]

---

[64] Gordon J. Wenham, *Genesis*, Word Bible Commentary (Waco, TX: Word, 1994), 29.

[65] Wenham, *Genesis*, 29–32. For other recent discussions of the interpretation of the image of God, see J. Richard Middleton, *The Liberating Image: The Imago Dei in Genesis 1* (Grand Rapids, MI: Brazos, 2005); J. Wentzel van Huyssteen, *Alone in the World: Human Uniqueness in Science and Theology* (Grand Rapids, MI: Eerdmans, 2006), 111–62; and Richard Briggs, 'Humans in the Image of God and Other Things Genesis Does Not Make Clear', *Journal of Theological Interpretation* 4: 1 (2010). On Barth's account of the uniqueness of humanity in the context of other creatures, see Greggs, *Barth, Origen and Universal Salvation*, 145–6.

Wenham's preference for an interpretation of the image of God focusing on the role human beings play in representing God finds striking and widespread support among recent commentators.[66] This view is supported by its link to Psalm 8, where the distinctiveness of human beings is also linked to their role in relation to other creatures (v. 6). This is not to say that this line of interpretation is without difficulty: Richard Briggs notes Nathan Macdonald's worries that interpreting the image in this way gains most of its momentum from an ancient Near Eastern context outside the Genesis text.[67] What is striking in this debate is that both the representative interpretation preferred by Wenham and the relational interpretation adopted by Barth and Westermann share the conclusion that attempts to define the image of God by locating a particular characteristic of humanity that is shared with God – the second group of interpretations considered by Wenham – are misguided. In the terms used by J. Wentzel van Huyssteen, this marks a shift away from a substantialist to a functionalist or relational interpretation of the image of God.[68] With this shift away from substantialist interpretations of the *imago Dei,* the long theological enterprise of seeking to identify a particular unique human characteristic with the divine image has been brought to an end. There are many reasons to welcome such a development: feminist theologians have argued that the link between rationality and the image of God was a way of privileging male over female[69] and those concerned to affirm the personhood of those with severe learning disabilities have recognized that the association of rationality with the divine image threatens to make such persons marginal human beings.[70] In the context of reflecting on the theological foundations for discussing differences between human and other creatures it is notable that as far as a doctrine of creation goes, the rejection of substantialist interpretations of the *imago Dei* is the abandonment of the attempt to locate a statement of human difference in the doctrine of the image of God. If a functional interpretation is right, then the *imago Dei* is a distinctively human task or vocation: a role that the

---

[66] See, for example, Victor P. Hamilton, *The Book of Genesis, Chapters 1–17*, NICOT, ed. R. K. Harrison (Grand Rapids, MI: Eerdmans, 1990), 1:135; Walter Brueggemann, *Genesis* (Louisville, KY: John Knox Press, 1982), 32; von Rad, *Genesis*, 58; Middleton, *Liberating Image*, 93–145; van Huyssteen, *Alone in the World*, 157.

[67] Briggs, 'Humans in the Image of God' citing Nathan Macdonald, 'Review of J. Richard Middleton, *the Liberating Image: The Imago Dei in Genesis 1*', *Review of Biblical Literature* (2005). For Westermann's objections, cited by Wenham, see Westermann, *Genesis 1–11: A Commentary*, 146–58.

[68] van Huyssteen, *Alone in the World*, 126. Van Huyssteen also identifies existential and eschatological interpretations.

[69] See van Huyssteen's survey in van Huyssteen, *Alone in the World*, 128–32.

[70] Hans S. Reinders, *Receiving the Gift of Friendship: Profound Disability, Theological Anthropology, and Ethics* (Grand Rapids, MI: Eerdmans, 2008), 227–44.

human creature is called on by God to play.[71] If the relational interpretation is correct, then God determines to have a particular kind of relationship with this creature. In neither case does the image of God denote any particular difference between the human creature and other creatures: both interpretations instead identify the unique human image bearing with a divine decision about how humans are to live. The task of locating human difference is not abandoned, but it is deferred: it is a question no longer to be addressed with reference to the characteristics of creatures as God created them.

There is a powerful supporting argument for such a deferral of a theological account of human difference beyond the text of Genesis. An adequate theological account of the *imago Dei* must reckon with the definitive New Testament statements that the primary account of the image of God is Christological (Col. 1.15; 2 Cor. 4.4). The image of the invisible God is not humanity, according to these texts, but the particular creature Jesus Christ. No doubt we can see a way of relating these claims – that through Christ human beings might be enabled to image God in the world – but this is again to defer interpretation of the *imago Dei* from the doctrine of creation to the doctrine of the incarnation. An appreciation of the Christological foundation of the doctrine of the image of God in a theological context, therefore, supports the growing consensus among commentators that it is a theological mistake to ground an account of human uniqueness among other creatures in the doctrine of creation. A judgement about the significance of the *imago Dei* for the relationship between human and other creatures must therefore await the discussion of the doctrine of the incarnation in the next chapter.[72]

While the doctrine of the image of God has been a very widespread way of giving a theological location to discussions of human uniqueness, it has not been the only basis theologians have considered for reflecting on what is unique about

[71] Morwenna Ludlow suggests there may be support for this vocational interpretation of the *imago Dei* in the thought of Gregory of Nyssa: 'Gregory of Nyssa's recasting of the idea of the image of God less in terms of reason/soul (which has a tendency to separate humans from other animals) and more in terms of qualities or virtues which enable human beings as psychosomatic unities to perform a role *in* creation might be a helpful way to reflect on the notion of the *imago dei* while maintaining an emphasis on the interconnectedness of creation.' (Morwenna Ludlow, 'Power and Dominion: Patristic Interpretations of Genesis 1', in David Horrell, Cherryl Hunt, Christopher Southgate and Francesca Stravrakopoulou (eds), *Ecological Hermeneutics: Biblical, Historical and Theological Perspectives* (London: T & T Clark, 2010), 152, italics in original).

[72] The doctrine of the fall is also clearly relevant here: Luther, for example, considered that human beings had lost their dominion over other animals with their original transgression and this would not be regained until the image was restored in their redemption (see Clough, 'The Anxiety of the Human Animal', 44). (This theme will be addressed in Chapter 5).

human beings in creation. A crucial use of the Great Chain of Being concept discussed earlier in the chapter was to situate human beings amidst God's other creatures. Clearly, a hierarchy with God at the top meant that human beings were not the masters in this context. Nor were they close to the summit: after God came all kinds of orders of angels and other celestial spiritual beings. Human beings found their place about halfway down: the most elevated of material beings. This did not prevent philosophers and theologians finding a special significance in the place of human beings in the Great Chain. Very frequently, they were pictured as the creature that uniquely bridged the spiritual and material realms. This is particularly clear in early Jewish thought. The Talmud states that human beings have three characteristics that make them like angels – they understand, walk erect and speak in the holy tongue – and three characteristics that make them like beasts – they eat and drink, procreate and excrete.[73] In *Genesis Rabbah* human beings are used by God to make peace between the celestial and terrestrial worlds by taking on immortality from the celestial sphere and the ability to procreate from the earthly sphere (12:8). Later this is developed along similar lines to the Talmud but with two sets of four characteristics: like animals, humans eat and drink, procreate, excrete and die; like angels they stand upright, speak, understand and see (14:3).[74] *Leviticus Rabbah* also pictures the creation of the human as God's union of the lower and upper spheres, through being made from dust but enlivened by the breath of God (9:9).[75]

This line of thought was taken up by Christian theologians. Augustine saw humanity as a combination of beasts and angels in the same way as the earlier Jewish authors:

> For example, man is a kind of mean between beasts and angels. The beast is an irrational and mortal animal, the angel is a rational and immortal one, and man is between them, lower than the angels but higher than the beasts: a rational and mortal animal, having mortality in common with the beasts and reason in common with the angels.[76]

This idea of human beings uniquely combining qualities from other creatures was readily developed into the concept of human beings as a microcosm of the universe: representing all its disparate parts within one unified being. This was

---

[73] Hagiga 16a, *Babylonian Talmud*, cited in Eilon Schwartz, 'Mastery and Stewardship, Wonder and Connectedness', in Hava Tirosh-Samuelson (ed.), *Judaism and Ecology: Created World and Revealed Word*, Religions of the World and Ecology, (Cambridge, MA; London: Harvard University Press, 2002), 98.

[74] Cited in Cohen, *Sa`ar Ba`aley Hayim* (Jerusalem: Feldheim Publishers, 1976), 32.

[75] Cited in Cohen, *Sa`ar Ba`aley Hayim*, 32.

[76] Augustine, *City of God*, 9.15.

implicit in Aristotle's contention that human beings possessed a vegetative soul like plants, a sensitive soul like other animals and, uniquely, a rational soul.[77] It was adopted by Origen and Gregory the Great and found full expression in the work of Maximus the Confessor, who, according to Andrew Louth, saw the human person as binding together all manner of divisions within the universe: intellectual and sensible, heaven and earth, paradise and the inhabited world, male and female, even – given his doctrine of deification – created and uncreated.[78] Maximus states that 'humanity clearly has the power of naturally uniting at the mean points of each division since it is related to the extremities of each division in its own parts' and gives this as the reason why humanity was created last 'as a kind of natural bond mediating between the universal extremes through their proper parts and leading into unity in itself those things that are naturally set apart from one another by a great interval'.[79] The idea of humanity as a microcosm became a medieval commonplace: for Bonaventure humankind 'is placed between the two principal realms of creation, namely between the corporeal and the spiritual world'[80] and Aquinas cites the Aristotelian divisions of the soul in order to argue that '[i]n some way or another all things are in man' since reason is shared with the angels, sense (*vires sensitivas*) with other animals, natural vital forces (*vires naturales*) with the plants and the body itself with inanimate things.[81]

Attempting to identify human beings uniquely through the invocation of the idea of microcosm depends on their unique possession among earthly creatures of some attribute that they have in common with God and other spiritual beings. The medieval Jewish philosopher Maimonides recognized this in his *Guide of the Perplexed* when he noted that but for the human intellect, one could just as easily call an ass or a horse a microcosm.[82] While for Maimonides and other medieval philosophers and theologians it seemed unproblematic to restrict rationality to human beings among the earthly creatures and to believe

---

[77] See Sorabji, 'Body and Soul'.

[78] Andrew Louth, 'The Cosmic Vision of Saint Maximus the Confessor', in Philip Clayton and Arthur Peacocke (eds), *In Whom We Live and Move and Have Our Being: Panentheistic Reflections on God's Presence in a Scientific World* (Grand Rapids, MI; Cambridge: Eerdmans, 2004), 192, cited in Dominic Coad. 'Creation's Praise of God: An Ecological Theology of Non-Human and Human Being'. PhD thesis. University of Exeter, 2010, 224. For other patristic uses of the idea, see Peter Harrison, 'The Virtues of Animals in Seventeenth-Century Thought', *Journal of the History of Ideas* 59: 3 (1998), 466.

[79] Maximus the Confessor, *Ambigua 41*, (Patrologia Graeca 91: 80a), translated in Louth, 'Cosmic Vision', 192.

[80] Schäfer, 'Position and Function of Man', 279.

[81] Aquinas, *Summa Theologica*, 1.96.2.

[82] Maimonides, *Guide of the Perplexed*, ch. 72, p. 190.

that this capacity gave them something in common with God, both claims can now be seen as questionable. In the first place, it is clear that on any sensible definition the capacity for rational thought is a continuum across species rather than a binary division with only human beings counting as rational. As noted at the beginning of the previous chapter, we know that sheep can recognize hundreds of faces, crows make tools to solve problems, chimpanzees are better than humans in some numerical memory tasks, dolphins can process grammar, parrots can understand abstract concepts and so on. The point here is not that human mental abilities are not impressive and unique, but that any assemblage of mental tasks that only humans can do – such as novel writing or abstract calculus – fails to identify the kind of discontinuous ability that would be plausible as the unique linkage between the earthly and heavenly realms the human-as-microcosm argument demands. To reliably identify rationality uniquely with human beings, for example, one is forced to the kind of solution by definition employed by Jonathan Bennett: 'I use "rationality" to mean "whatever it is that humans possess which marks them off, in respect of intellectual capacity, sharply and importantly from all other known species".'[83] Any substantive definition of rationality will either fail to identify a difference of kind rather than degree between humans and other animals – e.g. 'capacity for abstract thought' – or will not plausibly identify an attribute sufficiently weighty to unite the earthly and heavenly realms – e.g. (despite my respect for mathematicians) 'capacity to perform abstract calculus'. For this reason, among others,[84] the attempt to identify human beings as unique on the basis that they play a pivotal role between earth and heaven must fail.

[83] Jonathan Bennett, *Rationality: An Essay Towards an Analysis* (Indianapolis, IN: Hackett, 1989), 5, cited in Donna Yarri, *The Ethics of Animal Experimentation: A Critical Analysis and Constructive Christian Proposal* (Oxford: Oxford University Press, 2005), 33. Bennett's book explores the basis of the 'common knowledge' that the difference between human and all other creatures is one of degree rather than kind, so that: 'Any possible creature whose intellectual level was higher than that of normal apes and lower than that of normal men – so the common belief runs – either would or would not have that special something which puts humans importantly above other animals: possessing the "special something", it would be essentially up with us; lacking the "special something", it would be down with the apes; it could not be half-way between the apes and us in respect of the gap between apes and ourselves which we regard as most important' (4). My argument here is that any successful definition of such a 'special something' would be merely the arbitrary naming of an attribute humans happen to like about themselves, which is far from what we need to enable the cosmic union the human-as-microcosm arguments require.

[84] For example, we could name any number of attributes of non-human creatures that humans do not possess, such as the ability to photosynthesize like plants or employ echo-location like bats. It is not clear why these attributes do not need to be part of the creature that comprehends all other creatures within itself.

There are no shortage of alternative candidates for identifying the key difference between humans and other animals. Pollux and others identified humans as the animals that laugh; Xenophon believed that only humans grasp logical consequences; Xen and Plato judged that humans alone are religious; Hesiod stated that humans alone have justice; other ancient Greek authors picked on peculiarities of hair or smell, or judged humans as uniquely divine or uniquely an imitation of the deity;[85] Aristotle suggested that humans are the only animal with ears that cannot move them;[86] Minucius Felix took up the widespread ancient observation that four-legged beasts look down towards the earth whereas humans walk erect and look towards the heavens, followed by many others;[87] Lactantius judged the only two attributes humans do not share with other animals are their spiritual nature and use of fire;[88] Hobbes considered humans to be unique in their proclivity to do wilful hurt to one another;[89] Marx thought that humans were the only species to produce universally, rather than just for immediate need;[90] Nietzsche proposed the capacity to promise, the possession of conscience, self-control and the ability to assess and value – as well as supreme arrogance and vanity;[91] Heidegger contrasted 'world-forming' humanity with the 'poverty in world' of other animals;[92] Mark Twain argued for the descent of human beings from the 'higher' animals, claiming that

[85] These examples are collected by Robert Renehan in Robert Renehan, 'The Greek Anthropocentric View of Man', *Harvard Studies in Classical Philology* 85 (1981), 246–51.

[86] Aristotle, *Historia Animalium*, 492 a.

[87] Minucius Felix, 'The Octavius of Minucius Felix', in A. Cleveland Coxe, James Donaldson and Alexander Roberts (eds), *The Ante-Nicene Fathers: Translations of the Writings of the Fathers Down to AD 325*, vol. 4, (Edinburgh: T & T Clark, 1997), ch. 17. Among many other examples, Basil of Caesarea and Martin Luther make the same point (Basil, 'Hexaemeron', Homily 9, §2; Luther, *Luther's Works*, 1.46).

[88] Lactantius, *Divine Institutes*, bk 2, ch. 9.

[89] Richard Ashcraft, 'Hobbes's Natural Man: A Study in Ideology Formation', *The Journal of Politics* 33: 4 (1971), 1091n.

[90] Karl Marx, *Early Writings*, Penguin Classics, trans. Rodney Livingstone and Gregor Benton (London: Penguin Books, 1992), 329, cited in Peter Scott, 'Thinking Like an Animal: Theological Materialism for a Changing Climate', *Studies in Christian Ethics* 24: 1 (2011), 64.

[91] Friedrich Wilhelm Nietzsche, *The Genealogy of Morals: A Polemic*, The Complete Works of Friedrich Nietzsche, vol. 13, ed. Oscar Levy, trans. Horace B. Samuel (Edinburgh; London: T. N. Foulis, 1910), Second Essay, §§1–8; Friedrich Wilhelm Nietzsche, *Human, All Too Human (1878)* (Cambridge; New York: Cambridge University Press, 2007), 307.

[92] Quoted in Giorgio Agamben, *The Open: Man and Animal*, trans. K. Attell (Stanford, CA: Stanford University Press, 2004), 50. Agamben's short book provides a wealth of other characterizations of differences between humans and other animals.

humans are uniquely avaricious, miserly, blushing, cruel and warlike;[93] Noam Chomsky claimed that language use is uniquely human;[94] Richard Leakey and Roger Letwin thought that it was the development of our consciousness based on symbol making that made humans a new kind of animal;[95] Fukuyama followed Hegel in stating that it was *thymos* or spiritedness that differentiates humans and animals;[96] Derrida lists clothes, speech, reason, the logos, history, laughing, mourning, burial, the gift as examples of the many attempts to construe the traits of the human, commenting that such a list is never closed.[97] Self-consciousness has often been used as an alternative to rationality to uniquely identify human beings, although this is becoming increasingly implausible with experimental evidence of self-consciousness in other animals.[98] The astonishing range of these attempts to identify the key difference between humans and other animals is sufficient evidence that no such account can succeed: instead, we must recognize that human/animal difference is being used as a trope for discussion of the authors' preferred features of human beings.

My argument here is not that there are no differences between human beings and other animals: clearly, it only makes sense to speak of human beings at all because such differences identify us uniquely among other creatures. Nor am I trying to minimize our sense of the differences between humans and other animals: it seems to me that these differences are significant and worth of careful comparative investigation. My objection is to the routine and thoughtless, theological or philosophical, drawing up of a list of attributes supposedly possessed by all human beings, and excluding all non-human beings. In the first place, many of the entries on such lists are inaccurate: the more we understand about the lives of other creatures the more obvious it becomes that intelligence, rationality, self-consciousness, relationality, morality, culture, and so on, and so on, define at best a spectrum of ability on which different creatures can be placed at different points. To believe ourselves to be the unique possessors of such attributes misleads us, both by underestimating the capabilities of the

---

[93] Mark Twain, *What is Man? And Other Philosophical Writings*, Paul Baender ed. (Berkeley and Los Angeles, CA: University of California Press, 1997), 80–5.

[94] Noam Chomsky, *Language and Mind* (New York: Harcourt Brace Jovanovitch, 1968), 69.

[95] Richard Leakey and Roger Letwin, *Origins Reconsidered: In Search of What Makes Us Human* (New York: Anchor Books, 1992), 304.

[96] Richard H. Roberts, *Religion, Theology and the Human Sciences* (Cambridge; New York: Cambridge University Press, 2002), 21.

[97] Jacques Derrida and David Wills, 'The Animal That Therefore I Am (More to Follow)', *Critical Inquiry* 28: 2 (2002), 373.

[98] For a survey of evidence in this area, see Marc Bekoff and Paul W. Sherman, 'Reflections on Animal Selves', in *Animal Passions and Beastly Virtues: Reflections on Redecorating Nature* (Philadelphia, PA: Temple University Press, 2006).

creatures erroneously denied possession of these attributes and by inaccurately characterizing the particularity of the human. In response to this objection, we could work at improving the accuracy of such lists – as noted above, we could reasonably expect humans uniquely capable of abstract calculus and novel-writing – although such a move only exacerbates a second concern that some human beings cannot be characterized as intelligent, rational, moral or self-conscious, let alone abstract mathematicians or novelists. This drives us back to the question of our motivation in drawing up such lists. If our aim is to characterize the difference between humans and other animals in order to understand what it is to be human, it seems that the more accurate and detailed our list becomes, the less likely it is that we can claim it to be universally true of human beings, and the harder it is to attribute significance to the differences we find. In his 1956 *Dictionary of Anthropology* Charles Winick describes the characteristics distinguishing human beings from monkeys, apes and lemurs: 'the nose's prominent bridge and well-developed tip, a median furrow in the upper lip, possession of the chin, ... large brain (2 1/2–3 times the size of the gorillas') ... outrolling of the lips and visibility of the mucous membrane as a continuous red line, long life span, ... symbolic expression, educability, and advanced culture'.[99] This list aptly indicates the combination of the accurate but unenlightening – e.g. the visibility of the mucous membrane – with the potentially interesting but inaccurate – e.g. educability, which has been observed in numerous studies on rats and birds, as well as in sophisticated primate examples such as Koko the gorilla learning American Sign Language and chimpanzees learning to memorize numbers in sequence better than human adults.[100]

[99] Charles Winick, *The Dictionary of Anthropology* (New York: Philosophical Library, 1956), 339, quoted in H. Peter Steeves, 'The Familiar Other and Feral Selves: Life At the Human/Animal Boundary', in Anagela N. H. Creager and William Chester Jordan (eds), *The Animal–Human Boundary: Historical Perspectives* (Rochester, NY: University of Rochester Press, 2002), 232.

[100] F. Patterson and E. Linden, *The Education of Koko* (New York: Holt, Rinehart & Winston, 1981); Inoue and Matsuzawa, 'Working Memory'. It is important to note that my argument here is not dependent on how differences between humans and other animals came into being. Emergence theory, for example, claims that it is possible for qualitatively new characteristics of particular creatures to develop through a continuous evolutionary process (see, for example, Arthur Peacocke, 'Biological Evolution – A Positive Theological Appraisal', in Robert John Russell, William R. Stoeger and Francisco J. Ayala (eds), *Evolutionary and Molecular Biology: Scientific Perspectives on Divine Action* (Vatican City State; Berkeley, CA: Vatican Observatory and Center for Theology and the Natural Sciences, 1998), 358). This identification of a possible route to explain how a particular qualitative difference came into being, however, does not help in the identification of a particular capacity that reliably discriminates between human and non-human animals.

A further problem with the project of contrasting human and non-human characteristics is the way it masks differences between non-human animals. Derrida recognized the difficulty here:

> Confined within this catch-all concept, within this vast encampment of the animal, in this general singular, within the strict enclosure of this definite article ('the Animal' and not 'animals'), as in a virgin forest, a zoo, a hunting or fishing ground, a paddock or an abattoir, a space of domestication, are all the living things that man does not recognize as his fellows, his neighbors, or his brothers. And that is so in spite of the infinite space that separates the lizard from the dog, the protozoon from the dolphin, the shark from the lamb, the parrot from the chimpanzee, the camel from the eagle, the squirrel from the tiger or the elephant from the cat, the ant from the silkworm or the hedgehog from the echidna. I interrupt my nomenclature and call Noah to help insure that no one gets left on the ark.[101]

It is obviously the case that human beings have vastly more in common with chimpanzees than chimpanzees do with rabbits, let alone birds, fish, insects or protozoa. Yet in our human/non-human comparisons we lump together chimpanzees, rabbits, birds, fish, insects and protozoa as a meaningful category in opposition to the human. We treat 'human' and 'non-human' as parallel categories, instead of recognizing that 'human' names one species of animal and 'non-human' names about 1,250,000 species. It would be interesting to examine the results of a similar attempted bifurcation of the animal universe on the basis of common British black garden ant and non-common British black garden ant, or Herring Gull and non-Herring Gull. No doubt the ants and the gulls in question would be more interested in the results than we are, and therefore it is understandable that humans have more interest in marking out the human and non-human boundary, but we should recognize that there is no obvious species-neutral reason that the human/non-human boundary should considered of greater magnitude to most other species boundaries.

Following Peter Singer's manifesto claim in 1976 that 'All animals are equal',[102] some have worried that giving up on the ways of rendering differences between humans and other animals that this chapter has brought into question would lead to a terrible flattening in our view of human and non-human

---

[101] Derrida and Wills, 'Animal', 402.

[102] Peter Singer, 'All Animals are Equal', in Tom Regan and Peter Singer (eds), *Animal Rights and Human Obligations* (Eaglewood Cliffs, NJ: Prentice Hall, 1989).

animal life.[103] This concern is most easily illustrated in ethical quandary cases: if we had to choose between saving an ant and a human infant from drowning in a pond, an affirmation of species egalitarianism threatens to leave us with no reason to prefer rescuing the baby.[104] This work will discuss the theological ethics of human relationships with animals in the second volume, but it should already be clear that the kind of attentiveness to the differences between animals I have argued for in this chapter will not lead to arguments for treating all creatures in the same way.[105] Such egalitarianism seems to me to be ruled out in a theological context by the occasions where Jesus affirms God's care for non-human creatures as a way of giving his human listeners confidence in God's providential care for them. In the Sermon on the Mount he invokes God's abundant provision for the birds of the air and the lilies of the field and asks his hearers 'Are you not of more value than they?' (Mt. 6.25–30 ‖ Lk 12.24–28). Later in Matthew's gospel he reminds them that although two sparrows are sold for a penny, not one falls 'apart from the Father' and states 'Do not be afraid: you are of more value than many sparrows' (Mt. 10.29–31 ‖ Lk. 12.6–7). In his debate with the Pharisees on whether healing is lawful on the Sabbath, he argues that they would pull their only sheep out of a pit on the Sabbath and 'How much more valuable is a human being than a sheep!' (Mt. 12.11–12 ‖ Lk. 14.5). These passages provide a clear and consistent basis in the teaching of Jesus both for an emphasis on God's universal providential care for every animal but also for believing that God values human life more highly than that of birds and that humans should value human life more highly than that of sheep. The passages do not suggest a rationale for such judgements: in this sense they parallel the undetermined content of the image of God noted above. They do not posit rationality, or intelligence, or self-consciousness, or any other attribute as a basis for moral regard. Nor do they provide support for the metaphysical speculations of the Great Chain of Being we have had

---

[103] David Schmidz surveys key objections to such species egalitarianism in David Schmidz, 'Are All Species Equal?', *Journal of Applied Philosophy* 15:1 (1998).

[104] In fact, Singer's preference utilitarianism does not find it hard to deal with this case: the preferences of creatures with the capacity to see themselves as existing over time can be considered more weighty than those without such a capacity (Peter Singer, *Practical Ethics*, 3rd edn (Cambridge: Cambridge University Press, 2011), 111). If it is the case that newly born infants do not have such a capacity, however, it is not clear that Singer would be able to justify saving a very young human infant over an ant, so long as the preferences of others did not favour the infant. He judges that Western attitudes to protecting infants have roots in a distinctively Christian view of things, rather than being a universal ethical value (Singer, *Practical Ethics*, 153–4).

[105] Singer himself noted that the equality for which he advocated would not lead to equal treatment: a pig could not have the right to vote because a pig cannot vote (Singer, 'All Animals are Equal', 75).

reason to reject earlier in the chapter. They do, however, suggest that when we move from doctrine to ethics, we will need to attend to this form of human/ non-human difference.

In the end, the unique identification of human beings among others of God's creatures will require the rehearsal of a range of characteristics indicating the ways we are like and unlike other creatures: unlike birds but like rabbits we cannot fly; like whales but unlike sharks we are warm-blooded; like crows but unlike protozoa we can engage in problem-solving activity; like monkeys but unlike fish we use tools; and so on. As far as the doctrine of creation goes – the focus of this part of the book – the only theological supplement to the identification of human particularity in this way is that we believe human beings to have been called on by God to image God among the other creatures. This human difference relates primarily to ethics rather than doctrine, however, and suggests that theologically the human/non-human difference is vocational. God has called human beings to be creatures in a particular way and take responsibility for the lives of other creatures. Here then we have the authentic theological construal of the difference between human beings and other creatures: we have been given our task to live as human creatures and they have been called to be creatures in their very many different ways.

Attending to Difference

Attending carefully to the differences between animals is both a joy and a responsibility: a joy because taking notice of the intricate detail of the lives of other animals is one way in which we celebrate the magnificently varied and mysterious creative work of God; a responsibility because the unique role humans are called to play in relation to other creatures in imaging God to them requires as full an understanding of them as is possible of the nature of their lives and what they may need from us. For the Christian, therefore, the origin of zoology in natural theology is not a historical curiosity but a reminder of the role of this science in the worship of God and the project of Christian discipleship.

Any adequate theological account of animals will balance the commonality of their lives before God, set out in the previous chapter, with an alertness to their very different modes of life and therefore the diversity of their needs, emphasized in this one. The differences between animals are complex, manifold and irreducible, and cannot therefore be comprehended in any simplistic binary human/non-human categories, nor in a notional unilinear scale of being from the greatest to the least. To affirm animals as creatures of God is to recognize and attend to the particularity of the lives they are called upon by their creator to live. Christian theology has often been alert to the demands of this task, as evidenced in Basil's *Hexaemeron* with which the chapter began, and must continue to recognize this as one among its many responsibilities.[106]

Looking forward to the ethical reflection that will be the focus of the second volume of this work, it is important to note that the identification of sameness or difference between human and non-human animals does not predetermine the significance of this relationship for particular moral judgements. For example, an argument in favour of human consumption of other animals could either be based on our similarity with other animals – lions eat gazelles so we can do likewise – or our difference from other animals – our distinctive human characteristics mean it is justifiable to consume other animals while unjustifiable to eat fellow human beings. Similarly, vegetarianism could either be grounded on a rhetoric of sameness – other animals are like us so we should not kill them for food – or on a rhetoric of difference – unlike other animals, humans have the capacity to make the moral decision not to consume other creatures. This makes clear that beyond the complexity of identifying the similarities and differences between humans and other animals lies the equally demanding task of how these similarities and differences are to be interpreted in an ethical context.

These first three chapters have enquired concerning the place of animals in the doctrine of creation. Chapter 1 explored the relationship of animals to the purpose of creation and argued that theologians have reason to affirm God's good creation of every animal creature independent of its utility to fellow creatures. Chapter 2 attempted a theological account of what it means to occupy the place of an animal creature before God, examining the common features of distinctive modes of animal life and arguing that animals exist in a particular and unsubstitutable realm as creatures radically dependent on other creatures for their being, but capable of independent response to their creator in ways particular to them. This third chapter then addressed the reciprocal question of how to discuss the ways in which animals differ in a theological context, affirming the value of creaturely diversity and noting difficulties with many ways in which animal differences have been rendered philosophically and theologically. We are now ready to pass beyond the doctrine of creation to ask about the place of animals in the doctrine of reconciliation in Part II of this book: considering the incarnation in Chapter 4 and the atonement in Chapter 5.

---

[106] Notable in this context is Colin Gunton's attention to the importance of maintaining particularity, which he identified with the work of the Spirit, as opposed to the unifying work of the Son (Colin Gunton, *The One, the Three and the Many: God, Creation and the Culture of Modernity* (Cambridge: Cambridge University Press, 1993), chs 6–7).

Part II

RECONCILIATION

Chapter 4

INCARNATION

While creation seemed a good place to begin a systematic theology of animals, as I did in Part I of this book, it is in approaching the person and work of Jesus Christ that we come to the heart of the matter. This has already been evident in the cross-referencing forward from the doctrine of creation to the doctrine of the incarnation that has been necessary: theology cannot give an adequate account of the purpose of creation (Chapter 1) without speaking of Jesus Christ, nor can we speak fully of what it means for human beings to be images of God (Chapter 3) without referring to Jesus Christ as the true image. Much of moment, therefore, has been deferred to this point. Even if the arguments of the first part of this book are accepted – that on the basis of the doctrine of creation human beings should understand themselves as part of a creative and redemptive process that does not find its goal in them alone (Chapter 1); that human beings are one creature among many, with significant features of their life in common with other animals, their nearest neighbours (Chapter 2); that in identifying their uniqueness, human beings should not resort to grand binary typologies but attend to the particulars of their lives and the lives of other creatures (Chapter 3) – in relation to the doctrines of the incarnation and atonement everything is again at stake. For in the scandalous particularity of God becoming incarnate in the man, Jesus of Nazareth, and defeating sin and death through the cross of Calvary and resurrection from the tomb, it seems that all labours up to this point have been in vain. Here, it seems, is the final and decisive evidence that God is concerned with one species, rather than the multitude of creatures I have been seeking theologically to remember, and that Christianity will never be able to escape a blinkered preoccupation with only one kind of animal: God became human. Not only that, but God became human in order to overcome human sinful disobedience and reconcile Godself with humanity: the choice of creature in which to become incarnate – human; the cause of the ill that needed remedying – human; and the beneficiaries of the divine act of incarnation and atonement – human. If in this part of the book there is nothing more to be said, other animals will have been relegated to a subsidiary and insignificant theological category even more decisively by the doctrine of reconciliation than they seemed to have been by the doctrine of creation.

One possible theological move immediately presents itself. If God became human for human beings, perhaps God became or will become dolphin for dolphins, gorilla for gorillas, ostrich for ostriches, herring for herrings, ant for ants and plankton for plankton. We know nothing of such incarnations – why should we? – but our ignorance is not a disproof of the thesis. Such a theory of multiple incarnations would allow us to keep Jesus Christ as God's human project, while remaining open to the idea that other animals may also have their Messiah. This proposal does not seem attractive to me, for a number of reasons. First, if we believe in the integrity of God's creative and redemptive project, it seems odd and over-complex to affirm a single creator of all creatures and then to divide God's work of reconciliation into millions of species-specific acts. Second, as is discussed below, New Testament texts and later Christian theologians saw the Christ-event as having a universal and cosmic significance. Having glimpsed this great vision, it is disturbingly anticlimactic to restrict the work of Christ to one among the myriad creatures of God: God's mighty work of reconciliation seems to be rendered curiously incapable of transcending species boundaries. Third, if we were to accept such a narrowing of our vision, we would have to become agnostic about God's purposes for other creatures: without knowledge of other incarnations we would have to say we know God cares about us; as for the rest, we cannot tell.[1] Such an agnosticism seems unwarranted given the many biblical texts in which God's care for other creatures is affirmed, both in the Old and New Testaments.[2] Fourth, evolutionary biology makes clear that species boundaries are surprisingly hard to define and are not static, so it would be a serious theological mistake to make the salvation of creatures dependent on their neat sorting into species-sized boxes.[3] For all these reasons, I judge it theologically unpromising to pursue a species-by-species programme of incarnation.[4]

---

[1] This agnosticism about the place of other creatures before God is frequently asserted by Barth, as noted later in the chapter.

[2] Many of these have been reviewed in earlier chapters, but a small representative sample would include Pss. 104, 136, 144; Job 38–41; Mt. 6.25–30 ‖ Lk. 12.24–28; Mt. 10.29–31 ‖ Lk. 12.6–7.

[3] For an introduction to the complexities of this topic, see John S. Wilkins, *Defining Species: A Sourcebook From Antiquity to Today* (New York: Peter Lang, 2009).

[4] The question of whether there could be multiple incarnations has been discussed from at least Aquinas onwards. Oliver Crisp reviews key arguments in Oliver D. Crisp, 'Multiple Incarnations', in Martin Stone ed. *Reason, Faith and History: Philosophical Essays for Paul Helm* (Aldershot; Burlington, VT: Ashgate, 2008). Crisp's view is that Brian Hebblethwaite is wrong that multiple incarnations are metaphysically impossible, but that God has not in fact done so. Paul Tillich's view is that humanity 'cannot

The position that the incarnation of God in Christ demonstrates God is concerned only with human beings, and that other incarnations of God would be necessary for other creatures, rests on the assumption that incarnation is species specific – of significance only for the species of creature in which God was incarnated. This assumption seems remarkably implausible to me, so the remainder of this chapter is an attempt to explore an alternative possibility: that God's single incarnation in a particular creature could be of significance to all creatures. The next section examines the question of appropriate ways of construing the incarnation. Rethinking the incarnation in this way will clearly have systematic implications for other theological doctrines, so the following section explores the wider doctrinal ramifications of this move, taking the structure of Karl Barth's theological project as a case study. The final section of this chapter reflects on the significance of this Barthian case study for construing the relationship between the doctrine of the incarnation and other doctrines more generally.

Reading the Particularity of the Incarnation

In becoming incarnate in a particular creature, God chose to become one thing and not another. God became a Jew rather than a Gentile, a man rather than a woman, an inhabitant of Palestine rather than one of South America, a creature alive in the first century AD rather than the twenty-first, a human being rather than a dog. Working through this list, we note that even within the New Testament canon, the church argued about the significance of the Jewishness of Jesus Christ and of his disciples,[5] but it eventually came to the conclusion that the religious identity of the incarnate God should not be construed as defining a boundary of salvation. One interpretation of church debates in the past two centuries about the role of women in the church, is as an argument concerning the significance of the maleness of the creature in whom God became incarnate. While some still argue for the exclusion of women from the clergy on the basis

---

claim to occupy the only possible place for Incarnation', although he thinks such a possibility cannot be proved or disproved (Paul Tillich, *Systematic Theology*, vol. 2, 95–6; Brian Hebblethwaite, 'The Impossibility of Multiple Incarnations', *Theology* 104 (2001)). In discussing Karl Rahner's perspective on extra-terrestrial intelligence (ETI) Christopher Fisher and David Fergusson conclude that Rahner's cautionary approach is justified: 'Until concrete evidence emerges of ETI it seems prudent for the moment to remain skeptical about the need for other incarnations' (Christopher L. Fisher and David Fergusson, 'Karl Rahner and the Extra-Terrestrial Intelligence Question', *Heythrop Journal* 47: 2 (2006), 288).

[5] See, for example, Acts 11.1–18.

of the gender of Jesus Christ, few theologians would be prepared to use the doctrine of the incarnation as grounds for gender discrimination. I am not aware of any attempt to argue for discrimination between creatures on the basis of the geographical or chronological location of the incarnate God.[6] The final element of God's choice noted in the list above, however – God's choice to become incarnate as a human being rather than any other creature – in contrast to all the other aspects of the particularity of the incarnation, is still widely considered to be decisive in delimiting the significance of God's action in Christ. This incongruity suggests that arguments relying on the incarnation to discriminate between human and non-human animals are structurally flawed: if we judge it illegitimate to discriminate between Jews and Gentiles or women and men on the basis of the kind of creature in whom God became incarnate, it seems that we should also consider it illegitimate to discriminate between humans and other animals on this basis.[7] Theological positions employing the doctrine of the incarnation to create a boundary between humans and other animals are misreading the particularity of creature we know as Jesus of Nazareth.

The traditional affirmation of the creeds of Nicaea, Constantinople and Chalcedon that God became human is accurate, therefore, but risks misleading by understating the significance of the incarnation, just as saying that God became male could do so. To supplement such formulations we will need to think bigger and affirm that 'God became an animal' or, most comprehensively, 'God became a creature'. The shock of such innovations may be ameliorated by recalling the basic Johannine formula 'the Word became flesh' (John 1.14), which can be paraphrased as the Word of God taking on the life-substance

---

[6] It is notable in this context that Rudolf Bultmann stresses that the time and place of the incarnation are unimportant at the same time as insisting on a solely human interpretation of the incarnation (Rudolf Bultmann, *The Gospel of John: A Commentary*, (eds) R. W. N. Hoare and J. K. Riches, trans. G. R. Beasley-Murray (Oxford: Blackwell, 1971), 65).

[7] Stephen Webb makes a similar argument in Stephen H. Webb, *On God and Dogs*, 170. Adam McIntosh also objects to inappropriate use of the particularity of the incarnation, and uses Barth's language of the history of Israel and the church as a microcosm of Christ's redemption to guard against interpreting the humanity of Christ as grounds for thinking God is only concerned for human beings in redemption (Adam McIntosh, 'Human and Animal Relations in the Theology of Karl Barth', *Pacifica* 22: 1 (2009)). I previously explored this line of argument in David Clough, 'All God's Creatures: Reading Genesis on Human and Non-Human Animals', in Stephen Barton and David Wilkinson (eds), *Reading Genesis After Darwin* (Oxford: Oxford University Press, 2009) and David Clough, 'Interpreting Human Life by Looking the Other Way: Bonhoeffer on Human Beings and Other Animals', in Ralf K. Wüstenberg, Stefan Heuser and Esther Hornung (eds), *Bonhoeffer and the Biosciences: An Initial Exploration*, International Bonhoeffer Interpretations (Frankfurt am Main: Peter Lang, 2010).

common to humans and other animals.[8] 'Flesh' translates the Greek *sarx* here as well as in other New Testament passages treating the incarnation (Eph. 2.14; 1 Tim. 3.16; 1 Jn 4.2). While it is sometimes used by Paul to emphasize human moral weakness, the Christological context here rules out this interpretation.[9] It is instead an inclusive term for all living things, with roots in the Hebrew *basar*, used frequently in the Old Testament to refer to all living creatures: God determines to destroy 'all flesh' in the flood (Gen. 6.13), without God's spirit 'all flesh' would perish (Job 34.15) and the Lord is proclaimed as the God of 'all flesh' (Jer. 32.27).[10] In John's gospel, the Greek translation of this Semitic phrase is used in John 17.2: 'you have given him authority over all flesh'. The fundamental New Testament assertion concerning the incarnation, therefore, is not that God became a member of the species *Homo sapiens*, but that God took on flesh, the stuff of living creatures.[11] That the Word became flesh means

[8] This is John Robinson's understanding of the Hebrew *basar*, which he takes to be semantically equivalent to the Greek *sarx* (John A. T. Robinson, *The Body: A Study in Pauline Theology*, Studies in Biblical Theology (London: SCM, 1952), 13, 17).

[9] John Calvin, *The Gospel According to John*, Calvin's Commentaries, (eds) T. F. Torrance and D. W. Torrance, trans. T. H. L. Parker (Edinburgh; London: Oliver and Boyd, 1959), 20.

[10] See David Cunningham, 'The Way of All Flesh', in *Creaturely Theology: On God, Humans and Other Animals*, (eds) Celia Deane-Drummond and David Clough (London: SCM, 2009), 113–17; Andrew Linzey, *Christianity and the Rights of Animals* (London: SPCK, 1987), 79–80. Linzey's position is discussed in Celia Deane-Drummond, *The Ethics of Nature*, New Dimensions to Religious Ethics (Malden, MA; Oxford: Blackwell, 2004), 63–5.

[11] Commentators on John 1.14 have tended to interpret 'the Word became flesh' as God becoming human: see, for example, R. H. Lightfoot, *St John's Gospel: A Commentary*, ed. C. F. Evans (Oxford: Clarendon, 1956), 85; Rudolf Schnackenburg, *The Gospel According to John*, vol. 1, trans. Kevin Smyth (New York: Herder & Herder, 1968), 267; Bultmann, *The Gospel of John: A Commentary*, 63, 65; C. K. Barrett, *The Gospel According to John*, 2nd edn (London: SPCK, 1978), 165; F. F. Bruce, *The Gospel of John* (Grand Rapids, MI: Eerdmans, 1983), 40; Craig S. Keener, *The Gospel of John: A Commentary* (Peabody, MA: Hendrickson Publishers, 2003), 408. A few follow Calvin in asking the question why John says that God became flesh rather than human (Calvin, *Gospel According to John*, 19–20; see also Schnackenburg, *The Gospel According to John*, 267) and some note that the usage of *sarx* reflects a Semitic usage, also found in John 17.2, Ps. 145.21 and Jer. 32.27 (see, for example, Keener, *The Gospel of John: A Commentary*, 408. None recognize, however, that the strong link between the Greek *sarx* and Hebrew *basar* make interpreting *sarx* in solely human terms questionable. It seems most likely that the question of whether the incarnation could have a more than human referent did not arise for these commentators. John's use of *sarx* in identifying what was assumed in the incarnation is especially striking given the repeated human-specific references in preceding verses (vv. 4, 9, 13). There remains the possibility that *sarx* is used here

therefore that God in Christ became a fleshly creature. The particular creature God became was a human, male, Jewish, Palestinian, first-century one, but none of these specifics seem to have been first in the mind of the New Testament authors who chose the term 'flesh' to characterize the event.

Incarnation as a Cosmic Event

We have noted the oddity of taking one aspect of the creature in which Christ became incarnate – its species – as of definitive significance for interpreting the meaning of the doctrine of the incarnation, and the striking image of the Word taking flesh as one of the foundational accounts of the incarnation. These arguments for a more-than-human understanding of the incarnation are supported by a much more general one: the authors of the New Testament believed the event of Jesus Christ had a significance that was nothing less than cosmic.

The obvious starting point in reviewing the New Testament Christologies that see the incarnation as significant for the whole of creation is the early Christian hymn in Colossians 1.15–20. Here Jesus Christ is identified as 'the firstborn of all creation' in whom 'all things in heaven and on earth were created, things visible and invisible, whether thrones or dominions or rulers or powers – all things have been created through him and for him' (vv. 15–16). In Christ 'all things hold together' (v. 17) and through him 'God was pleased to reconcile to himself all things, whether on earth or in heaven, by making peace through the blood of the cross' (v. 20). The repetition of 'all things' (*ta panta*) here is striking, together with the clarifications that under this heading belong everything 'visible and invisible', 'whether thrones or dominions or rulers or powers', 'on earth and in heaven'. At the heart of the hymn is the affirmation that Christ is the beginning and the end of creation and that there is nothing beyond the scope of his creative and redemptive work.[12]

---

to represent the human by synecdoche, but there seems no good reason to prefer this interpretation.

[12] For discussion of the hymn, see Markus Barth and Helmut Blanke, *Colossians: A New Translation with Introduction and Commentary*, The Anchor Bible, vol. 34B, (eds) William Foxwell Albright and David Nowell Freedman, trans. Astrid B. Beck (New York: Doubleday, 1994), 193–218; R. McLachlan Wilson, *A Critical and Exegetical Commentary on Colossians and Philemon*, International Critical Commentary (London; New York: T & T Clark International, 2005), 123–59; Eduard Schweizer, *The Letter to the Colossians: A Commentary*, trans. Andrew Chester (London: SPCK, 1982), 55–88; F. F. Bruce, *The Epistles to the Colossians, to Philemon, and to the Ephesians*, The New International Commentary on the New Testament (Grand

Colossians is by no means unique among New Testament texts in viewing the incarnation as significant for the whole of creation. Elsewhere in the epistles the first chapter of Ephesians is an obvious parallel, where God's salvific plan, 'set forth in Christ' is 'to gather up all things (*ta panta*) in him, things in heaven and things on earth' (Eph. 1.9–10), and where 'all things' have been put under Christ's feet and Christ is head of 'all things' (1.22). Just as in the Colossians hymn, the author is concerned here to emphasize the full universal scope of *ta panta*.[13] The opening of the letter to the Hebrews affirms that Jesus Christ is the 'heir of all things' and 'sustains all things' (Heb. 1.2–3). In the first letter to the Corinthians, Paul writes that for Christians 'there is one God, the Father, from whom are all things and for whom we exist, and one Lord, Jesus Christ, through whom are all things and through whom we exist' (1 Cor. 8.6). The opening of John's gospel also declares that 'all things' came into being through Christ (Jn 1.3) and Revelation 3.14 repeats the claim of Christ's role in

Rapids, MI: Eerdmans, 1984), 54–76; Eduard Lohse, *A Commentary on the Epistles to the Colossians and to Philemon*, Hermeneia – a Critical and Historical Commentary on the Bible, ed. Helmut Koester (Philadelphia, PA: Fortress Press, 1971), 41–61. Despite the clear cosmic scope of the passage, it is notable that some commentators insist on an anthropocentric interpretation: Eduard Lohse, for instance, ends his discussion with the unsupported claim that 'The great drama, wherein the principalities are stripped of their power and the reconciliation of all things has taken place, is for the sake of man alone' (Lohse, *Colossians and to Philemon*, 61). James Dunn notes the clear influence of Wisdom literature in New Testament Christology here and elsewhere (James D. G. Dunn, *Christology in the Making: A New Testament Inquiry Into the Origins of the Doctrine of the Incarnation*, 2nd edn (London: SCM, 1989), 163–212). See also the extensive discussion of the use of Col. 1.15–20 in an ecological context in David Horrell, Cherryl Hunt and Christopher Southgate, *Greening Paul: Rereading the Apostle in a Time of Ecological Crisis* (Waco, TX: Baylor University Press, 2010), 87–115.

[13] For discussion of this passage, see John Muddiman, *The Epistle to the Ephesians*, Black's New Testament Commentaries (London; New York: Continuum, 2001), 75–6; Ernest Best, *A Critical and Exegetical Commentary on Ephesians*, International Critical Commentary (Edinburgh: T & T Clark, 1998), 138–43, and Markus Barth, *Ephesians: Introduction, Translation and Commentary on Chapters 1–3*, The Anchor Bible, vol. 34, eds William Foxwell Albright and David Nowell Freedman (Garden City, New York: Doubleday, 1974), 86–92. Best concedes that 'As far as early Christianity is concerned it must be allowed that there is also a strain, a more widely found strain, in scripture which sees part of creation as finally remaining outside the love and care of God and Christ, perhaps acknowledging his sovereignty but not willingly offering any allegiance; where this holds, the stress lies on the defeat of evil and not on its summing up in Christ' (142). His conclusion is that the Ephesians strain 'represents more closely the central drive of the NT'.

creation.[14] We can see, therefore, that recognition of the universal significance of the incarnation is widely evident in the New Testament.[15]

These passages make clear that, even in the period in which the New Testament was being written, Christian theologians recognized that in the life

---

[14] Best lists the references to '*ta panta*' elsewhere in the New Testament and discusses the development of the relationship between Jesus Christ and creation (Best, *Ephesians*, 139, 142). See also Bruce, *Colossians, Philemon, and Ephesians*, 56.

[15] Jürgen Moltmann locates the beginning of the modern discussion of the 'cosmic Christ' in Joseph Sittler's 1962 address to the World Council of Churches (Joseph Sittler, 'Called to Unity', *Ecumenical Review* 14: 2 (1962), reprinted with others of Sittler's writings in Joseph Sittler, *Evocations of Grace: The Writings of Joseph Sittler on Ecology, Theology and Ethics*, (eds) Steven Bouma-Prediga and Peter Bakken (Grand Rapids, MI: Eerdmans, 2000), 38–50), but notes that Sittler acknowledges he was only expanding on the 1951 book Allan D. Galloway, *The Cosmic Christ* (Nisbet & Co., 1951). J. A. Lyons traces the beginning of 'cosmic Christ' language back to a Swiss schoolmaster Leonhard Usteri the Younger in 1832 (J. A. Lyons, S. J., *The Cosmic Christ in Origen and Teilhard de Chardin* (Oxford: Oxford University Press, 1982), 11). Moltmann develops the theme in the penultimate section of *The Way of Jesus Christ* (Jürgen Moltmann, *The Way of Jesus Christ: Christology in Messianic Dimensions* (San Francisco, CA: Harper, 1990), 274–312). Andrew Linzey makes clear that such a broad view of the incarnation is by no means an innovation in the theological tradition: Irenaeus states that the Word of God 'contains all things created, and is inherent in the entire creation ... and hung upon the tree, that He might sum up all things in Himself' (Irenaeus, 'Against Heresies', bk 5, ch. 18, §3); Athanasius sees the Logos as illuminating and containing all things giving 'life and everything, everywhere, to each individually and to all together' (Athanasius, *Contra Gentes and de Incarnatione*, ed. and trans. Robert W. Thompson, (Oxford: Clarendon, 1971), 115–17); St John of the Cross writes that in God's union with humanity God was united with the nature of all creatures, leaving them 'all clothed with beauty and dignity' (St John of the Cross, *The Complete Works*, ed. and trans. A. E. Peers, (Wheathampstead: Anthony Clarke, 1974), vol. II, V, p. 49) (all cited in Linzey, 'Neglected Creature', 196, 158, 202). Paul Blowers and Robert Wilken present an overview of the theme of cosmic Christology in Maximus the Confessor in their introduction to Maximus the Confessor, Paul M. Blowers and Robert Louis Wilken (eds), *On the Cosmic Mystery of Jesus Christ: Selected Writings From Maximus the Confessor* (Crestwood, NY: St Vladimir's Seminary Press, 2003), 13–43. Lyons notes that the most extensive development of the theme has been in the work of Teilhard de Chardin, who became convinced that the cosmic nature of Christ must be asserted as a third term in parallel to his divinity and humanity (Lyons, *Cosmic Christ*, 5). George Maloney traces the roots of cosmic Christology in the Christian tradition in defence of Teilhard in George A. Maloney, S. J., *The Cosmic Christ From Paul to Teilhard* (New York: Sheed & Ward, 1968). My aims are at some distance from and considerably less radical than Teilhard's: I am suggesting instead that the creatureliness of Christ is an appropriate gloss on traditional affirmations of his humanity, so that the humanity of Christ can be recognized as a synecdoche for his taking on of creatureliness.

and death and resurrection of this one creature, Jesus Christ, was contained the origin, destiny and meaning of the entire universe. God became incarnate in one creature, but this incarnation revealed the meaning and transformed the being of every creaturely life. In this context, to think of the incarnation as bearing significance only for human beings seems an odd theological oversight, requiring the setting aside or convoluted reinterpretation of key New Testament discussions of the person of Christ. The texts put the discussion of the purpose of creation in Chapter 1 in a new context, presenting a vision of creation centred on God's work in Jesus Christ. It is clear from these texts that it would be a mistake to think that a Christocentric interpretation of creation is thereby an anthropocentric one. The focus here is not the humanity of Christ but the universality of his creative and reconciling work: when our thoughts are being directed to all things, visible and invisible, in heaven and on earth, to become fixated on the species of the creature in which God became incarnate is a clear case of missing the point. As I noted at the beginning of the chapter, everything is at stake for our theological thinking about animals in our interpretation of the incarnation, but the stake is returned doubled and redoubled because the New Testament so clearly and so frequently makes clear that the scope of the doctrine of the incarnation can be no less than the doctrine of creation, and that creation can only properly be understood in the light of incarnation.

Karl Barth and the Limits of the Creature

While the position developed in the two preceding sections, that the incarnation has a more than human significance, seems to be coherent and well-informed by New Testament texts, we should also recognize that such a position seems to be at significant odds with many established formulations of Christian doctrine. As we saw in Chapter 1, Karl Barth's theology is a good example of a tendency to identify the work and person of Jesus Christ with humanity so closely that the rest of creation seems to suffer from neglect. Jesus Christ is defined by Barth as God in movement towards humanity and the history of creation only has meaning as the playing out of the primal history between God, the man Jesus Christ and his people.[16] The reason for creation is that God's eternal son willed to be not an animal or angel but human, and the purpose of creation is to make possible God's covenant with humanity.[17] Jesus Christ is interested only in the salvation of human beings, nothing else, and only human beings

---

[16] Barth, *CD* II/2, 7–8.

[17] Barth, *CD* III/1, (eds) T. F. Torrance and G. W. Bromiley, trans. J. W. Edwards, O. Bussey and Harold Knight (Edinburgh: T. & T. Clark, 1958), 18, 42.

are determined by God as covenant-partners.[18] Humanity is 'the partner in the covenant of grace which is the whole basis and aim of creation'.[19] This exclusive emphasis on the humanity of Christ in combination with Barth's Christological focus means there is little space for consideration of other creatures. It is true that Barth accompanies this line of argument with repeated recognitions of ignorance concerning the place of other creatures before God, but this agnosticism does not prevent him from asserting human uniqueness in countless respects.[20] It is also accompanied by surprising sensitivity to appropriate treatment of other animals, including never killing them 'except under pressure of necessity'.[21] Finally, however, these qualifications cannot undo the impact of the narrow interpretation of the incarnate God in relation to the species in which God chose to become incarnate.

The implication of the argument I developed in the first section concerning misreadings of the particularity of the incarnation is that Barth is no more justified in claiming grounds for discriminating theologically between humans and other animals on the basis of the incarnation, than he would be in claiming that discrimination on grounds of gender or religion is justified on this basis.[22] It seems, therefore, that we must reject the argument he makes for the privileging of the human over all other creatures on the basis of the species of the creature in whom God became incarnate. In order to assess the consequences of this judgement, we must consider whether there are other considerations that could provide an alternative foundation for the unique status Barth attributes to human beings. It is notable that Barth rejects many of the strategies other theologians and philosophers use in this context. In relation to humans being

---

[18] Barth, *CD* III/1, 208–9, 352, cf. Barth, *CD* III/4, 336–7.

[19] Barth, *CD* III/2, (eds) G. W. Bromiley and T. F. Torrance, trans. Harold Knight et al. (Edinburgh: T. & T. Clark, 1960), 14.

[20] Barth observes that we do not know how the lordship and praise of God are exercised in the cosmos (Barth, *CD* III/2, 17), we do not know what it means that other creatures have the same divine counterpart as humans, what it means to say they are with God or what constitutes the glory of other creatures (137–8), we do not know how other animals are also souls of their bodies (359), we do not know whether the life of an animal is the life of a specific subject (374), we do not know about the particularity of independent animal life (394–5), we do not know whether other animals think (399), we do not know whether they are rational beings (419–20), we do not know whether the being of the world is known by other creatures and we do not know whether the world speaks to other creatures (Karl Barth, *Church Dogmatics*, vol. IV/3.1, (eds) G. W. Bromiley and T. F. Torrance, trans. G. W. Bromiley (Edinburgh: T. & T. Clark, 1961), 140–1).

[21] Barth, *CD* III/2, 354.

[22] Barth does assert that the male comes before the female, but does not defend this judgement on the basis of the incarnation (Barth, *CD* III/2, 169).

made in the image of God, he argues that the doctrine does not exalt human beings among the other creatures: humans are first among equals (*primus inter pares*) and other creatures are external partakers of the divine image in humanity.[23] Barth considers carefully and then rejects attempts to define what is specifically human with reference to natural science, ethics, existentialism or theistic philosophy,[24] arguing in relation to scientific accounts that we should not make the mistake of judging humans to be superior to other animals on the basis of scales of values constructed according to what humans value. Only when we already know that we are human, he observes, can we identify characteristics that differentiate us: otherwise we read attributes of animals as a foreign alphabet.[25] Rationality in particular, is an inadequate way to distinguish between humans and other animals: there is no abstract interest in the rational nature of humanity in the Bible, and we cannot judge concerning the rationality of non-human animals because we only have an external view of them.[26] The particularity of the human is therefore rooted in the ontological determination of human beings in Jesus Christ.[27] Once Barth has established this foundation for understanding humanity, he is prepared to make a number of claims that other features of human beings are distinctive: only human beings can thank God, be responsible before God, be determined by God's Spirit for the covenant and be known as possessors of independent life, souls of their bodies, with awareness of others, active before God.[28] What is notable about these claims, however, is Barth's striking and repeated agnosticism concerning the capacities of other animals. All these formulations are structured in the form that we only know human beings to have this capacity: as regards other animals, we cannot say. Obviously this agnosticism cannot be the basis of reliably differentiating between one creature and another, let alone for making absolute categorizations concerning their place in God's creative and redemptive purposes. Therefore Barth's argument concerning the theological distinctiveness of the human stands or falls on whether it can be built on the humanity of Jesus Christ, and therefore, on the basis of my argument above, it falls.

Those less sympathetic than I to the wider shape of Barth's theological project might judge that this problem in the structure of his thought provides

---

[23] Barth, *CD* III/1, 187.

[24] Barth, *CD* III/2, 121, 127, summarizing §44.

[25] Barth, *CD* III/2, 89.

[26] Barth, *CD* III/2, 402, 419–20. Others, of course, would argue that evidence is available that other animals are capable of what we consider to be rational thought: for a variety of approaches to the question, see Susan Hurley and Matthew Nudds (eds), *Rational Animals?* (Oxford: Oxford University Press, 2006).

[27] Barth, *CD* III/2, 136.

[28] Barth, *CD* III/2, 169, 176, 359, 374–5, 394–5, 399, 406–7.

ample grounds to look elsewhere for resources to develop an adequate account of the place of other-than-human creatures in relation to the doctrine of the incarnation.[29] The route I prefer is to seek instead to examine the work necessary in revising Barth's theology to avoid interpreting the incarnation as privileging the human above all other creatures. Obviously, there is more than one route to overcome this difficulty. One could, for example, set aside all that Barth says about rooting an understanding of what it is to be human in Christology. Then one would be free to accept traditional modes of differentiating between humans and other creatures on grounds of their bearing of the divine image or their supposedly unique abilities to reason, use language, behave responsibly, etc. This would result in a theology that had retained the elevation of the human at the cost of Barth's Christological foundation for theology. My judgement is that it is preferable to do the opposite: to retain Barth's Christological foundation for theology at the cost of the elevation of the human, on the grounds that it both results in a theology that is true to the basic structure of his project and gives a more adequate account of the place of non-human creatures. One justification for this judgement is that 60 years on from Barth it is no longer an adequate theological argument to claim we do not know about other animals. Thomas Nagel may be right that we will never know what it is like to be a bat,[30] but copious recent studies demonstrate capacities for thinking in non-human animals that are surprising, and certainly would have been surprising to Barth.[31] In addition to this rationale for revision external to Barth's work, there are at least two indications that he might have had some sympathy with this way forward. In the Preface to the second part of volume III of the *Church Dogmatics* he notes:

> I also think it conceivable that, in spite of the counter-arguments adduced, the limits of the term 'creature' may with the necessary boldness and

---

[29] It is notable that both Paul Santmire and Andrew Linzey engaged in detail with Barth's theology in relation to creation beyond the human in their doctoral theses and judged it lacking: see Santmire, 'Creation and Nature' and Linzey, 'Neglected Creature'.

[30] Thomas Nagel, 'What is it Like to be a Bat?', *Philosophical Review* 83: 4 (1974).

[31] See, for example, Marc Bekoff, *Minding Animals: Awareness, Emotions, and Heart* (New York: Oxford University Press, 2002); Marc Bekoff, *Animal Passions and Beastly Virtues: Reflections on Redecorating Nature* (Philadelphia, PA: Temple University Press, 2006); Frans de Waal, *Good Natured* (Cambridge, MA: Harvard University Press, 1996); David DeGrazia, *Taking Animals Seriously: Mental Life and Moral Status* (Cambridge: Cambridge University Press, 1996); Donna Haraway, *The Companion Species Manifesto: Dogs, People, and Significant Otherness* (Chicago, IL: Prickly Paradigm Press, 2003).

sobriety be more widely drawn than I have dared attempt. At these points, and in relation to other things which may be missed or censured, others may now take up the threads and draw them further.[32]

Later, in volume IV part 3.2, he considers whether it is appropriate to think about Jesus Christ not just as 'the One He is alone with God' and 'the One He is with and in His community':

> Does He not already exist and act and achieve and work also as the Pantocrator, as the κεφαλὴ ὑπὲρ πάντα, as the One who alone has first and final power in the cosmos? Concealed though He may be in the cosmos and not yet recognised by it as by His community, does He not already exist in it with supreme reality, with no less reality than He does at the right hand of God the Father or in His community?[33]

Barth does not develop the point, stating that his present concern is with Jesus' relationship with his community, so 'we may raise but cannot answer this stimulating question'.[34] In both passages, therefore, Barth seems already to have anticipated and to be open to the line of thought we are pursuing here. What follows is therefore a case study in relation to this key theological figure in order to explore what it might mean to reconsider a systematic theological account in the context of a new understanding of the theological significance of non-human animals.

The task of re-envisioning the scope of the incarnation must begin, as Barth suggests, with the limits of the term 'creature', which in many contexts Barth takes to be synonymous with human creatures.[35] Instead of accepting this narrow circumference, we must recognize that all things made by God are creatures of God: mountains, clouds, rocks, rivers, seas, trees, grasses, fish, insects, dinosaurs, birds, reptiles and mammals (including humans), to name but a few. To generate such a list is to make clear the diversity among creatures, but let us stay with this broad definition of the category for the present. The key question is how such a revision impacts the structure of a theological project such as Barth's: what are the systematic implications of changing our usage of 'creature' to encompass all that God has made?

---

[32] Barth, *CD* III/2, Preface. Linzey quotes this passage in Linzey, 'Neglected Creature', 184.

[33] Karl Barth, *Church Dogmatics*, vol. IV/3.2, (eds) G. W. Bromiley and T. F. Torrance, trans. G. W. Bromiley (Edinburgh: T. & T. Clark, 1962), 756, cited by Jürgen Moltmann (Moltmann, *Way of Jesus Christ*, 279).

[34] Barth, *CD* IV/3.2, 756.

[35] For an analysis of this difficulty, see Linzey, 'Neglected Creature', 23, 124–6.

Barth begins the *Church Dogmatics* with two part-volumes treating the doctrine of the Word of God. This opening focusses on God's revelation to human beings, but does not attempt to confine God's activity in relation to creation to this mode. Barth is not here suggesting equivalence between Jesus Christ, the Word of God and God's revelation, which would identify the work of Christ entirely with the human: this would exemplify the modalist heresy by thinking of the second person of the trinity simply with God's activity of revealing.[36] He does discuss the role of the incarnation in revelation in terms that identify it with the human – 'God's revelation takes place in the fact that God's Word became a man and that this man has become God's Word'[37] – but, again, this can be construed as an aspect of God's dealing with human beings in particular rather than as exclusive of other creatures. Writing and reading theology is a human enterprise, and Barth cannot be faulted for attending to its presuppositions and limits on that basis.[38]

The second volume of the *Dogmatics* concerns the doctrine of God. The first part-volume discusses human knowledge of God, before summarizing the Christian doctrine of God as the One who loves in freedom.[39] There are no consequences of widening the definition of the creature in relation to the doctrine of the incarnation here. In the second part-volume, however, we come immediately to the heart of the matter with Barth's doctrine of election. Barth states that God's election of humanity is 'the sum of the Gospel' and is a part of the doctrine of God because Jesus Christ is the electing God and the elected human being in one.[40] Election 'is the eternal beginning of all the ways and works of God in Jesus Christ' and in Jesus Christ God determines Godself for

---

[36] For Barth revelation is a trinitarian act: see Karl Barth, *Church Dogmatics*, vol. I/1, (eds) G. W. Bromiley and T. F. Torrance, trans. G. W. Bromiley (Edinburgh: T. & T. Clark, 1975), §8.

[37] Karl Barth, *Church Dogmatics*, vol. I/2, eds G. W. Bromiley and T. F. Torrance, trans. Knight, G. T. Thomson and Harold Knight (Edinburgh: T. & T. Clark, 1956), §1.

[38] Santmire disagrees, judging that a theology construed as the Word of God cannot adequately represent the biblical view of nature (Santmire, 'Creation and Nature', 368–9). But this construal is of the nature of theology, not of the nature of the content of theology or the content of God's revelation concerning the natural world. There is no structural reason why this Word of God to humanity cannot be received as an affirmation of God's creative and redemptive purposes in relation to all creatures.

[39] Karl Barth, *Church Dogmatics*, vol. II/1, ed. G. W. Bromiley and T. F. Torrance, trans. T. H. L. Parker et al. (Edinburgh: T. & T. Clark, 1957), §28.

[40] Barth, *CD* II/2, 3.

humanity, takes on Godself the rejection of humanity and elects humanity to participation in God's glory.[41]

Here we need to consider a bold innovation to Barth's project. Election is too significant a part of the structure of his theology to suggest that human beings could be elect and the remainder of creation have some other role in God's purposes. As we shall see, God's election and the accompanying covenant with the creature is the very reason for creation in Barth's account. If human beings are the only creatures elected by God in Christ, then non-human creation will remain the after-thought and scenery that the passages surveyed above suggest. Instead, in recognition of the confession that the Word became flesh, we must state that in Jesus Christ God determines Godself for God's creatures, takes up creatures gone astray and elects God's creatures to participation in God's glory.[42] That this represents a revision rather than a contradiction of Barth's aim in setting out the doctrine of election is clear at several points. Barth is quite prepared, for example, to talk about God's love for the world in the context of election, following John 3.16:

> What takes place in this election is always that God is for us; for us, and therefore for the world which was created by Him, which is distinct from Him, but which is yet maintained by Him. The election is made with a view to the sending of His Son. And this means always that in Him and through Him God moves towards the world. It means not merely that He creates and sustains the world, but that He works on it and in it by (miracle of all miracles) giving Himself to it. It means that the will

---

[41] Barth, *CD* II/2, 95.

[42] In *The Travail of Nature* Santmire moots the possibility of the kind of revision in Barth's work I develop here: 'Would it be impossible, in a Barthian mode, to think of God electing nature, as well as humanity, in Christ? Would it be impossible to picture a community of many creatures, not just persons, gathered in the ark of eternity, as it were, as the ultimate beginning and the ontological foundation of all the ways and works of God? Would it be anything but an enhancement of God's grace, from a Barthian perspective, not to begrudge the generosity of God, rather to confess that the creatures of nature also have an external determination, that God intends to have a history also with the galaxies and the dinosaurs and the birds of the air, that they also, in due proportion, along with all our fellow human beings, are our "covenant partners"?' (Santmire, *Travail of Nature*, 171–2). Kathryn Tanner comments that while Barth's theology has an anthropocentric cast because it is centred on Christ, it is important to remember that he believes 'Christ is to have a worldwide effect – not only on all people, but on the whole world' and that the special task assigned to human beings 'does not exclude other creatures from having their end in Christ; it merely specifies the manner of their inclusion' (Tanner, 'Creation and Providence', 125–6).

for fellowship, which is His very being and to which the world owes its existence, is actively demonstrated to the world in a way which surpasses anything that could be expected or claimed. If we describe this movement as election, then it is only because we would thereby emphasise that it is the active demonstration of His love. Would it be love – the love of the personal God, and as such real love – if it were not an electing? As electing love it can never be hatred or indifference, but always love. And the active demonstration of that love is this: 'God so loved the world, that he gave his only begotten Son, that whosoever believeth in him should not perish, but have everlasting life.' (Jn 3.16)[43]

Elsewhere Barth claims that God 'elects creation, man, the human race, as the sphere in which He wills to be gracious'.[44]

Despite these promising signs, however, we should not overlook potential difficulties in such a shift concerning the object of God's election. The first issue concerns the parameters of a broader view of election. The logic of the argument drawing on 'flesh' vocabulary would suggest that animals, human and non-human, should be understood as recipients of election in Christ, but other creatures such as plants and rocks should be excluded. As was argued in Chapter 2, there is certainly merit in attending to the particularity of animate creatures: they have significant features in common with one another that differentiate them from other creatures. In biblical terms as well as being fleshly, they also are all creatures with the breath of life (*nephesh hayyah*, e.g. Gen. 2.7, 19; Ps. 104.27–30; Eccl. 3.18–21). Barth says that with them the history of creation begins, 'the establishment of a covenant between God and His creation which moves independently like Himself and renews itself by procreation after its kind'.[45] To establish a boundary here, however, between animate and inanimate creatures, seems very likely to repeat Barth's mistake in failing to appreciate the breadth of God's purposes in relation to creation. The Psalms call the whole of creation to join in the praise of God (Ps. 66.1–4; 98.7–8; 145.9–16; 148), God is frequently affirmed as the God of all creation rather than just its animate parts (e.g. Gen. 1; Job 38–41; Ps. 104) and the inclusion of 'all things' in the cosmic vision of Ephesians and Colossians seems to allow for no half-measures (Eph. 1.10; Col. 1.15–20). It is notable in this context that Barth states that even plants and trees were created for their own sake by God, with their own dignity and justification independent of their usefulness to animals.[46] In Barthian terms, if we

---

[43] Barth, *CD* II/2, 25–6.
[44] Barth, *CD* II/2, 11.
[45] Barth, *CD* III/1, 170.
[46] Barth, *CD* III/1, 143, 152.

understand God to be radically 'for' creation, nothing less than the election of all creation can give it an adequate place in his theology. At this point, therefore, we must attend to God's purposes in relation to animal creatures without constructing a new barrier between animal and non-animal creatures.

The second question that might be raised at this point relates to the broad inclusivity of this new vision of election: is it plausible to speak of God's relationship with whales, cats, gnats, trees, plankton, viruses, cliffs, streams, clouds and red dwarfs in terms of election? Certainly it stretches the language that arose in the context of the calling of Abram and his descendants and which was taken up by Christian theologians. It seems to me, however, that the most significant innovation necessary between the theological tradition to which Barth is heir and my proposal here, is accomplished by Barth himself. Barth transformed a doctrine that had been used to maintain fences between groups of human beings into an expression of God's radically inclusive graciousness towards all human creatures. In Barth's account, election is no longer a means of God choosing some and abandoning others: Jesus Christ is the only human being determined to be rejected by God and the hope of all humanity is to be made elect in Jesus Christ.[47] We may pause at the implication that broadening our understanding of the creature in the context of the doctrine of election threatens to collapse the distinction between creation and election: if our hope is that all creatures may be elect in Jesus Christ it seems their election is effected in their creation. Yet it is Barth who made clear the close relationship between these categories in calling creation the external basis of the covenant of grace.[48] If Barth is right that 'the creature's right and meaning and goal and purpose and dignity lie – only – in the fact that God as the creator has turned toward it with His purpose'[49] then the existence of all creatures is properly dependent on their place in God's covenantal purposes and we cannot finally separate God's acts of creation and election. The shift I am proposing, to include other creatures alongside the human ones Barth had in mind, is an innovation of smaller magnitude than that effected by his grand vision of the scope of God's grace in creation and election.

A third potential difficulty in widening the definition of the creature in the context of the doctrine of election concerns Barth's emphasis on the corporate aspect of election. God's election is of Jesus Christ as representative of 'the whole people that hastens towards this man and derives from Him', equipping them 'to be "a light of the Gentiles", the hope, the promise, the invitation and the summoning of all peoples'.[50] Here Barth links the Christian doctrine of

---

[47] Barth, *CD* II/2, 94–125.
[48] Barth, *CD* III/1, 94–229.
[49] Barth, *CD* III/1, 94.
[50] Barth, *CD* II/2, 53.

election with the election of Israel, yet moving to an affirmation of the election
of all God's creatures threatens to invalidate the idea of God's chosen people
through its inclusiveness.[51] Barth's account is instructive here, however, in
locating the primary object of election as Jesus Christ, rather than a particular
group of human beings, in order to do justice both to the particularity of God's
election and the radical inclusive possibility that none but Christ are rejected by
God.[52] If it is through Christ that those human beings that God determined to
be with are elected to participate in God's glory, then there seems little objection
to claiming that, through Christ, God's other creatures are elected to this
participation. The basis of this election in God's determination to be for God's
creatures means that we do not need to claim that other-than-human creatures
are elect only secondarily, through the election of human beings: all creatures,
human and non-human, are elect through Christ's taking on of creatureliness.
This also makes clear that understanding God's incarnation in Jesus Christ
as significant for all creatures is not anthropocentric, but Christocentric:
it is through the assumption of creatureliness by the divine Christ that all
creatures may be saved; other animals are not saved through Christ's taking
on humanness any more than women are saved by the taking on of maleness.
Considering the corporate aspect of election also opens the question of what
becomes of the church under an interpretation of the incarnation as Christ
becoming creature: such an understanding must have implications for how we
are to understand the church as the body of Christ. However, the vocation of
this group of humans who have received God's Word in the person of Jesus
Christ may be interpreted as enabling rather than excluding the redemption
of other human and non-human creatures,[53] thus broadening rather than
abandoning the corporate dimension of election to humanity in solidarity with
the whole of creation.

With this revision of Barth's doctrine of election, the most significant work
necessary within Barth's theological framework to broaden the definition

[51] To mention Israel in relation to the Christian doctrine of election obviously
raises the issue of Christian supersessionism, which Mark Lindsay discusses in
relation to Barth's theology in Mark R. Lindsay, *Barth, Israel, and Jesus: Karl Barth's
Theology of Israel* (Aldershot: Ashgate, 2007).

[52] Karl Barth, *Church Dogmatics*, vol. IV/1, (eds) G. W. Bromiley and T. F. Torrance, trans.
G. W. Bromiley (Edinburgh: T. & T. Clark, 1956), 92. Tom Greggs treats universalism
in relation to Barth's theology in Greggs, *Barth, Origen and Universal Salvation*.

[53] Stephen Webb recognizes this issue in arguing that the church is 'both a particular
institution, the people who follow Jesus, and the sign of the body of Christ, which
has no limits' (Webb, *On God and Dogs*, 172–3). Adam McIntosh argues that
Barth's eschatology encourages a view of the church as 'a people whose life is the
microcosmic witness to God's creative purposes for all life forms and not only human
beings' (McIntosh, 'Human and Animal Relations', 30).

of the creature is accomplished. The remainder of the second volume of the *Dogmatics* discusses the response of the creature to this election in obedience to the command of God. Barth's discussion might be broadened here to explore biblical accounts of commands to non-human and non-animate creatures, but clearly there will remain a need for a substantive account of how human beings in particular live in response to their election. Barth's doctrine of creation, the third volume of the *Dogmatics*, will require significant revision to allow a wider definition of the creature, but most of the changes here are merely the outworking of the broader doctrine of election. The covenant for which creation is the external basis becomes a covenant with all creatures, a concept with explicit biblical precedent in Genesis (Gen. 9.1–17) and Hosea (Hos. 2.18), as well as more generally in the many examples of God's providential care for all creation. Barth's discussion of the particularity of the human will therefore be revised to establish human beings more clearly in the context of the other creatures of God. This does not mean failing to attend to the distinctiveness of the human, although treating this topic adequately will require advancing beyond the almost complete agnosticism concerning the capabilities of the other creatures Barth espouses. Revising Barth's doctrine of creation also does not mean the relationship between God and the human creature can no longer receive more intensive examination than God's relationships with other creatures: theology is – as far as we know – a human enterprise with a human audience. This attention to the human must be done in such a way that it enables human beings to see their place among God's other creatures as well as appreciate their particular vocation among them. In relation to the ethical topics Barth discusses under the doctrine of creation, it is interesting to note that the fundamental orientation of his discussion of the ethics of human relationships with other parts of creation needs no revision. Barth's position that there is no biblical basis for speaking of a determination of human beings towards their fellow-creatures must be corrected,[54] but the core of his treatment of plants and other animals is in alignment with seeing them as joint covenant partners. In relation to plants, Barth says that human beings may use their superfluity for food but should not wilfully destroy them;[55] in relation to other animals, Barth says they can be killed only as a matter of necessity, and then as a sacrificial act with gratitude and repentance.[56] In a modern context where few humans need to kill other creatures for food, this is a radical ethical stance.

---

[54] Barth, *CD* III/2, 332–3.

[55] Barth, *CD* III/2, 351.

[56] Barth, *CD* III/2, 355. Commenting on this passage, James Gustafson writes: '[t]here is a kind of piety in these remarks' but 'while there is great sensitivity to the natural order as the sustaining environment for human life the focus is on God's relation to man, who is then related to nature, and not on the ordering of the relationships

Barth's doctrine of creation was to have been followed by volumes devoted to the doctrines of reconciliation and redemption; although the former was not completed and the latter not begun before he died. In the next chapter I give consideration to the implications for the doctrine of reconciliation of defining the creature more broadly, considering how the concepts of sin and atonement refer to human and other-than-human animals. The incompleteness of Barth's project means it is harder to think through the implications of the doctrine of redemption in his company, but Part III of this book argues that broadening our understanding of creatures in the doctrine of election will mean a parallel expansion in our understanding of God's redemptive acts.

The preceding pages have considered the implications of following the path Barth identified but left unexplored – drawing the limits of the term 'creature' more broadly than he did. It is clear that there are significant revisions necessary to his theological project, the most significant of which concern his doctrine of election. These revisions do not, however, threaten the theocentric and Christocentric focus of his theology and do not threaten the coherence of the structure of his theology. Nor do they weaken Barth's affirmation of God's grace to human beings. Rather, they place the significance of the incarnation for humanity in a wider context, extending the scope of God's graciousness to God's creatures in a way wholly in keeping with Barth's deepest theological insights and motivations. It seems, therefore, that this experiment with Barth's theology suggests that a broader interpretation of the incarnation can be given without jeopardizing aspects of the doctrine that are theologically fundamental.

Rethinking the Image of God in a Christological Context

The Colossians hymn surveyed in the second section of this chapter begins with the identification of Jesus Christ as 'the image of the invisible God' (1.15), which recalls us to the task deferred from Chapter 4 of reconsidering the significance of the identification of humans as the *imago Dei* in a Christological context. Alongside the Colossians text, we must also note Paul's reference in 2 Corinthians to 'the gospel of the glory of Christ, who is the image of God' (4.4).[57] Also relevant here are two references Paul makes to bearing the image of Christ: in Romans 8 he states that God predestined some to be 'conformed to

in nature and man's place in it' (James M. Gustafson, *Ethics From a Theocentric Perspective*, vol. 2 (Chicago, IL: University of Chicago, 1984), 36). The reworking of Barth's thought proposed here may go some way to addressing Gustafson's concerns.
[57] James Dunn notes the link to Wisdom literature in this discussion of divine image, citing Wisdom 7.26: 'For she is a reflection of eternal light, a spotless mirror of the working of God, and an image of his goodness' (Dunn, *Christology in the Making*, 165).

the image of his Son' (v. 29) and in 1 Corinthians 15 he describes resurrection as exchanging the image of Adam for that of Christ: 'Just as we have borne the image of the man of dust, we will also bear the image of the man of heaven' (v. 49). In 2 Corinthians Paul describes how Christians see 'the glory of the Lord as though reflected in mirror' and how they 'are being into the same image' (3.18). Colossians 3 describes being clothed with the new self 'which is being renewed in knowledge according to the image of its creator' (v. 10). In assessing the significance of these passages, we should note first that in the passages identifying Christ as the image of God the focus is on Jesus Christ revealing God, making visible what would otherwise be invisible. This is explicit in Colossians 1.15, but is also evident from the context of 2 Corinthians 4, where Paul is discussing the way knowledge of God has been veiled from those who are perishing, so that they cannot see Christ, the image of God (vv. 3–4). Jesus Christ is the true image of God, therefore, the unique revelation of the unseen God. If this is the case, our understanding of the *imago Dei* in Genesis 1 must be revised. For it is not the humanness of Christ as such that images God; otherwise God would be equally well revealed in any other human being. Christ reveals God uniquely because Christ uniquely is God incarnate. It is the unique event of divinity taking up creatureliness that results in the unique imaging of God. In this one creature is God truly revealed. This makes it clear that we can no longer speak without qualification of human beings as images of God. Instead we must recognize our capacity to image God as being present only in and through Jesus Christ, fully realized in our resurrection (1 Cor. 15.49) and for now a process rather than a static reality (Col. 3.10; 2 Cor. 3.18).[58]

The account of the image of God evident in these New Testament texts makes clear that the *imago Dei* cannot function as a theologically significant marker between humans and other animals as a reading of Genesis 1 might suggest. There is no difficulty with the versions of functional or relational interpretations of the *imago Dei* discussed in the previous chapter: human beings are called to image God and in Christ they are being transformed into creatures that may image God more fully. There is no difficulty in acknowledging a particular mode of imaging God that is unique to the particular assemblage of capacities that are characteristic of human beings: only human beings can serve God in human-specific ways. What is made problematic by the New Testament discussions of the image of God is the idea that humanness

---

[58] The only New Testament reference to imaging God that sits oddly with this line of interpretation is 1 Cor. 11.7, where the text states that a man does not need to veil his head because he is the image and reflection of God, whereas the woman is the reflection of the man. For a discussion of the difficulties in interpreting this text, see Gordon D. Fee, *The First Epistle to the Corinthians*, The New International Commentary on the New Testament (Grand Rapids, MI: Eerdmans, 1987), 512–24.

as such – as distinct from other forms of creatureliness – reveals God in a unique way or that human beings have a superior standing in relation to other creatures because they represent or even resemble God. Reading the texts we have surveyed undermines such interpretations of the image of God because it becomes obvious that the key distinction is that between Christ and all other creatures, rather than particular groups of creatures that image God in different ways. Once this division between Christ and other creatures in relation to the image of God is clarified, we can consider in what ways different creatures may be partial images of God. Aquinas, for example, agreed with Augustine that a trace of the trinity can be found in all creatures.[59] Particular biblical references suggest more specific images: Isaiah 31, for example, records that the Lord will fight on Mount Zion as a lion growls over its prey and is not daunted by a band of shepherds called out against it (v. 4). It is hard to escape the conclusion that there is a sense in which the lion is an image of God in this case. Jesus' cry to Jerusalem that he longed to gather her children like a hen gathers her brood is a similar case (Mt. 23.37 ‖ Lk. 13.34) and John the Baptist's identification of Jesus as the Lamb of God (Jn 1.29) is only one of many New Testament instances in which lambs seem to function as images of Christ in some sense.[60] Augustine rejects the idea that the Spirit becomes incarnate as a dove at the baptism of Jesus,[61] but it seems hard to escape the idea that the dove is at least an image of the Spirit at this point. Perhaps we might say, then, that like human beings, other kinds of creature may become images of God in ways particular to them.[62]

God Became a Creature

To describe the event of the incarnation as God taking on creatureliness seems in the first instance a radical departure from the creedal confessions of the

---

[59] Thomas Aquinas, *Summa Theologica*, I.45.7, citing Augustine's *De Trinitate*.

[60] See, for example, Acts 8.32; 1 Cor. 5.7; 1 Pet. 1.19 and the extended metaphor in Revelation starting in Rev. 5.6 and extending throughout the book.

[61] Augustine, *The Trinity (de Trinitate)*, The Works of Saint Augustine: A Translation for the 21st Century, ed. John E. Rotelle, trans. Edmund Hill, O.P. (Hyde Park, NY: New City Press, 1991), bk II, ch. 2, §10, cited in David Grumett, 'Christ the Lamb of God and the Christian Doctrine of God', paper presented at the Annual Conference of the American Academy of Religion (2010).

[62] Kathryn Tanner explores the idea of human imaging of God as a task and responsibility, as well as ways in which other creatures image God, in Kathryn Tanner, *Christ the Key* (Cambridge: Cambridge University Press, 2010), ch. 1, 'Human Nature', 1–57.

church, but my argument in this chapter is that this interpretation of the incarnation is a supplement to rather than a contradiction of the affirmation that God became human. The Johannine characterization of the incarnation as the Word becoming flesh is a notable precedent for such a move, the New Testament Christologies that stress the universality of the event of the incarnation seem to demand nothing less and the worked example of revisiting the structure of Barth's theology with this in mind suggests the coherence of Christian doctrine would be retained in this rethinking. Raising the question of where other animals belong in relation to God's incarnation in Jesus Christ makes clear the danger of thinking in too small a box. Accounts of the doctrine of the incarnation that claim that it is of only human significance, or which attempt to use it as a boundary marker between human and non-human creatures not only fail to account for the place of the other creatures before God, but also come to be seen as a strangely blinkered underestimate of the scope and grandeur of God's creative and redemptive purposes. Not merely the being of one species of creature, but the being of every kind of creature is transformed by the event of incarnation. The doctrine of the incarnation does not therefore establish a theological boundary between humans and other animals; instead, it is best understood as God stepping over the boundary between creator and creation and taking on creatureliness. The theological commonality established between human and non-human creatures in relation to the doctrine of creation in Part I of this book is therefore confirmed and strengthened by recognizing the commonality of all animal creatures before God under the heading of incarnation. This leads us on to consider the place of animals in relation to the reconciling work of Christ, which I take up in the next chapter.

Chapter 5

ATONEMENT

In Anselm's work *Cur Deus Homo?* (Why did God become Human?) the answer he gives is that God became human in order to save human beings from their sins. Humanity through their sins had incurred a debt to God that justice required be settled by humanity, rather than merely set aside, but which humanity had no means of repaying. Only God had the resources to pay the debt, but the debt could only justly be settled by humanity. Therefore, Anselm argues, only a being both divine and human could save humanity from their sin, so God graciously took on humanity in Jesus Christ to pay their debt through death on the cross.[1] My aim in rehearsing Anselm's account of the atonement is not to revisit the well-trodden debate about its merits in relation to other alternative accounts, but to draw attention to the stark anthropocentrism of this explanation of the atonement. The problem of human sin is God's motivation in becoming incarnate and the effectiveness of the atonement depends on the humanity of Christ. In contrast to the wide reach of the Christology with which the previous chapter closed, we are here once more confronted with the apparent drastic narrowing of God's interests to the fate of a single species. If Anselm is right that the motivation of the incarnation is a response to human sinfulness, other creatures are mere bystanders. We may consider them lucky in this regard, if we believe that only human beings need the remedy that the incarnation provides. Other animals would then be like passers by at a serious road accident where the injured are being helped by paramedics, grateful to have been spared the necessity of such emergency care. In this case, God would be the *creator* of all things, as discussed in the first part of this book; God might be the *redeemer* of all things, the topic of the last part; but God would be the *reconciler* only of the single species who had turned away from God's purposes. Only humans need reconciliation in Christ, on this view, so Christ's work of reconciliation applies only to them.

A doctrine of the atonement that refers only to the human in this way depends on two problematic assumptions that I wish to challenge in this

[1] Anselm, 'Cur Deus Homo', in *Anselm: Basic Writings*, ed. Thomas Williams (Indianapolis, IN: Hackett, 2007).

chapter. In the first place, it is not clear to me that human beings are uniquely sinful and therefore the only creatures requiring the forgiveness of their sin. Second, even if sin were judged an inappropriate category to apply beyond the human sphere, it does not seem convincing to believe that other creatures do not have need of reconciliation, particularly in the light of the Colossians hymn discussed in the previous chapter. Beyond these two problematic assumptions, there is also a problematic consequence of limiting the doctrine of the atonement to humanity. If Anselm is right that a remedy for human sin is the explanation for the necessity of the incarnation, then it seems we must set aside the grand Christological visions of Colossians and Ephesians: not all things, but just human things are gathered in Christ according to God's plan. And even if Anselm is wrong that the atonement is a full account of the motivation for the incarnation and we retain the cosmic scope of the incarnation while making atonement a species-specific event, we seem to be left with a very unattractive asymmetry and separation between Christmas, Easter and Ascension. Christmas and Ascension on this account seem to be for all creation; Easter just for one kind of creature that has been badly behaved. For all these reasons, and despite the apparent obstacles, I propose that we need a doctrine of the atonement that follows the doctrine of the incarnation in encompassing all creatures.

Is Sin Uniquely Human?

Genesis 6 seems to be in two minds about how far responsibility extends for provoking the divine wrath that leads to the great flood. In verse 5, it is the wickedness of *adam,* humanity, that the Lord sees and in verse 6 the Lord is sorry he made *adam.* In verse 7a, the Lord determines to blot out *adam* from the earth, but the verse continues with a gloss that adds birds, creeping things and land animals to the creatures that will be blotted out and the verse concludes with the explanation that the Lord is sorry he has made 'them'. There is already ambiguity here about which creatures the Lord is sorry for making.[2] Verses 5–8 are generally attributed to the Yahwist source, with the Priestly source giving its explanation of the flood in verses 11–13. Here there seems to be less ambiguity: it is 'the earth' that is corrupt in God's sight and filled with violence (v. 11). God sees this corruption and sees that this is because 'all flesh' (*kol-basar*) has corrupted its ways (v. 12). God tells Noah, 'I have determined to

---

[2] Victor Hamilton notes that this verse suggests '[e]ither the other creatures contributed to the depravity in the world, or else they are innocent victims' (Hamilton, *Genesis 1–17,* 276).

make an end to all flesh [*kol-basar*], for the earth is filled with violence because of them; now I am going to destroy them along with the earth' (v. 13).

Commentators are divided as to how to interpret these passages. Philo of Alexandria discusses the question twice in his *Quæstiones in Genesin* ('Questions on Genesis'), asking what sin the birds and beasts committed for God to determine to kill them together with human beings. His answers match his robustly anthropocentric view of creation discussed in Chapter 1 – since the beasts were made to serve humanity, they were rightly destroyed when the reason for their existence had been destroyed[3] – but once this instrumental view of other animals is rejected, as Chapter 1 argued it should be, the question remains. Luther cites Nicholas of Lyra's view that 'the birds and the rest of the animals had also departed from their nature and crossbred with various kinds', speculating that he may have been influenced by Rabbinic sources. Luther's opposition to this view is blunt:

> I do not believe this. Among the beasts the creation or nature stayed the way it was created. They did not fall by sinning, as man did. No, they were created merely for this physical life. Therefore they do not hear the Word, and the Word does not concern itself with them; they are altogether without the Law of the First and the Second Table. Hence these words must be applied only to man.[4]

It is hard to escape the conclusion that Luther is bringing his opinion to the text at this point, rather than seriously seeking to interpret what is before him. Like Philo, however, he is aware of the apparent difficulty caused by the asymmetry between crime and punishment, and gives an answer very similar to that of Philo:

> That even the animals bore the punishment of sin and perished in the Flood, together with mankind, happened because God wanted to destroy man completely, not only in body and soul but also with his possessions and the dominion with which he had been created. Examples of similar punishments occur in the Old Testament ... In the very same manner, not only the human beings but also all their possessions were destroyed by the Flood, that there might be full and complete punishment for sin. The beasts of the field and the birds of the heaven were created for mankind;

---

[3] Philo, *Philo Suppl. I*, Loeb Classical Library, trans. F. H. Colson and G. H. Whitaker (London: Heinemann, 1929), I.94; II.9. For a longer survey of Philo's views of animals, see Clough, 'All God's Creatures'.
[4] Luther, *Luther's Works*, I.58.

these are the wealth and possessions of men. Accordingly, the animals perished, not because they sinned but because God wanted man to perish among and together with all those things that he had on the earth.[5]

Again, once the assumption that other animals were only created for the sake of human beings has been challenged, the question that Luther clearly feels the force of here is once more at issue. There is another difficulty with Luther's position, however. He states that among the other animals, everything stayed the way it was created, yet elsewhere in his commentary he claims that thorns, thistles, harmful worms, toads, flies and butterflies were a result of the fall, as were the savage dispositions of wolves, lions and bears.[6] Before the fall, there was harmony not just among human beings but between them and the other animals, and Adam would have handled lions and bears as we do puppies.[7] There is no difficulty in seeing why Luther needed to distinguish between life in Eden and life after the fall: he wanted to be able to demonstrate the life God intended human beings and other creatures to have in contrast to the life they are now subject to because of sin. This separation of states cannot be maintained, however, if things remained the same for other animals after the fall, so Luther must be corrected at this point in order to make his own position coherent. He could consistently maintain that the changes in the life of other creatures were a result of human sin, which seems his view in the rest of the commentary, but his statement that things remained the same for other creatures must be set aside.[8]

Modern interpreters are much more ready to consider the possibility that 'all flesh' means more than human beings. Dillman's 1897 commentary observes that 'Not men alone, but … even the animals, contrary to 1.28–30, had learnt to show enmity to one another, and to pursue and slay one another' and notes the parallels with accounts of the Golden Age in Porphyry and Virgil.[9] John Skinner agreed in 1910, suggesting that the other animals had begun to prey

---

[5] Luther, *Luther's Works*, I.58–9. Calvin also understands 'all flesh' in 6.12 as referring to human beings, giving the argument that the same word refers to human beings only in Isa. 40.5 and Zech. 2.13, though this is not obviously the case (Calvin, *Genesis*, 253).

[6] Luther, *Luther's Works*, I.38, 54, 77.

[7] Luther, *Luther's Works*, II.74; I.62.

[8] For a more detailed discussion of Luther's views of animals in this and other texts, see Clough, 'Anxiety of the Human Animal'. Willis Jenkins notes Aquinas's view that the nature of other animals was not changed by human sin (Willis Jenkins, *Ecologies of Grace: Environmental Ethics and Christian Theology* (New York: Oxford University Press, 2008), 146–7).

[9] A. Dillman, *Genesis Critically and Exegetically Expounded* (Edinburgh: T & T Clark, 1897), vol. I, 268.

upon each other and to attack human beings, citing the medieval Jewish scholar Rashi.[10] Claus Westermann's 1974 commentary cites A. R. Hulst's 1958 survey of interpreters, the 'overwhelming majority' of which see 6.12 as referring to other animals as well as humans, although Westermann follows Hulst in considering this improbable, for reasons that are not quite clear.[11] Victor Hamilton's 1990 commentary agrees with Rashi, Dillman and Skinner, noting that the usage of *kol-basar* elsewhere in the flood narrative makes an inclusive reference in 6.12 most probable.[12]

From this brief survey, it is evident that Genesis 6 is ambiguous about whether the activities of non-human animals could have been part of what provoked God to destroy the earth with the flood. Verse 5 asserts that human beings were the reason for the flood; verse 7 is ambiguous; and any straightforward interpretation of verse 12 suggests that all living creatures shared in the corruption that provoked God's wrath. Some commentators may have been motivated to interpret verse 12 as referring to human beings in order to harmonize it with verse 5. Others may have believed for reasons external to the text that other-than-human animals could not be morally at fault and interpreted verse 12 in the light of this belief. With reference to the Genesis 6 text, however, it seems that these two possibilities are both present. Beyond the question of how widely we should spread responsibility for provoking God's wrath, there is also the question of how widely the corruption had spread. Here there is less difficulty: whether or not humans are solely responsible for the corruption, verses 12 and 13 give the corruption of 'all flesh' as an explanation for the corruption of the earth. This gives a clear sense of contagion in the corruption, even beyond the 'all flesh' sphere of humans and other animals. There seems little doubt that the whole earth shares in the corruption, however we construe its cause.

One path beyond the ambiguity of Genesis 6 about sin in animals other than humans is to look elsewhere in the biblical text. As proximately as Genesis Chapter 3, we are confronted by the serpent, 'more crafty than any other wild animal that the Lord God had made' (v. 1), who leads Eve and through her, Adam into their fateful transgression. Many theologians have followed Calvin in blaming Satan, rather than the snake, for this evil act, but there is no doubt in the text that – even in Eden – there is a non-human animal that is acting in opposition to God's purposes.[13] In Genesis 9, God tells Noah that God will demand a reckoning for human life from humans and from other animals

[10] John Skinner, *A Critical and Exegetical Commentary on Genesis*, International Critical Commentary (Edinburgh: T & T Clark, 1910), 159.
[11] Westermann, *Genesis 1–11: A Commentary*, 416.
[12] Hamilton, *Genesis 1–17*, 279.
[13] Calvin, *Genesis*, 140.

(v. 5), which is clearly a punishment for wrongdoing both by humans and by other animals. This is confirmed by the repeated emphasis that the blessings of the Noahide covenant – which seems in reciprocal relationship with the duties imposed in vv. 4–6[14] – apply to every living creature as well as human beings (vv. 10, 12, 15, 16, 17). The same shared responsibility is evident in the prohibitions on going on to Mount Sinai in Exodus 19, where any human or other animal that touches the mountain is required to be stoned or shot with arrows (v. 13; recalled in Heb. 12.20). Prominent in the legislation of Exodus that follows the return of Moses from Sinai is the provision that if an ox gores a man or woman to death, it shall be stoned to death (21.28). This does not seem to be a punishment for the owner, who is specifically said not to be liable. It could be construed as a means of preventing future accidents or eradicating ritual impurity, but the manner of death seems closer to a punishment for the animal itself, following the Genesis 9.5 stipulation. Non-human animals are also culpable for sexual misconduct: if a man or woman has sexual relations with an animal both shall be put to death, for 'their blood is upon them' (Lev. 15–16). In response to Jonah's call to Nineveh to repent, both humans and other animals are covered with sackcloth and stop eating and drinking (Jon. 3.7–10).[15] It seems, therefore, that the attribution of guilt before God to non-human animals is by no means unknown in the Bible beyond Genesis 6.

It is interesting to note that the tradition of holding non-human animals responsible under the law, inspired by the Exodus 21.28 text and by Old Testament prohibitions of witchcraft, continued until comparatively recently. In his remarkable book *The Criminal Prosecution and Capital Punishment of Animals*, Edward Payson Evans collected accounts of nearly 200 court cases in which non-human animals were prosecuted, starting with the prosecution of moles in the Aosta Valley in modern Italy in the year 824 and ending with the prosecution of a dog in Switzerland in 1906 (the date of the book's publication).[16] Most of the trials took place across Europe, although Evans also records examples from the United States, Canada and South America. The

---

[14] David VanDrunen argues that the covenant imposes moral obligations on human beings in David VanDrunen, 'Natural Law in Noahic Accent: A Covenantal Conception of Natural Law Drawn From Genesis 9', *Journal of the Society of Christian Ethics* 30: 2 (2010), 137–9.

[15] We could also note the call in Psalm 68 that the wild animals in the reeds be rebuked, although it is not clear for what they are to be rebuked (Ps. 68.30). Revelation pictures dogs together with fornicators, murderers and idolaters outside the new Jerusalem (Rev. 22.15), although this could be on the basis of a belief that they are unclean, rather than that their actions have caused this exile.

[16] E. P. Evans, *The Criminal Prosecution and Capital Punishment of Animals* (London: William Heinemann, 1906).

animals involved are diverse: locusts, snakes, mice, caterpillars, flies, eels, pigs, bulls, beetles, horses, oxen, rats, cows, goats, weevils, cocks, snails, dogs, asses, mules, dolphins, doves, termites and wolves. The trials were of two kinds: secular tribunals which applied capital punishments to domestic animals such as pigs, cows and horses as a punishment for murder, following the Exodus legislation, and proceedings in ecclesiastical courts against vermin causing a nuisance by devouring crops or infesting buildings, such as rats, mice, locusts and weevils, by means of exorcising or excommunicating them.[17]

One example will serve to indicate the seriousness with which the court proceedings against animals were taken. Evans records the case of wine-growers of St Julien in 1545, who complained that weevils were ravaging their vineyards.[18] The official, François Bonnivard, heard the arguments of Pierre Falcon for the plaintiffs and Claude Morel in defence of the weevils, before deciding to issue a proclamation rather than passing sentence. The proclamation was as follows:

> Inasmuch as God, the supreme author of all that exists, hath ordained that the earth should bring forth fruits and herbs not solely for the sustenance of rational human beings, but likewise for the preservation and support of insects, which fly about on the surface of the soil, therefore it would be unbecoming to proceed with rashness and precipitance against the animals now actually accused and indicted; on the contrary, it would be more fitting for us to have recourse to the mercy of heaven and to implore pardon for our sins.[19]

The official then provided instructions for public prayers and masses for all the households to participate in. These were done and the insects disappeared. In April 1587, however, a complaint was made to the Bishop of Maurienne on behalf of the inhabitants of St Julien, stating that the weevils had resumed their destructive behaviour and asking that they be excommunicated. The bishop appointed Antoine Filliol as procurator for the weevils and Pierre Rembaud as their advocate. In a hearing on 6 June, Rembaud argued that the action was not maintainable because his clients had kept within their rights and not made themselves liable to excommunication, since in Genesis they were instructed by God to multiply and given every green thing to eat. In consuming the vines of the plaintiffs, therefore, his clients were only exercising their God-given rights. Furthermore, he argued that it is unreasonable to use canonical law

---

[17] Evans, *Criminal Prosecution*, 2.
[18] Evans, *Criminal Prosecution*, 38–50.
[19] Evans, *Criminal Prosecution*, 38–9.

against brute beasts subject only to natural law and the impulses of instinct, and dismissed the arguments of the plaintiffs that the lower animals were made subject to humanity as untrue and irrelevant to the case. Following this hearing a series of adjournments are requested for various reasons until 27 June, when François Fay argued for the plaintiffs that although animals were created before human beings they were intended for his use and had no other *raison d'être*, citing Psalm 8 and Paul's dismissal of God's concern for oxen (1 Cor. 9.9). In a further hearing on 4 July, Filliol argued that any subordination of other creatures to humanity did not include the right to excommunicate them and noted that the opposing counsel had not responded to the argument that the insects were subject solely to natural law. In an 18 July hearing he demanded that the case be closed, but the prosecutor successfully applied for a new term.

Meanwhile, extra-legal measures were being taken. At the end of June a public meeting was called after mass to consider the provision of alternative ground that might sustain the weevils without devastating the vineyards. As the result of a popular vote, an area of land was identified and the springs of water on the land put at the service of the weevils, although the inhabitants of St Julien reserved rights to pass through the land, make use of the springs and work the mineral mines there, providing they do not harm the means of sustenance of the weevils. On 24 July the procurator of the plaintiffs asked the court to order the defendants to move to this new land and not return to the vineyards on pain of excommunication. Filliol, on behalf of the defendants, asked for an adjournment to consider the offer, which was granted. Troops passing through the territory caused further adjournments until 3 September, when Filliol declared the land on offer was not suitable as it did not provide appropriate food for the defendants. The procurator for the plaintiffs insisted the land was admirably adapted for the defendants, and the official reserved his decision until experts had examined the place and submitted a written report. Evans then records, somewhat anticlimactically, 'The final decision of the case, after such careful deliberation and so long delay, is rendered doubtful by the unfortunate circumstance that the last page of the records has been destroyed by rats or bugs of some sort.' He speculates that perhaps 'the prosecuted weevils, not being satisfied with the results of the trial, sent a sharp-toothed delegation into the archives to obliterate and annul the judgment of the court'.[20]

Once we have recovered from our astonishment that such events could ever have taken place, what are we to make of this judicial application of the biblical

---

[20] Evans, *Criminal Prosecution*, 49. For further discussion of animals trials, see Peter Dinzelbacher, 'Animal Trials: A Multidisciplinary Approach', *Journal of Interdisciplinary History* 32: 3 (2002).

traditions concerning the legal responsibilities of other-than-human animals? In the first place, we should note that the biblical material we have surveyed concerning the responsibility of non-human animals under the law is clearly interpreted in this tradition as meaning that these animals are subjects responsible for their actions. This is not to say that this view represented a consensus. Thomas Aquinas, for example, believed animals to be irrational and therefore incompetent subjects of guilt or punishment. He therefore judged it to be vain and unlawful to curse them and if they were cursed as creatures of God he considered it blasphemous.[21] He also argued that animals could not have oaths imposed upon them, except insofar as they are moved by God or the devil.[22] Nonetheless, we need to reckon with an alternative tradition in which the Bible was interpreted to indicate that non-human animals were capable of wrongdoing, even to the point of the considerable expense of putting them on trial. Second, we should not rush past the phenomenon of animal excommunications itself, which seems inescapably to carry with it the implication that the animals concerned were in some sense communicant members of the church in order for excommunication to be a possibility.[23] Again, we may find it hard to share this view, but it is striking to be confronted by a longstanding ecclesiastical tradition in which it was taken seriously. Third, the arguments used by the advocates in these cases, an example of which we have seen in the case above, are perhaps one of the few places where serious consideration has been given to understanding the theological place of animals and further research of these sources with this question in mind would be fascinating. Finally, the existence of these trials challenge us with the foreignness of the categories they work with and perhaps make us a little less sure of our views about other animals and the nature of the Christian traditions of thinking about them.

Beyond these biblical and historical approaches to the question of whether non-human animals may be understood to behave in a sinful way, we might also look at evidence from studies of animal behaviour. For example, in 1975 Jane Goodall was observing chimpanzees in Tanzania. Tanzanian field staff observed an adult female, who had been named Passion, take an infant from a mother, Gilka, kill the infant by biting its forehead and consume its body, with Passion's daughter Pom. In 1976, Gilka became pregnant again and gave birth to a son that the staff named Orion. Goodall wrote about what happened next in a letter home to her family. ('Prof' was the name given to Passion's elder son.)

---

[21] Aquinas, *Summa Theologica*, 2-2.76.2.
[22] Aquinas, *Summa Theologica*, 2-2.90.3.
[23] Peter Dinzelbacher makes this observation in Dinzelbacher, 'Animal Trials', 409.

Passion attacked Gilka, Pom helped for a bit, and then while Passion continued, Pom seized the baby, went off with him, and – just as Passion did before – deliberately killed him, biting into his forehead. Then the cannibalistic family fed on his remains for 5 hours, Passion taking charge of the body, Pom and Prof begging ... Sparrow ... came alone, picked up a bit of meat, after staring and staring, sniffed it, flung it down and vigorously wiped her fingers on the tree trunk. Her daughter, Sandi, did exactly the same. Poor Gilka. She was badly hurt this time, and couldn't use her hand the rest of the day – maybe longer.[24]

Goodall reports in another letter that she 'just cried and cried' when she heard the news.[25] These were not isolated incidents: a year earlier staff found the body of the baby of Melissa, another female in the community, with the same bite mark, surrounded by Melissa, Passion, Pom and a group of adult males. In November 1976 Passion and Pom killed and ate Melissa's next baby, who was three weeks old. Only the intervention of staff and researchers prevented the family stealing the baby of Little Bee in August 1977 and Melissa's twins in November of the same year. Passion attacked another mother even after her own son was born; although with the birth of Pom's son in 1978, the infant killing came to an end.[26]

How should we decide whether this sad story in the life of a chimpanzee group is an example of sin? If we chose to link our definition of sin to deliberate evil choices, we would have to consider how far Passion and her family were capable of such choices or whether they were merely acting without deliberate intent. Unless we resorted to a Cartesian understanding of non-human animals as instinct-driven machines, however,[27] we could not avoid the conclusion that the actions of the chimpanzees were some combination of free and forced choices. In most or all human examples of murder we would similarly find actions were to some extent free and some extent driven by emotion or instinct. We might argue for a difference of degree between the human and chimpanzee cases, but it seems implausible to defend a position that these actions are different in kind. Under this consideration, therefore, we would have to

---

[24] Jane Goodall, *Beyond Innocence: An Autobiography in Letters: The Later Years*, ed. Dale Peterson (Boston, MA; New York: Houghton Mifflin, 2001), 207.

[25] Goodall, *Beyond Innocence*, 206.

[26] Goodall, *Beyond Innocence*, 193–5. Goodall reported her findings in Jane Goodall, 'Infant Killing and Cannibalism in Free-Living Chimpanzees', *Folia Primatologica* 28: 4 (1977).

[27] See René Descartes, *Discourse on Method and Other Writings*, trans. Frank Edmund Sutcliffe (Harmondsworth: Penguin, 1968), Discourse 5, 73–6.

conclude that to the extent the chimpanzee infanticides were not merely actions forced by instinct or emotion, they were sinful.[28]

An alternative approach to whether these acts of infanticide could be understood as sinful might be to ask whether this behaviour was 'natural' for chimpanzees, with the thought that if non-human animals are behaving 'naturally' their behaviour could not be sinful. Such judgements are fraught with difficulty – what is 'natural' human behaviour? – but it is clear that Goodall was shocked by the unusual features of this case. We might even go so far as finding in the account evidence of shock and disgust in the reactions of other chimpanzees in the group, such as the reactions of Sparrow and her daughter to witnessing the consumption of Orion's body and the response of the adult male chimpanzees to the killing of Melissa's first baby. While the details in this case are unusual, infanticide has been widely observed in chimpanzees – where males are most commonly the perpetrators – and many other species. Sarah Hrdy published a study of infanticide among langurs in 1977,[29] arguing that this was not merely aberrant as previously believed. Hrdy suggested there were four ways in which infanticide could be adapted to evolutionary success – exploiting the infant as a resource (usually by cannibalism), reducing competition for resources, eliminating dependent offspring of a prospective mate, or parental elimination of particular offspring in order to improve the chances of other offspring – as well as pathological examples where infanticide reduces reproductive fitness.[30] A 2008 book Hrdy co-edited with Glenn Hausfater treats infanticide in various birds, carnivores, fish, amphibians, invertebrates, monkeys, baboons, gorillas, langurs, mice and gerbils, together with some studies of the phenomenon in human societies.[31]

If we interpret 'natural' here as compatible with reproductive success, we are presented with the question of whether animal behaviour that is natural

---

[28] Beyond the particular example I have considered here, recent studies of primate groups point to differences of degree rather than kind in relation to human experience of virtue and vice. For consideration of this issue, see Bekoff, *Animal Passions*; and, in a theological context, Celia Deane-Drummond, 'Are Animals Moral? Taking Soundings Through Vice, Virtue, Conscience and *Imago Dei*', in Celia Deane-Drummond and David Clough (eds), *Creaturely Theology: On God, Humans and Other Animals* (London: SCM, 2009).

[29] Sarah Blaffer Hrdy, 'Infanticide as a Primate Reproductive Strategy', *American Scientist* 65: 1 (1977).

[30] These are listed in Glenn Hausfater and Sarah Blaffer Hrdy, 'Comparative and Evolutionary Perspectives on Infanticide: An Overview', in Glenn Hausfater and Sarah Blaffer Hrdy (eds), *Infanticide: Comparative and Evolutionary Perspectives* (Piscataway: NJ: Transaction Publishers, 2008), xix.

[31] Glenn Hausfater and Sarah Blaffer Hrdy (eds), *Infanticide: Comparative and Evolutionary Perspectives* (Piscataway: NJ: Transaction Publishers, 2008).

in this sense is for this reason to be judged not sinful. On this account, if the actions of Passion and her family, or the more common actions of male chimpanzees killing the young of potential mates, were part of a potentially successful reproductive strategy, they could not be judged sinful. This position seems very implausible in that it excludes from moral censure actions done for selfish reasons by non-human animals, when actions done from this motivation by humans are most of what concerns ethics in the normal run of things. We do not consider in mitigation of a human murder whether a reproductive advantage was gained thereby and it would be strange to turn our moral methodology upside down at the boundary of the human species. We may be able to understand the motivation of a male chimpanzee who kills the dependent offspring of a potential mate, but that does not mean we thereby remove it from the area of permissible moral enquiry. We may similarly understand the motivation of human murderers who kill for all kinds of selfish ends, but this does not mean we do not make moral judgements of their actions. It seems clear, therefore, that resolving the question of whether these infanticides were 'natural' in the sense of contributing to the reproductive success of Passion and her family would not resolve the question of whether the infanticides were sinful.

In response to the question of whether these chimpanzee infanticides were sinful, neither considering the question of free and intentional action, nor reflecting on whether these actions were 'natural', rules out the judgement that they were sinful. Perhaps orienting ourselves by looking briefly at biblical and theological understandings of sin may help take our assessment of this question further. A focal Old Testament passage for understanding the dimensions of sin is Psalm 78, where the Ephraimites are portrayed as kindling God's rage because they failed to keep God's covenant, forgot what God had done for them and rebelled against God by questioning God's provision for them (vv. 9–20). In the New Testament, the word most commonly used for sin is *hamartia* and means missing the mark. Sin is seen as a power under which people are universally bound and from which they need salvation through Jesus Christ (e.g. Rom. 3.9–18; Col. 1.13–14). This power has cosmic dimensions, entering the world in Adam and leading to the entry of death into the world (Rom. 5.12). Key emphases in the doctrinal development of the theme were Augustine's understanding of sin as disordered desire resulting from a privation of the good,[32] Reinhold Niebuhr's interpretation of this disordered desire in a

---

[32] For a recent account of Augustine's doctrine of sin, see Alistair McFadyen, *Bound to Sin: Abuse, Holocaust and the Christian Doctrine of Sin* (Cambridge: Cambridge University Press, 2000), 167–199.

modern context as the sin of pride[33] and the feminist challenge to this position, suggesting sin is better characterized as a slothful loss of self or a breakdown in right relationship.[34]

Some of these perspectives on sin seem to be straightforwardly applicable to the situation of non-human animals. We have seen in previous chapters that the Noahide covenant was made with the descendants of Noah and of every animal that came out of the ark and that non-human animals are specified as being accountable for not killing human beings (Gen. 9.5–17). Sin characterized as covenant-breaking, therefore, seems applicable to other animals. For this to be the case we do not need to engage in lengthy disputes concerning the extent to which particular non-human animals have the cognitive capacity to understand and respond to a covenant, let alone the issue – also relevant to human beings – of whether or not the terms of the covenant have been made clear to them. The biblical view, evident in Genesis 9 and other texts such as Job 38–41 and Psalm 104, is that each creature has been given its place within God's creation and the Genesis 9 covenant is an expression of a divine expectation that creatures will live within the boundaries God has established for them. While non-human infanticide is not prohibited in the Genesis 9 covenant, we could extend the metaphor of covenant to propose that infanticide as practised by Passion and her family is outside the boundaries of creaturely flourishing envisaged in the commands to be fruitful and multiply (Gen. 1.22, 8.17). The characterization of sin as forgetting God's ways in Psalm 78 is applicable in a similar way: for non-human animals to depart from the mode of flourishing God intended for them could be described as their forgetting God's ways. Similarly, the portrayal of humans living under the power of sin in the New Testament seems readily relevant to the situation of non-human animals: all creatures suffer from the violence that fills the earth in Genesis 6 (v. 11) and Romans 8 pictures the liberation of all creation (v. 21). The Augustinian characterization of sin as distorted desire and the feminist image of sin as the breakdown of right relationships are both clearly apt representations of the chimpanzee infanticides. The other images of sin seem less plausible to interpret in a non-human context. It is hard to conceive of other animals rebelling against God, as Psalm 78 describes. The New Testament image of missing the mark could be rendered in a way similar to not fulfilling the part in creation envisaged by God, but seems also to express

---

[33] Reinhold Niebuhr, *The Nature and Destiny of Man: A Christian Interpretation*, Library of Theological Ethics (Louisville, KY: Westminster John Knox Press, 1996), vol. 1, 186–203.

[34] See Judith Plaskow, *Sex, Sin and Grace: Women's Experience and the Theologies of Reinhold Niebuhr and Paul Tillich* (Lanham, MY: University Press of America, 1980) and McFadyen's survey of feminist approaches to sin in McFadyen, *Bound to Sin*, 131–66.

failing to meet an intentional objective. The discussion between Niebuhr and his feminist critics on the relationship between pride and sloth also seems difficult to apply in a non-human context.

From the exercise of mapping key Christian understandings of sin in a non-human context, it is clear that some, but not all, images of sin are applicable beyond the context of human persons. We should note that not all images of sin are obviously applicable to all human beings, either: infants may seem rebellious at times, but not in the Psalm 78 sense, surely, and probably are not slothful or prideful either. To take a different example, some of the images of sin may also not be relevant to those with severe learning difficulties. It would clearly make no sense, therefore, to exclude non-human animals from the application of language of sin because not all the biblical images of sin were relevant to them. It would make more sense to say that in some ways some animals other than humans do manifest signs of sinfulness, whereas there are other modes of sinfulness that seem to be particular to humanity.

Another objection to attributing sin to non-human animals relates to the question of whether or not their actions could properly be understood as intentional acts of will. The argument might go as follows: if Passion did not decide to kill and eat the chimpanzee babies and if her action was not deliberate, then her action did not meet the threshold for sinful acts. We might go further and say that if she did not know that what she was doing was wrong, she has not committed a sin. The difficulty with restricting the scope of sin in this way is that it fails to reflect the complexity of the relationship between the concepts of sin, guilt and responsibility in the Christian tradition. At the root of the doctrine of original sin is the recognition that we do not begin life with a clean slate and then make a series of deliberate choices that result in our being awarded good or bad marks. This would be to side with Pelagius rather than Augustine in their disputes about the relationship between sin, grace and free-will. Instead we must acknowledge that by the time we are able to exercise what we think of as free choices, we are already deeply compromised by our pre-rational desires and actions, our complicity in social and historic acts of injustice and the many ways in which our lives are shaped by networks of relationships that frequently exhibit pride, selfishness and greed, together with any number of other sinful tendencies.[35] In relation to any particular act, therefore, it is impossible to trace the extent to which it is free and deliberate and the extent to which it is forced or unthinking. Yet to respond to this complexity with the claim that we must

---

[35] For an instructive account of the issues at stake in a theological treatment of sin and free-will, see Wolfhart Pannenberg, *Anthropology in Theological Perspective* (Edinburgh: T. & T. Clark, 1985), 104–19 and Pannenberg, *Systematic Theology*, 231–75.

exclude all such mixed acts from the category of sin would be to exclude all human action from being identified as sinful. Sin as applied to human actions therefore must encompass a messy complexity in which we recognize that our actions are both our own and influenced by forces that are beyond us. There seems no good rationale for analyzing the actions of chimpanzees in a way that is discontinuous from this analysis. What caused Passion and her family to embark on and continue their infanticide? Presumably a complex combination of genetics, nurture and circumstance made Passion consider the possibility of acting in this way and assent to the possibility, when other chimpanzees would not have considered the action as a possible one or would have considered and rejected it. Unless, as noted above, we subscribe to the strange Cartesian view that other animals are automata and humans are absolutely discontinuous from them in their capacities for thought, it seems that we would have a similar task in seeking to penetrate the actions of a human serial killer. We might judge the ability of chimpanzees to make considered choices about their actions to be closer to the capacity of a human child than a human adult, but we do not believe that children go from automata to responsible subjects at a particular age and so this judgement of degree is not a reason for considering chimpanzees outside the boundary of sinful action.

If these biblical, historical and doctrinal considerations suggest that sin is an appropriate category to apply to animals other than humans, there remains a significant objection from a very different direction: whether it is fair to other animals to attribute sin to them. We might instead picture a creation that is entirely innocent apart from the human species. If we take into account a twenty-first century awareness of the ecological damage caused by human activities, so that it seems that the earth is suffering from a 'plague of people' in James Lovelock's words,[36] we might judge there is something to be said for maintaining the innocence of the non-human realm and locating sinfulness squarely with the human. If I think of our family cat, the blue tit that cheeps in the garden or the spider I rescue from the bath, there seems to be little sense in sharing responsibility for what is wrong in the world: instead it seems that I am part of a community that has contributed to and can recognize problems that confront us, whereas they are not. On this account, other animals may do things that are problematic or destructive – such as the chimpanzee infanticides – but they act innocently, whereas human beings act sinfully when they do similar things within or beyond their own species.

In response to the objection that attributing sin to other animals is unjust to them, we need to take into account two further points. First, to say that

---

[36] James E. Lovelock, *The Revenge of Gaia: Earth's Climate Crisis and the Fate of Humanity* (New York: Basic Books, 2006), 3.

the language of sin is applicable beyond the human realm is not to say that responsibility is equally shared. The latter is clearly not the case: human beings are not the only animal capable of manipulating their environment, but they do so on a scale that is greater and in a manner that is more complex than other animals. To say that the lives of other animals may also be subject to sin is not to diminish human responsibility in any way. Second, we should note the danger of a prideful desire to emphasize human significance, even in this negative mode. Jürgen Moltmann comments that this seems like hubris: 'if human beings cannot be like God the Creator, then they want at least to be the reason for creation's ruin'.[37]

In discussing the question of whether sin is uniquely human, we have examined the creaturely actions that provoked the flood in Genesis 6, other biblical discussions of human and non-human action in opposition to God's purposes, legal traditions that held other animals accountable for their actions, possible analogues to human sin in the lives of chimpanzees, biblical metaphors for sin, and questions of the relationship between freedom and moral responsibility. Provided we recognize the defects of the Cartesian binary categorization of humans as ensouled moral subjects and other animals as machines, there seems to be no good theological grounds for believing that human responsibility for actions before God is discontinuous from the responsibilities of other creatures. Some forms of sin will be particular to human beings – perhaps other forms will be particular to other creatures – and the capacity for sin will depend on the degree to which a particular creature is able to respond to God and to its environment. There seems, however, no clear biblical or theological case for considering all non-human creatures free from the possibility of sinful actions.[38]

Who Needs Reconciliation?

Sinful creatures stand in need of reconciliation with God, so if the argument of the preceding section is correct, it is already clear that God's action in Christ of reconciliation cannot be understood as merely human in its motivation or impact. It is important to note, however, as we did above, that the question

[37] Moltmann, *The Way of Jesus Christ*, 375–6 n.
[38] It may be helpful to emphasize here that I am not arguing that the attribution of sin to non-human animals provides any kind of justification for the suffering they undergo. The innocent suffering of animals other than humans has often been advanced as a particular aspect of the problem of evil, as I discuss in Chapter 6. I do not believe the suffering of human beings can be justified with respect to individual sinful acts, let alone the suffering of non-human beings.

we have been discussing of whether non-human creatures are able to sin is separable from and much more controversial than the question of whether these creatures suffer from the consequences of sin. Even if we judged that non-human creatures were not able to sin in the way I have argued, therefore, we might still judge them to be in need of reconciliation.

Merely suffering as a result of sin does not seem to relate immediately to reconciliation. It is clear that other-than-human animals can and do suffer from the consequences of human sinfulness whether or not they are themselves capable of sin. Whenever any non-human animal is treated cruelly by a human it suffers the effect of human sin and stands in need of rescue from the impact of sin on its life. Properly speaking, however, we should probably say that such victims of sin need redemption rather than reconciliation: their victimhood does not separate them from God in a way that requires the work of Christ to overcome. They need an immediate salvation or liberation, and possibly a final one – as will be explored in the final part of this book – but such innocent suffering in itself is not well understood as requiring reconciliation, since suffering evil does not create an obstacle between creature and God.

There is another sense of suffering from the result of sin, however, that seems more applicable to the category of reconciliation. We can approach this question by returning to the opening chapters of Genesis. At the end of the sixth day of creation, God assigns plants yielding seeds and trees with seeds in their fruit as food for human beings (1.29). To the beasts of the earth, birds of the air and everything that creeps on the earth, God gives every green plant for food (1.30). In Eden, therefore, no animal – including human beings – preys on another animal. Animals consume plants but live in harmony with one another. In Genesis 6, it is clear that this harmony was lost with the expulsion of Adam and Eve from Eden: as we have seen, the earth had become filled with violence and 'all flesh' (*kol-basar*) had corrupted its ways (6.11–12). After the flood, human beings are given permission to kill other animals for food for the first time (9.3) and other animals are prohibited only from killing human beings (9.5), suggesting that humans and other animals are allowed to be predators, killers of other creatures for food, for the first time. Beyond Genesis, prophetic visions look forward to a time when there will be peace once again between humans and other creatures (Isa. 2.4; 11.6–9; 65.25–6; Mic. 4.3) and the foundational importance of peace to God is shown in that one of the names of the Messiah is the 'Prince of Peace' (Isa. 9.6). In the New Testament, Jesus teaches that peacemakers will be called the children of God (Mt. 5.9) and that his followers should turn the other cheek when attacked, love their enemies and pray for those who persecute them (Mt. 5.39–45). This praise of peacemakers is echoed in Paul's letter to the Romans and the letter of James (Rom. 12.14–21; Jas 3.18), while the letters to the Hebrews and 1 Thessalonians refer to the 'God of peace' (Heb. 13.20; 1 Thess. 4.23). The work of Christ itself is described in Colossians as God making peace through the blood of the cross (Col. 1.20) and the Revelation of St John pictures this peace as a new heaven and new earth where there will be no more death, crying or pain (Rev. 21.4).

The most obvious reading of these texts concerning the God's will for peace and harmony between creatures is that relationships of predation where the life of one creature is sustained only at the expense of the lives of others are not original or final indications of God's creative and redemptive will. The era inaugurated by Genesis 9, where humans have explicit permission to kill other animals for food, seems in this context to be a concession by God to the human inability to live within the original constraints envisaged in Genesis 1 and 2. Prophetic voices look forward to the end of this interim time when the harmony with other creatures will be restored again and suffering will be no more, a prophecy that seems echoed and extended in Paul's majestic vision of a groaning creation set free from its bondage to decay (Rom. 8.21–2).[39] Here, then, predatory relations between creatures seem to be one of the consequences of the fall and the creation is promised liberation from the present time of groaning in which lives are subject to suffering and cut short by death. Whether or not it makes sense to say that non-human creatures are capable of sin, this reading of the fall suggests that many or most creatures are caught up in structures of predation and competition for resources that mean they are in need of reconciliation with God in an analogous way to humans caught up in situations of structural sin.[40] In Eden, God gave lions green plants for food; for now they are forced to prey on other animals to survive; the prophets look forward to the time to come when they will eat straw like the ox and live in peace with other creatures.[41]

[39] For a discussion of the hermeneutical issues concerning the use of this passage in an ecological context, see Hunt et al., 'An Environmental Mantra?'.

[40] Andrew Linzey cites Thomas Torrance's sensitivity to the predator prey process and pain in other animals: 'Are these only ingredients in the functioning of animal survival-mechanisms and of orderly development, or do they contain elements which we cannot but regard as evil? What of the fact that creatures exist by devouring one another, and of the endless waste of life in the universe at all levels of sentient and organic life? What of needless arbitrary suffering like cruelty which shocks our sense of rightness and goodness? It is difficult not to think that somehow nature has been infiltrated by an extrinsic evil, affecting entropy for ill, corrupting natural processes, and introducing kinks into their order, so that it is hardly surprising that even the ablest scientists can be overwhelmed by the pointlessness of it all' (Thomas Forsyth Torrance, *Divine and Contingent Order* (Oxford: Oxford University Press, 1981), 122–3, cited in Andrew Linzey. 'The Neglected Creature', 294–5).

[41] The discussion in Chapter 3 concerning the possibility that Israelite food laws were informed by the uncleanness of predatory animals provides additional support

There is, however, an important difficulty in relating the doctrine of the fall to the conditions of non-human life if we take the theory of evolution to be broadly accurate in characterizing the development of life on earth, as I do. If non-human predation and suffering are judged to be intrinsically evil, it seems that creation was fallen long before human beings had any opportunity to respond positively or negatively to God. Even if we allow sin to be applied beyond the human, it seems implausible to attribute agency to the creatures that would first have consumed other creatures, which would have been very simple creatures indeed.

One response to this difficulty is to deny the doctrine of the fall altogether and instead affirm that the world was always intended by God to contain the predation and suffering we see about us.[42] This provokes the obvious question of how to reconcile the goodness of God with such a world, particularly given the strength of biblical witness concerning God's desire for peace between creatures we have just recalled. The only promising route here seems to be to claim, with Christopher Southgate that 'the sort of universe we have, in which complexity emerges in a process governed by thermodynamic necessity and Darwinian natural selection, and therefore by death, pain, predation, and self-assertion, is the only sort of universe that could give rise to the range, beauty, complexity and diversity of creatures the Earth has produced'.[43] Southgate

for this position. Robert Grant notes that one homily erroneously attributed to Basil states that 'at first even the panther and the lion ate fruits, but after men fell and God allowed them to eat meat the animals took the same liberty' so that '[t]he lion turned carnivorous and vultures began to eat cadavers' (Grant, *Early Christians*, 78).

[42] This is the position of Christopher Southgate, who judges that believing that creation has been corrupted by the rebellious action of free moral agents is incompatible with scientific understandings of the development of life. In support of this position, he cites John Polkinghorne's view that impermanence and death are the prerequisite of new life, so that the blind alleys and malfunctions of the physical world will produce 'what humans perceive as the physical evil of disease and disaster'. In this sense, Polkinghorne comments 'the universe is everywhere "fallen" and it has always been so' (John Polkinghorne, *Reason and Reality* (London: SPCK, 1991), 99, cited in Southgate, *Groaning of Creation*, 28). Southgate notes that Arthur Peacocke also shares his view: 'The traditional interpretation of the third chapter of *Genesis* that there was a historical "Fall", an action by our human progenitors that is the explanation of biological death, has to be rejected…There was no golden age, no perfect past' (Arthur Robert Peacocke, *Theology for a Scientific Age: Being and Becoming – Natural, Divine, and Human*, Enlarged edn (Minneapolis, MN: Fortress Press, 1993), 222–3 (italics in original), cited in Southgate, *Groaning of Creation*, 29) The position I am defending here is not one that depends on the literal interpretation of the Eden story that Peacocke rejects, nor one that sees biological death as a consequence of the fall.

[43] Southgate, *Groaning of Creation*, 29 (italics removed from original).

terms this the 'only way' argument. In this view, then, God does not like the suffering that creating in this way entails, but accepts it as the least bad way of making creatures like us and those around us. Southgate is aware of the diffi-culties of this position, the most acute of which is the challenge given dramatic expression in Dostoyevsky's *The Brothers Karamazov*, where the older brother Ivan shocks the young Alyosha with his reasons for refusing to give allegiance to the Christian God. Ivan describes a range of terrible stories of cruelty to children – and a horse – that he has found in the newspapers. He recognizes that these evils may be part of some bigger divine plan: 'I want to see with my own eyes the hind lie down with the lion, and the murdered man rise up and embrace his murderer. I want to be there when everyone suddenly finds out what it was all for.'[44] He cannot accept, however, that the suffering of these children is worth this 'higher harmony' and therefore he says he must return to God his entrance ticket to this divine drama.

The application of Ivan's rebellion to God's purported decision to create complex, beautiful and diverse creatures through 'death, pain, predation and self-assertion' is clear: it is not at all obvious that a god who planned to use this means of creating even the most wonderful creatures would be worthy of worship. This is not to say that retaining a doctrine of the fall invalidates Ivan's challenge: in such a scheme the god in question must still permit the suffering of creatures, and this must remain uncomfortable for Christians to confront. To say that the gracious and loving God directly intended the creation of creatures in this way, however, makes Ivan's position a much more fundamental argument against Christian belief. Under this theodicy-driven redescription, God has become the sort of mono-maniacal biological engineer familiar from science-fiction stories, struggling with recalcitrant materials to achieve a particular desired outcome, in the belief that this goal outweighs all the devas-tation and suffering caused along the way. Southgate judges that his emphasis on God's co-suffering with creatures ensures his account is not susceptible to this kind of challenge,[45] but acknowledges the question of what difference it makes to the suffering creature that God also suffers. He responds that God's presence 'at some deep level takes away the aloneness of the suffering creature's experience'.[46] It is a crucial consequence of the interpretation of incarnation and atonement presented in the previous chapter and this one that God becomes intimate with creaturely suffering, but this is not to say that this suffering can be utilized in the context of theodicy to justify God's infliction of suffering on

[44] Fyodor Dostoyevsky, *The Brothers Karamazov*, trans. Richard Pevear and Larissa Volokhonsky (New York: Farrar, Strauss and Giroux, 1990), 244.
[45] Southgate, *Groaning of Creation*, 16, 50–4, 56–7.
[46] Southgate, *Groaning of Creation*, 52.

creatures. The pain inflicted on an individual by a surgeon, for example, may or may not be judged to be justified on the basis of benefit to the patient or to others, but if the surgeon decided to inflict the same pain on themselves, it would not materially alter the judgement one way or another. On this account, God becomes both the intentional perpetrator of suffering and the co-victim of it, but the latter does not alter the conclusion generated from the former that this God is unworthy of worship.

There is an additional weighty consideration against taking the path that God creates through suffering because that is the 'only way' God can do it. The very idea of materials being resistant to God's purposes and therefore only usable by God in a particular way sets aside the doctrine of *creatio ex nihilo* – God's creation of all things from nothing – and thereby the possibility of a God transcendent in relation to the created order.[47] This is a God who is either unable to create in any other way – and is therefore not omnipotent – or chooses to create through suffering and predation when creating without these evils was a possibility – and is therefore not good.[48] Genesis 1–2 reveal a God who has ordered a good creation in which diverse creatures live in harmony with one another; Genesis 3 makes clear that something happened which means we can no longer read off God's purposes by observation of the world in its current state. To insist against this that the life of the world we see around us is a reliable indication of God's creative purposes is to privilege our own independent observation of the world over basic affirmations concerning the doctrine of God that are biblically rooted and defended throughout the Christian tradition. Attempting to solve the problem of the relationship between the fall and evolution by denying the fall, therefore, is by no means an attractive option for Christian theology.

In order to develop an alternative way of understanding the relationship between the Christian doctrines of creation, fall and redemption with the evolution of life on earth, we need to find a different starting point. We must interpret the fall Christologically and through the doctrine of the atonement – which is why discussion of the topic appears in this chapter. The opening of the letter to the Colossians, discussed in the previous chapter, proclaims that through Christ 'God was pleased to reconcile to himself all things, whether on earth or in heaven, by making peace through the blood of his cross' (Col.

---

[47] For a summary of the significance for Christian doctrine of the affirmation that God created from nothing, see Gunton, 'The Doctrine of Creation', 141–2.

[48] Southgate acknowledges the problem for his account posed by the doctrine of *creatio ex nihilo* but judges that the difficulties with the other options he identifies mean we should accept the 'only way' argument in spite of this problem (Christopher Southgate, 'Reading Genesis, John, and Job: A Christian Response to Darwinism', *Zygon* 46: 2 (2011), 387–8).

1.20). Here it is immediately clear that 'all things' have become separated from God such that they need reconciliation, which rules out an exclusively human account of the atonement.[49] Beyond this, however, the verse also makes clear that we need to think about time in a way very different from the way it functions in evolutionary timelines. The 'all things' reconciled to God cannot be understood as merely those things present at the time of Christ's death and resurrection: the verse understands these events as trans-temporal in their significance, effecting reconciliation for all creatures, at every point in time. If this is the point in the history of creation where creation is reconciled to God, the effects of the event of the cross must reverberate through cosmic history from the moment at which it took place forward to the end of time and backward to its very beginning. At every point in time its effect is felt, undoing the estrangement of creatures from God. There is no alternative to finding a different way of thinking of time such as this if we are to do justice to the cross as a trans-temporal event.

The question that now arises is to ask what this understanding of the cross in relation to time means for our understanding of the fall. Here there is reason to follow Karl Barth's advice that sin is only known in the encounter with God's grace.[50] We should avoid an account of the fall that is detached from the work of Christ: instead, the primary evidence for the fall is that Christ came to effect reconciliation between all things and God. Once we have recognized the trans-temporal character of the cross and resurrection, however, it seems we must consider that the estrangement that is revealed in the work of Christ must be understood in the same way. It is as the estrangement of creaturely life is overcome and reconciled to God in Christ that we recognize its depth and extent. This estrangement is represented most obviously in the wrongful execution of the incarnate God, but that is merely one focal instance of the myriad ways in which creatures before and since have turned from their creator. Just as we understand creaturely reconciliation centred on the death and resurrection of Christ and radiating backwards and forwards through time, so too we can understand the estrangement of creaturely life from God as typified in the cross, but illuminated by the inbreaking of God's grace backwards and forwards through time. In recognizing the depths of human sin represented at Calvary, we come to see how humans and other creatures have departed from God's way and become trapped in patterns of sin. The fall is therefore seen to be historical – it is

---

[49] The deduction from this verse that all things have become estranged from God is made by F. F. Bruce (Bruce, *Colossians, Philemon, and Ephesians*, The New International Commentary on the New Testament (Grand Rapids, MI: Eerdmans, 1984), 74) and Lohse (Lohse, *Epistles to the Colossians and to Philemon*, 59), among others.

[50] Barth, *CD* IV/2, 381.

in history that God's creatures turn from God – but not in the sense that a single fateful decision is a temporal cause of all the sin that follows. Human sin is what God's grace in the death and resurrection of Christ primarily and most obviously reveals, but in lighting up the whole of creaturely history the ways in which the lives of other creatures have been distorted by sin is also made clear.[51]

Before moving on, it is worth acknowledging and responding to a significant objection to the position I have outlined. In Southgate's critique of Neil Messer's discussion of the fall in an evolutionary context, Southgate asks whether Messer's position privileges a concern for the goodness of God over a concern for God's sovereignty, since 'if creatures who do not (on our present understanding) have freedom of will commit acts of violence on each other and inflict suffering on each other, contrary to God's will, and God is unable to prevent this, then can this God really be regarded either as the *creator ex nihilo*, or indeed as the sovereign Lord of creation?'.[52] I have found Messer's account helpful in the development of my own position, and Southgate's critique is as valid a question to the account I have outlined as to Messer's. The argument developed in this chapter is sceptical that free choice or sin is particular to humanity and unconvinced that it makes sense to restrict the structure of Christian doctrine to temporal schemes of cause and effect.[53] The only account we can give in a theological context to the existence of evil is creaturely rebellion against God's graciousness in creation. It is not a full or complete explanation, and a great deal of creaturely suffering does not seem comprehensible under this heading. To acknowledge this is not to deny that God creates *ex nihilo* or that God is the sovereign Lord of creation, but to confess that we will not know how God's goodness, power and love relate to the darkest parts of creation until we are freed from doing theology as wayfarers (*theologia viatorum*) and are able to see as the angels do (*theologia comprehensorum*).[54]

---

[51] My judgement is that this trans-temporal and Christological account of the fall is preferable to that offered by an angelic fall before creation, as proposed in Michael Lloyd, 'Are Animals Fallen?', in Andrew Linzey and Dorothy Yamamoto (eds), *Animals on the Agenda: Questions About Animals for Theology and Ethics* (London: SCM Press, 1998), on the basis that we are better off interpreting the fall in relation to Christ rather than being dependent on speculative pre-histories of spiritual beings. Lloyd's position is criticized for different reasons by Southgate (Southgate, *Groaning of Creation*, 29–32).

[52] Southgate, 'Reading Genesis, John, and Job: A Christian Response to Darwinism', 381–2, (italics in original), critiquing Neil Messer, 'Natural Evil After Darwin', in Michael Northcott and R. J. Berry (eds), *Theology After Darwin* (Milton Keynes: Paternoster, 2009).

[53] Southgate himself allows the possibility of free choice in primates (Southgate, 'Reading Genesis, John, and Job: A Christian Response to Darwinism', 385).

[54] For discussion of this theme in the context of Barth's theology, see David Clough,

To take this path rather than the one Southgate takes is to prefer a confession of ignorance to attributing suffering to God's original intention in creation.

The answer to the question of who needs reconciliation can therefore be answered quite straightforwardly: in Christ, God reconciles all things to Godself; God does not effect reconciliation where there is no need; therefore all things need the reconciliation God brings in Christ. We see the clearest examples of the consequences of this estrangement in the sin of human beings, but the lives of other creatures are also subject in many different ways to the impact of turning from God. In particular, the predator/prey relationships between creatures that characterize life in these days are not part of God's original creative purpose and the prophets look to a time in which creatures will live in harmony once more. For now we exist in the time between the times in which we look back to God's reconciling act in Christ and look forward to the new creation when harmony between creatures will be fully and finally established.

An Animal Sacrifice

In one of the remarkable images of the passion collected by James Marrow, from the twelfth century Mosan Floreffe Bible, Christ is depicted on the cross in the main upper panel of the picture, while below a calf is being sacrificed. Writing on the arch above the scene leaves the viewer in no doubt as to the significance of what is being portrayed: 'For the blemish of sin a calf is given, worship's sacrifice; this inscription teaches that Christ is the calf.'[55] Marrow makes clear that the imagery of Christ as a sacrificial calf is no isolated instance: traditions that Christ was led over a rough and stony way are traceable to Deuteronomy 21.3–4, which gives instruction to the elders concerning how to kill a heifer in order to absolve themselves of the bloodguilt of a murder in which the culprit has not been identified.[56] The link between the blood of Christ and the blood of sacrificed goats, calves and heifers is made directly in Hebrews 9, where Christ is the high priest who 'entered once for all into the Holy Place, not with the blood of goats and calves, but with his own blood, thus obtaining eternal

---

[55] James H. Marrow, *Passion Iconography in Northern European Art of the Late Middle Ages and Early Renaissance: A Study of the Transformation of Sacred Metaphor Into Descriptive Narrative* (Kortrijk, Belgium: Van Ghemmert Publishing Company, 1979), 100, commentary on Figure 72, 'Crucifixion and the Sacrificial Calf' taken from the British Library, Add. MS 17783.

[56] Marrow, *Passion Iconography*, 99.

redemption' (9.12). In medieval exegesis, Marrow notes, Christ was the paschal lamb roasted on the Passover following 1 Corinthians 5.7, the unyoked red heifer without blemish to be sacrificed in Numbers 19.2, and all of the calves, rams, lambs and scapegoats of Numbers 25 sacrificed as expiation for the sins of the people.[57] The widespread portrayal of Christ as a sacrificial lamb is rooted in the prophecy of Isaiah depicting the servant of the Lord 'like a lamb that is led to the slaughter' (53.7), in the description of Christ's blood in 1 Peter as 'like that of a lamb without defect or blemish' (1 Pet. 1.19) and in the imagery of Christ in Revelation 5.6 as a slaughtered lamb at the centre of the heavenly throng. Marrow makes the case that more subtle features of passion iconography, such as Christ being pulled, dragged, prodded, led on a rope and maltreated in various ways, are also references to his being treated as if he were an animal being led to sacrifice.[58] David Grumett and Rachel Muers note that in John's Gospel Jesus' death is portrayed in terms of the Passover sacrifice of a lamb. Just as required in Exodus 12, none of Jesus's bones were broken (Exod. 12.46; Jn 19.33, 36), his body is removed before the morning (Exod. 12.10; Jn 19.31). The sponge lifted to Jesus lips is held on a branch of hyssop, the plant to be used to spread the blood of the Passover lamb on the lintels and doorposts of the Israelites (Exod. 12.22; Jn 19.29). Jesus's body is pierced with a spear (Jn 19.34) just as the body of the Passover lamb would have been pierced to be roasted over the fire (Exod. 12.9) and some commentators suggest that Christ's death took place at the time of the lamb sacrifice in the Temple. Grumett and Muers observe that Christian liturgical practices emphasize this identification: the *Agnus Dei* before the Eucharist in which the death of Christ is recalled affirms that the lamb of God takes away the sins of the world; Catholic metropolitans and archbishops wear a pallium woven from wool from lambs offered at the church of St Agnes on her feast day.[59]

Here we have a very different mode of considering the place of animals in relation to the atoning work of Christ. Up to this point in considering atonement, we have been considering what kinds of creatures are the beneficiaries of the atonement; we are now returned to the question of the previous chapter in asking what kind of creature is sacrificed on the cross. If we are right to understand that God takes on creatureliness and animality in the incarnation, then it is as a creature and an animal that Jesus Christ is put to death on the cross. This places the texts and traditions linking animal sacrifice to the crucifixion of Christ in a very particular light: Christ's death is not merely *like* an animal sacrifice – it *is* an animal sacrifice. On the cross a human animal

[57] Marrow, *Passion Iconography*, 117.
[58] Marrow, *Passion Iconography*, 163–4.
[59] Grumett and Muers, *Theology on the Menu*, 120.

creature is put to death in a way that the New Testament and later Christian traditions have interpreted in terms of the Jewish sacrifice of a non-human animal creature. The interpretation of Christ's death as an animal sacrifice in the New Testament points strongly to the view that Christ's death means that the sacrificing of other animals is no longer necessary: this is especially clear in Hebrews 9.12. The sacrificial system in which animals are put to death is brought to a conclusion in the death of the animal in which God was enfleshed. The atonement enacted in the death of this divine and human animal is sufficient to take away the sins of the whole world.[60]

We should note that to acknowledge this continuity between the death of Christ and the ritual sacrifice of animals does not necessarily imply that animals other than humans are among the beneficiaries of Christ's action, as this chapter has argued. Indeed, it could suggest the opposite: if Israelite animal sacrifices were rituals that functioned in the context of the relationship between human beings and their God, then to interpret Christ's death in this context may be seen to suggest that it also has significance only for the relationship between humanity and God. The problem with this argument is that it misses the way that even to affirm that salvation in Christ is effective for 'everyone who believes in him' (Jn 3.16) is already to recognize that the significance of the atoning work of Christ must be expanded beyond the context of Israel. Christ came to save the world (Jn 3.17) so the beneficiaries of his sacrifice cannot be delimited by those who were beneficiaries of the animal sacrifices of Israel. Once we have recognized that the Christian identification of Christ's death as an animal sacrifice cannot avoid an expansion of those whose sins are reconciled by this atonement, the only question is how inclusive this expansion should be. This chapter has made clear that creatures beyond the human are in need of the reconciliation offered in Christ and that the cosmic visions of Colossians and Ephesians make any species-specific boundaries on his work entirely improper. For Israel, therefore, non-human animals were sacrificed for the sake of humans; in Christ, a human animal was sacrificed not for humans but for the sake of all creatures.

[60] David Grumett and Rachel Muers make clear that although the fourth-century Christianizing of the Roman Empire led to the prohibition of animal sacrifice, the practice continued, even among Christians. They point to examples from the ancient church of Armenia, where the sacrificial liturgy called the *matal* persist to the present day; the twelfth-century papal court, where a lamb sacrifice was observed; sacrificial rituals of British Christians in the seventh century; and the continuation of animal sacrifice by Orthodox Christians in Georgia, Bulgaria, Palestine, Jordan, Syria, Egypt and Ethiopia (Grumett and Muers, *Theology on the Menu*, 109–14). The implications of interpreting Christ's death as the end of animal sacrifice, therefore, is an intra-Christian issue as well as an obvious locus of dialogue between Christians and Jews.

Reconciliation with Animals in Mind

To argue, as this chapter has done, that God's atoning work in Christ is not limited in its effects to the human is not to suggest that human beings are not particular and significant objects of God's atoning work in Jesus Christ. Because God became incarnate as a human being, the human dimensions of this event are particularly obvious; because theologians are human, a human preoccupation in outlining this doctrine, as others, is understandable. If this chapter is right, however, human beings are not uniquely sinful or uniquely in need of reconciliation, and we therefore need to understand atonement as God taking up the lost cause of God's creatures and carrying it through to rescue creation from its bondage and free it for the life of the children of God.

These two chapters on the place of animals, human and other-than-human, in the doctrines of the incarnation and atonement have argued that God's great work of reconciliation in Jesus Christ cannot be understood as a merely human event. As Part I argued that there are good theological reasons to recognize that God's purpose in creation extended far beyond the human, so Part II has shown that our vision of reconciliation must be similarly broad. God so loved the world that God graciously determined to save the world by taking on fleshy creatureliness in Jesus Christ (Jn 3.16–7; 1.14). In Christ all things are held together (Col. 1.17) and 'through him God was pleased to reconcile to himself all things, whether on earth or in heaven, by making peace through the blood of the cross' (Col. 1.20). The reign of God in which this reconciliation is established is already here, but not yet fully present: for now, animal creatures still suffer and prey upon one another. The final part of the book addresses the place of animals in what is to come, under the heading of the doctrine of redemption.

Part III

REDEMPTION

Chapter 6

THE SCOPE OF REDEMPTION

The first two parts of this volume have surveyed the place of animals in God's work of the creation of the universe and the reconciliation of all things to God; in this third and final part I turn to the place of animals in God's work of redemption. This chapter examines the scope of God's redemptive project: the question of what God redeems. The following chapter explores the question of the shape of the lives of redeemed creatures, especially as it relates to relationships between them.

Wesley: Non-Human Animals Need Redemption

In 1781 John Wesley preached a sermon on Romans 8.19–22 entitled 'The General Deliverance'. He quotes from the King James version that the 'earnest expectation of the creature waiteth for the manifestation of the sons of God', that 'the creature was subjected to vanity' and that 'the creature itself shall be delivered from the bondage of corruption into the glorious liberty of the children of God'.[1] Wesley's sermon is structured around a theological problem. He begins with the statement that 'Nothing is more sure' than that God is merciful towards 'all that have sense, all that are capable of pleasure or pain, of happiness or misery'. In support of this position Wesley quotes psalms 104, 145 and 147, that God's mercy is over all his works, providing all things with plenteousness, preparing food for cattle as well as human beings, feeding the young ravens when they cry to God, and sending springs into rivers to give drink to beasts of the field and even wild asses.[2] The problem Wesley identifies is how to reconcile the providential care of God for all creatures proclaimed in these psalms with what we see around us every day: 'If the Creator and Father of every living thing, is rich in mercy towards all; if he does not overlook or

---

[1] John Wesley, *Sermons on Several Occasions*, vol. V (New York: Ezekiel Cooper and John Wilson, 1806), 117.
[2] Wesley, *Sermons*, 117.

despise any of the works of his own hands: if he wills even the meanest of them to be happy, according to their degree: how comes it to pass, that such a complication of evils oppresses, yea, overwhelms them?'[3]

To answer this animal particularization of the problem of evil, Wesley sets out a sermon in three parts: what the original state of non-human animals was, what their state is at present and what their state will be when Paul's prophecy in Romans 8 comes to pass.[4] Originally, in Paradise, Wesley argues that non-human animals were blessed with self-motion, a degree of understanding and a power of choice guided by this understanding.[5] They even had some resemblance to moral goodness.[6] Humans were also blessed with these capacities, although to a higher degree. The factor separating humans and other animals was not reason, Wesley argues, which is another word for the understanding that is common to human and non-human animals. Rather, what separates humans from other kinds of animals is that humans are capable of knowing, loving and obeying God, while other animals are not.[7] Therefore he argues that the perfection of humanity in Eden was obedience to God, whereas the perfection of other animals was obedience to humanity. This unique human capacity meant that human beings were the only channel of communication between God and the other animals, so that when humanity became incapable of transmitting God's blessings through their disobedience, the rest of creation was 'subjected to vanity'.[8] As a result, the current state of other animals is far from their original one: they have lost vigour, strength and swiftness, but even more have substantially lost their understanding and power of will so that they are now 'utterly enslaved to irrational appetites'.[9] This is the reason, Wesley contends, that non-human animals are now savage and cruel to their fellow creatures, that many of them have become horrid in appearance and why so many of them suffer, not least at the hands of humans.[10]

Wesley reaches the climax of his sermon in the question: 'But will the *creature*, will even the brute creation always remain in this deplorable condition?'[11] His answer is forthright:

> God forbid that we should affirm this, yea, or even entertain such a thought! 'While the whole creation groaneth together', (whether men

---

[3] Wesley, *Sermons*, 118.
[4] Wesley, *Sermons*, 118.
[5] Wesley, *Sermons*, 121.
[6] Wesley, *Sermons*, 122.
[7] Wesley, *Sermons*, 122.
[8] Wesley, *Sermons*, 123.
[9] Wesley, *Sermons*, 123.
[10] Wesley, *Sermons*, 124–5.
[11] Wesley, *Sermons*, 127 (italics in original).

attend or not), their groans are not dispersed in idle air, but enter into the ears of him that made them. While his creatures *travail together in pain*, he knoweth all their pain, and is bringing them nearer and nearer to the birth, which shall be accomplished in its season. He seeth *the earnest expectation* wherewith the whole animated creation *waiteth for* that final *manifestation of the sons of God*: in which *they themselves also shall be delivered*, (not by annihilation: annihilation is not deliverance), from the present 'bondage of corruption into (a measure of) the glorious liberty of the children of God'.

Nothing can be more express. Away with vulgar prejudices, and let the plain word of God take place. They 'shall be delivered from the bondage of corruption, into glorious liberty': even a measure, according as they are capable, of the liberty of the children of God.[12]

Wesley cites the final chapter of Revelation in support of his conclusion – God's declaration that 'I am making all things new' and the assurance that 'he will wipe every tear from their eyes' and that death, mourning and crying will be no more (21.4–5) – noting that the text does not limit these promises to humans alone.[13] Animals will exceed their former state, even in Paradise: 'As a recompense for what they once suffered, while under the *bondage of corruption*, when God has *renewed the face of the earth*, and their corruptible body has put on incorruption, they shall enjoy happiness, suited to their state, without alloy, without interruption, and without end.'[14] Wesley sees in this latter point an important response to 'a plausible objection against the justice of God, in suffering numberless creatures, that had never sinned, to be so severely punished', since such creatures 'receive ample amends for all their present sufferings'.[15] He also hopes that recalling God's mercies to all creatures may 'enlarge our hearts towards these creatures' so that we may 'habituate ourselves to look forward, beyond this present scene of bondage, to the happy time, when they will be delivered therefrom, into the liberty of the children of God'.[16]

In this sermon, Wesley sees no alternative to an interpretation of Romans 8 that includes all animals in its grand redemptive vision, but he also sees in Paul's image of a creation set free from its bondage both an answer to a systematic theological concern about the unjust suffering of sinless creatures and the inspiration for a change in Christian practice to avoid cruelty to other animals.

[12] Wesley, *Sermons*, 127 (italics in original).
[13] Wesley, *Sermons*, 128.
[14] Wesley, *Sermons*, 129 (italics in original).
[15] Wesley, *Sermons*, 131.
[16] Wesley, *Sermons*, 131–2.

The account I have presented of where animals belong in Christian doctrine does not agree with Wesley at every point. In particular, my assessment of commonalities between human and non-human animals in Chapter 2 suggests Wesley is wrong to think that humans are the only animals that are capable of obeying God: the whale commanded to swallow Jonah is one of many examples discussed where other animals do God's bidding. If human beings are not unique in this capacity, Wesley's argument that human beings are the unique channel for God's blessings to other animals also fails and, with it, his explanation for the plight non-human animals currently find themselves in. The perspective provided in Chapter 2 of humans as one of many of God's animal creatures, especially clear in the closing chapters of Job, provides additional grounds for thinking that Wesley is wrong to believe that God only blesses other creatures through humanity. Beyond these points, I am also less convinced than Wesley that it is helpful to discuss the redemption of animals as compensation, a point in which other authors follow him and which I discuss in more detail below. What is notable and important about Wesley's sermon, however, is that he is clear that the Romans 8 text requires a more-than-human view of redemption and that he recognizes that this view of the scope of redemption will have practical consequences for Christian treatment of other animals.

Wesley's belief in the place of non-human animals in God's redemptive purposes was not a fleeting whim. Eighteen years previously, in 1763, he published *A Survey of the Wisdom of God in Creation: Or a Compendium of Natural Philosophy* in which he summarized Bonnet's *The Contemplation of Nature*. Wesley includes an extensive footnote concerning whether 'brutes have a soul or not' which concludes that at the end of time brutes will return to their original immortal essence and humanity will have to give an account of their treatment of other animals.[17] Three years after the 'General Deliverance' sermon, in 1784, Wesley published, with a short preface, extracts from John Hildrop's work *Free Thoughts on the Brute Creation,* in which Hildrop argues against the Jesuit Guillaume Bougeant's position in the 1739 work *Amusement Philosophique sur le Langage des Bêtes.*[18] Bougeant's book was itself responding to a problem concerning the redemption of animals that had been famously but

[17] John Wesley, *A Survey of the Wisdom of God in the Creation: Or, a Compendium of Natural Philosophy, Containing an Abridgement of That Beautiful Work, the Contemplation of Nature By Mr Bonnet, of Geneva, Also, an Extract From Mr Deuten's 'Inquiry Into the Origin of the Discoveries Attributed to the Ancients'* (New York: N. Bangs and T. Mason, 1823), 129 n.

[18] John Hildrop, *Free Thoughts Upon the Brute Creation, Or, an Examination of Father Bougeant's Philosophical Amusement, &c.: In Two Letters to a Lady* (London: R. Minors, 1742); Guillaume Hyacinthe Bougeant, *Amusement Philosophique sur le Langage des Bêtes* (La Haye: Chez A. van Dole, 1739).

unsatisfactorily addressed by René Descartes. The following section traces the debate concerning the redemption of non-human animals in the period from Descartes to Wesley.

Descartes and Hildrop: Non-Human Redemption as a Theological Problem

René Descartes is well known to have concluded that non-human animals were irrational automatons. What is less well known is that he claimed to have been motivated in pursuing the question by his view that their place in eschatology was the second most important question in Christian apologetics. In his *Discourse on Method* he explains that he embarked on a lengthy discussion of the soul

> because it is of the greatest importance: for, after the error of those who deny the existence of God, which error I think I have sufficiently refuted above, there is nothing which leads feeble minds more readily astray from the straight path of virtue than to imagine that the soul of animals is of the same nature as our own, and that, consequently, we have nothing to fear or to hope for after this life, any more than have flies or ants; instead, when one knows how much they differ, one can understand much better the reasons which prove that our soul is of a nature entirely independent of the body, and that, consequently, it is not subject to die with it; then, since one cannot see other causes for its destruction, one is naturally led to judge from this that it is immortal.[19]

Two of Descartes' letters show this was an enduring concern. In a letter to Newcastle in 1646, nine years after the publication of the *Discourse* he observes that if brutes thought as we do, 'they would have an immortal soul like us. This is unlikely, because there is no reason to believe it of some animals without believing it of all, and many of them such as oysters and sponges are too imperfect for this to be credible.' He notes that such concerns are easy to ridicule, but they provoke a worry about human souls: 'If now even a single oyster or sponge also has an immortal psyche, the coin of individual worth is instantly devalued by a massive flooding of the market.'[20] Three years later he wrote to Henry More that he thought it 'more probable that worms, flies,

---

[19] Descartes, *Discourse on Method*, 76.
[20] Cited in Gareth B. Matthews, 'Animals and the Unity of Psychology', *Philosophy* 53: 206 (1978), 452–3.

caterpillars and other animals move like machines than that they all have immortal souls'.[21]

It may be that Descartes' thinking about the relationship between non-human animals and machines was not wholly motivated by a concern to defend the Christian doctrine of redemption in advancing his thesis that non-human animals were merely machines: he may instead have been seeking to defend himself against possible charges of heterodoxy.[22] What is significant here is the relationship between his philosophy and the redemption of animals other than human beings. Inspired by the mechanical advances of his day, Descartes argued in his *Discourse on Method* that 'if there were such machines which had the organs and appearance of a monkey or of some other irrational animal, we would have no means of recognizing that they were not of exactly the same nature as these animals'.[23] In contrast, he suggested, if there were machines that were like human beings, we could tell that they were machines because they would not be able to arrange words meaningfully and they would not be able to use reason to adapt to new situations. He develops the first point, concerning language, by arguing that while even the most stupid human beings can use words, no non-human animals can do so, and concludes from this that since so little reason is necessary to use language, other animals must have no reason at all.[24] Instead, he claims, non-human animals are like clocks: mechanisms without mind that behave in certain ways because of the way their parts are arranged. Human beings, on the other hand, must have a reasonable soul that has been created expressly by God, joined and united with the body in order to constitute a truly human being.[25]

Obviously, there are all kinds of reasons to reject Descartes' account of the relationship between body, mind and soul, quite independent of its application to non-human animals.[26] As it relates to non-human animals in particular, the Cartesian position that animals other than humans are mindless, insentient

[21] Descartes, *The Philosophical Writings of Descartes*, vol. III, *The Correspondence*, trans. John Cottingham et al. (Cambridge: Cambridge University Press, 1991), 366.
[22] Leonora Rosenfield notes: 'One sometimes suspects that the religious aspect of of Descartes' reasoning about the beast-machine was above all a self-defense and a means of gaining approbation for his revolutionary thesis', citing Etienne Gilson in support. She notes the view of Adrien Baillet, Descartes' seventeenth-century biographer, that Descartes was motivated in his philosophical work on non-human animals by his own dissections of animal brains (Leonara Cohen Rosenfield, *From Beast-Machine to Man-Machine* (New York: Oxford University Press, 1941), 23).
[23] Descartes, *Discourse on Method*, 73.
[24] Descartes, *Discourse on Method*, 74–5.
[25] Descartes, *Discourse on Method*, 74–5.
[26] For a recent survey of philosophical objections, see Gordon Baker and Katherine J. Morris, *Descartes' Dualism* (London: Routledge, 1996). For a survey of the issues

automata is wildly implausible, and there is good reason to believe that not even Descartes himself believed it.[27] The implausibility of the position that non-human animals were merely automata did not, however, prevent many of Descartes' followers from adopting it. Nicolas Malebranche claimed to have proved that non-human animals were incapable of sensation through the following argument: 'being innocent, as everyone agrees and I assume, if they were capable of feeling, this would mean that under an infinitely just and omnipotent God, an innocent creature would suffer pain, which is a penalty and a punishment for some sin'.[28] Since pain is a punishment, animals are innocent and God is not unjust, Malebranche reasoned, these animals cannot really be suffering pain. He lamented that he found it difficult to persuade people of this, since they interpret the actions and sensible movements that animals make as of more significance so that 'one risks exposing oneself to the laughter of superficial and inattentive minds if one pretends to prove to them, by moderately abstract arguments, that animals do not sense'.[29]

An alternative argument reasoned directly from existing ethical attitudes to the eschatological state of non-human animals. In the letter to More, cited above, Descartes commented that his position 'is not so much cruel to animals as indulgent to human beings – at least to those who are not given to the super-stitions of Pythagoras – since it absolves them from the suspicion of crime when they eat or kill animals'.[30] Cardinal Melchior de Polignac took up this point in his 1747 Latin verse defence of Cartesian dualism, arguing that if animals have immortal souls we commit murder daily, so it is more humane to believe that they suffer no pain.[31] Racine agreed.[32] Mostly, however, the argument in relation to ethics went in the opposite direction, with Cartesian doctrine used to defend new cruelties to animals newly believed to be insensate. During a visit from Fontanelle, Abbé Trublet records that Malebranche kicked a pregnant dog and when Fontanelle cried out in compassion Malebranche rebuked him saying

in a theological context, see the first two chapters of Stuart C. Brown, *Philosophy of Religion: An Introduction With Readings* (London: Routledge, 2001), 5–51.
[27] See John Cottingham, 'A Brute to the Brutes?' Descartes' Treatment of Animals', *Philosophy* 53 (1978).
[28] Nicolas Malebranche, *The Search After Truth*, Cambridge Texts in the History of Philosophy, (eds) Thomas M. Lennon and Paul J. Olscamp (Cambridge: Cambridge University Press, 1997), 323.
[29] Malebranche, *The Search After Truth*, 324.
[30] Descartes, *Philosophical Writings*, 366.
[31] Cited in Rosenfield, *From Beast-Machine to Man-Machine*, 51–2.
[32] Cited in Rosenfield, *From Beast-Machine to Man-Machine*, 59.

'What? Don't you understand that it doesn't feel anything?'[33] Other Cartesian cruelties were more systematic:

> They administered beatings to dogs with perfect indifference, and made fun of those who pitied the creatures as if they had felt pain. They said that animals were clocks; that the cries they emitted when struck, were only the noise of a little spring which had been touched, but that the whole body was without feeling. They nailed poor animals up on boards by their four paws to vivisect them and see the circulation of the blood which was a great subject of conversation.[34]

Pierre Bayle was convinced both of the theological motivation for the arguments of Descartes and by their inability to convince, observing 'It is a pity that the opinion of Descartes should be so hard to maintain, and so improbable; for it is otherwise very advantageous to religion, and this is the only reason which hinders some people from quitting it.'[35]

A further attempt to move beyond the Cartesian position was put forward by the Jesuit priest Guillaume Hyacinthe Bougeant in *Amusement Philosophique sur le Langage des Bêtes* (1739). He argued against Descartes that it is clear that non-human animals are more than mere machines, but saw the difficulty Descartes found in thinking the souls of other animals to be like those of human beings. If there were a spiritual element in other animals not differing essentially from a human soul, he wrote, it would seem arbitrary to exclude them from paradise, but the immortality of animal souls was contrary to Christian teaching. The solution he came to is that we must conclude that animals are incarnations of evil spirits, punished by God by being made into animals.[36] This

---

[33] Rosenfield, *From Beast-Machine to Man-Machine*, 70.

[34] Fontaine, cited in Rosenfield, *From Beast-Machine to Man-Machine*, 54. In a recent article, Justin Leiber argues that this story was a fabulation by Nicolas Fontaine, that this is made clear in Rosenfield's book, and that those such as Peter Singer and Stephen R. L. Clark who cite the story from Rosenfield are mistaken and unscholarly (Justin Leiber, 'Descartes: The Smear and Related Misconstruals', *Journal for the Theory of Social Behaviour* 41: 4 (2011), 365–76). Leiber provides no citation for his statement that 'Rosenfield says that the story has to be a fabulation', however, and I can find no evidence in the book that she takes this view. Rather, she presents evidence that the Cartesian thought-world provided a context in which such attitudes towards other animals were possible.

[35] Cited in Rosenfield, *From Beast-Machine to Man-Machine*, 50.

[36] Bougeant, *Amusement Philosophique sur le Langage des Bêtes* (La Haye: Chez A. van Dole, 1739). Hildrop discusses Bougeant's argument in the first letter of Hildrop, *Free Thoughts Upon the Brute Creation, or, an Examination of Father Bougeant's Philosophical Amusement, &C.: In Two Letters to a Lady* (London: R. Minors, 1742).

position may have been merely an amusement for Bougeant and not intended to be taken seriously, but this heightens, rather than lessens, the point that the association of non-human animals and eschatology seems to lead to theological absurdities that frequently disparage animals other than humans.

It seems that neither a Cartesian analysis of the relationship between sensation in non-human animals and their possession of a soul, nor the responses we have surveyed, provide a plausible account of the nature of other-than-human animals and their place in God's redemptive purposes. John Locke rejected the Cartesian position in recognizing that other animals are capable of thought, but was nonetheless convinced that to attribute immortal souls to them would be stretching plausibility. In response to a letter from the Bishop of Worcester in 1698, he writes:

> if your lordship allows brutes to have sensation, it will follow, either that God can and doth give to some parcels of matter a power of perception and thinking; or that all animals have immaterial and consequently, according to your lordship, immortal souls, as well as men: and to say that fleas and mites, etc. have immortal souls as well as men will possibly be looked on as going a great way to serve an hypothesis, and it would not very well agree with what your lordship says.[37]

John Hildrop's 1765 work 'Free Thoughts upon the Brute Creation' cites Locke's criticism of immortal souls for non-human animals, noting that since Locke others have improved on his arguments with reference to Robert Hooke's microscope observations of life on a previously unimagined scale, such as 'eels in vinegar' (probably nematodes).[38] Hildrop also discusses the arguments of Peter Browne against attributing immaterial souls to 'brutes'. Browne is concerned at the difficulty of deciding how these brute souls are to be disposed once their bodies have been dissolved. It is clear to Browne that brute souls cannot be of the same kind as human souls, because they would then be capable of happiness and misery, and liable to divine reward and punishment. He also sees difficulties in believing that the souls of non-human animals are of a different kind, because then there would have to be a different kind of

---

[37] John Locke, 'Mr Locke's Reply to the Bishop of Worcester's Answer to His Second Letter', in *Works of John Locke*, vol. IV, (London: Thomas Tegg et al., 1823), 466. Nicholas Jolley discusses Locke's argument in Nicholas Jolley, *Locke: His Philosophical Thought* (Oxford: Oxford University Press, 1999), 94.

[38] Hildrop, *Free Thoughts*. For details of Hooke's work in this area, including the illustration of 'eels in vinegar' from his 1665 work *Micrographia*, see Jordynn Jack, 'A Pedagogy of Sight: Microscopic Vision in Robert Hooke's Micrographia', *Quarterly Journal of Speech* 95: 2 (2009).

immaterial soul for every species of fly and insect, 'even down to the *Cheese Mite*'.[39]

Hildrop is unpersuaded by the arguments of Locke and Browne. In relation to these numberless creatures he argues there are two options: '*all these Effects of infinite Wisdom were intended to answer some end, to serve some purpose, or they were not: they contributed something to the Beauty and Harmony of the whole, or they did not: they were either useful and necessary in their several Ranks and Orders, or superfluous and useless*'.[40] Hildrop terms this choice a dilemma and states that to take the second horn is to consider some beings 'noxious and mischievous', merely 'By-blows, Excrescencies, or fortuitous Productions, with which *infinite Wisdom* had no manner of Concern'.[41] One must then believe either they should not have been created at all, or that they should immediately be 'struck out of the List of Beings'. Such a position, Hildrop exclaims, should strike one with a 'religious horrour': he asks his reader, 'Is not the Blasphemy as shocking to your Piety, as the Nonsense to your Understanding?'[42] If instead we take the first horn of the dilemma and accept that God had reason to create each creature, Hildrop argues that all creatures that God had a reason to create, God also has a reason to preserve, since any reason for their annihilation or extinction would be a reason that they should not have been created. Therefore, he concludes, not only every species but every individual creature will have a place in immortality, citing the universal restoration in Acts 3.21 and the liberation of creation in Romans 8.21.[43]

It is important to recognize that some aspects of Hildrop's argument depend on a static view of creaturely being such as the Great Chain of Being examined in Chapter 3. There it was noted that a scheme where each creature has its unique place in a grand harmonious and perfect whole cannot accommodate change, since such a change would either be towards perfection, in which case the prior state was imperfect, or away from perfection, in which case the resulting state would be imperfect. This is obviously incompatible with evolutionary theory where creaturely kinds are in a state of constant flux from generation to generation. In the context of evolution, it seems that there are even stronger arguments than those Hildrop counters for believing particular creatures to be superfluous or useless: those individuals who do not reproduce and therefore contribute their genetic inheritance to future generations seem

---

[39] Peter Browne, *The Procedure, Extent, and Limits of Human Understanding* (London: William Innys, 1729), 173–4 (italics in original), quoted in Hildrop, *Free Thoughts*, 55–6.
[40] Hildrop, *Free Thoughts*, 51 (italics in original).
[41] Hildrop, *Free Thoughts*, 52 (italics in original).
[42] Hildrop, *Free Thoughts*, 52.
[43] Hildrop, *Free Thoughts*, 53.

obviously to fall into this category; those species that have become evolutionary
dead ends through extinction similarly seem to be superfluous on a larger scale.
Beyond these kinds of examples of superfluity among creatures, we may be
tempted to believe that even those creatures that have contributed to the evolutionary developing of extant organisms but have themselves become extinct
have shown themselves to be disposable steps towards the kinds of creatures
we see about us today. Such interpretations of evolution could be marshalled
to support teleological anthropocentrism, identified in the Introduction and
argued against in Chapter 1, which claims that human beings were the goal of
God's creative project. For example, one could say that God used the process of
evolution to generate human beings, which implies that all creatures antecedent
to us, together with our creaturely contemporaries, are side-effects or merely
necessary ingredients on the way to the goal of the human.[44]

Despite the significant shifts of world-view between Hildrop and ourselves,
however, I do not believe his position on the redemption of other animals can
be defeated merely by the invocation of evolutionary change. If, as Chapter 1
argues, teleological anthropocentrism is bad theology, allying it with evolutionary theory does not make it better: since we have no theological grounds
to conclude that human beings were God's sole or central aim in establishing
creation and good theological reasons to deny such a claim, so we have no
theological stake in claiming humanity to be the climax of an evolutionary
process – even if such a concept were not problematic in itself.[45] Furthermore,
from a theological point of view, there seems no necessity in valuing organisms
that are later in time over those that are earlier. My great-grandmother is
not less important than me because she preceded me; the magnificence of the
stegosaur is no more reduced by its location in a time distant from mine than
the magnificence of the elephant is by the geographical distance of its homeland
from my own. One crucial theological perspective on the universe is that God

---

[44] Pierre Teilhard de Chardin's interpretation of evolution in the context of
theology (see, for example, Pierre Teilhard de Chardin, *The Phenomenon of Man*,
trans. Bernard Wall (New York: Collins, 1959)), where the trajectory of the universe
seems to be towards and then beyond the human as possessors of thought, is one
developed theological account manifesting this tendency. For a discussion of his
thought in the context of evolutionary theory, see Celia Deane-Drummond, *Christ
and Evolution: Wonder and Wisdom* (London: SCM, 2009), 36–40. Simon Conway
Morris's evidence of evolutionary convergence provides one possible model for how
God could be understood to use evolutionary processes to attain specific outcomes
(Simon Conway Morris, *The Crucible of Creation*).

[45] Such an account would both have to explain on what grounds a particular
moment in the incremental process of evolutionary development should be considered
climactic and then explain why evolutionary development beyond *Homo sapiens* was
either not possible or represented a decline from this human summit.

is transcendent with respect to its temporality as with respect to all its other aspects, so that all moments in time are equally present to God. This leads us to a vision of the grandeur and diversity of creaturely being that retains Hildrop's recognition of the unsubstitutable particularity of every creature while recognizing the temporal dimension in which kinds of creatures change over time. As Hildrop maintains, God had reason to bring into being every kind of creature and every individual creature that has existed and will exist in the universe. The temporal and causal relationship of one creature to another identified by evolutionary theory is not grounds to believe that God values only the final creature in any evolutionary series. To each creature is given a particular time and place; none is superfluous or useless. Just as we are accustomed to picturing human beings as being gathered up in Christ without regard to when they died, so we must become accustomed to think of other animals, too – ammonites and stegosaurs, dodos and Javan tigers – being gathered up in the divine plan of redemption.

We should, however, pause to assess Hildrop's claim that what God had reason to create, God has reason to redeem. The alternative is clear and widely stated, as Chapter 1 demonstrated: many or most of God's creatures were made by God to be disposable and only for life this side of the new creation; these were intended by God to be the scenery or supporting players for the redemption of the other creatures in which God was really interested; one of the discontinuities between this world and the next will be that only a subset of creatures are suitable or chosen by God for this latter blessed existence. In the chapters in the first part of this book exploring the contours of the Christian doctrine of creation, the implausibility of this position was made clear; the chapters exploring incarnation and atonement in the second part made clear the theological importance of retaining a connection between the doctrines of creation and reconciliation. Now in the context of the doctrine redemption, it is still clearer that, for Christian doctrine to be coherent, we cannot afford for creation, reconciliation and redemption to be disjoint, but instead must see them together as different aspects of a single divine act of graciousness by God towards all that is. Christians confess God, Father, Son and Spirit, not as the maker of some things, but all things; not as reconciling and gathering up some things, but all things (Col. 1.20; Eph. 1.10); not as bringing liberation to some things in creation, but all things (Rom. 8.18–23). What is at stake in the truth of Hildrop's affirmation, therefore, is the coherence of Christian theology as such.

Redemption as Compensation?

Hildrop's argument for the redemption of non-human animals is based in confidence in the wisdom of God's creative and providential purposes, but an alternative argument for the redemption of other animals begins almost from the opposite point of view: redemption is necessary not because of the goodness of God's purposes but because of the evils suffered by non-human creatures. In Wesley's 'General Deliverance' sermon with which this chapter began, we saw that he considered it 'a plausible objection against the justice of God' that God allows 'numberless creatures, that had never sinned, to be so severely punished'. He considered a view of redemption in which such creatures 'receive ample amends for all their present sufferings' an important response to this objection.[46] This is the same problem addressed by Malebranche, but where Malebranche dealt with it by denying that non-human animals suffer, Wesley proposes instead to acknowledge the suffering but make up for it with a future in which they can in recompense 'enjoy happiness suited to their state, without alloy, without interruption, and without end'.[47]

In his 1944 book *The Problem of Pain*, C. S. Lewis also discusses the question of the place of non-human animals in the new creation. He restricts the application of suffering to that of sentient creatures, arguing that only in this case is it meaningful to think of a self that is suffering.[48] However, Lewis recognizes that at least some non-human animals are conscious and sentient, and, because he considers them innocent of sin and that their suffering precedes any possibility of human sinfulness, he concludes that it must originate from a mighty created power working for ill on the universe before the suffering of any sentient creatures.[49] For creatures that are merely sentient, Lewis argues that immortality is almost meaningless:

> If the life of a newt is merely a succession of sensations, what should we mean by saying that God may recall to life the newt that died today? It would not recognize itself as the same newt; the pleasant sensations of any other newt that lived after its death would be just as much, or just as little, a recompense for its early sufferings (if any) as those of its resurrected – I was going to say 'self', but the whole point is that the newt probably has no self.[50]

In Lewis's view, the question of immortality for other creatures depends on their relationship to human beings: it is atheistic to think of other animals in themselves, instead: 'The beasts are to be understood only in their relation to man

[46] Wesley, *Sermons*, 131.
[47] Wesley, *Sermons*, 129 (italics in original).
[48] C. S. Lewis, *The Problem of Pain* (New York: Oxford University Press, 2002), 136–7.
[49] Lewis, *The Problem of Pain*, 138–9.
[50] Lewis, *The Problem of Pain*, 141.

and, through man, to God.'[51] Therefore, Lewis concludes, we can consider the possibility that some non-human animals have immortality through their masters; he does not judge that other animals may have immortality in their own right.[52]

Much of the discussion of the previous chapters tells against Lewis's position that non-human animals relate to God only through human beings, but Chapters 1 and 2 most clearly make the case that non-human animals live before and in response to God in their own right, rather than requiring mediation of God through humanity. For this reason, Lewis's view that the immortality of other animals should be conditional on their relationship to human masters must be rejected. Beyond this, it is interesting to note that his objection to the immortality of merely sentient creatures relies on the view that redemption is compensation for undeserved suffering: it is because merely sentient creatures could not experience recompense that their immortality makes no sense to Lewis. If the basis for redemption is not one of compensation, Lewis's objection loses its force: if God has reason to redeem what God has reason to create, the experience of being a redeemed newt is beside the point. Instead, it exists in the new creation for the same reason that it existed in the old, because God willed it to be so and because it contributes to the magnificence of the whole for it to be present rather than absent.

Moltmann agrees with Malebranche, Wesley and Lewis that the suffering of innocent creatures constitutes a moral problem and draws the conclusion that the victims of such suffering require compensation:

> There is therefore no meaningful hope for the future of creation unless 'the tears are wiped from every eye'. But they can only be wiped away when the dead are raised, and when the victims of evolution experience justice through the resurrection of nature.[53]

In Christopher Southgate's extended treatment of theodicy in the context of the suffering of non-human animals, *The Groaning of Creation*, he cites this

---

[51] Lewis, *The Problem of Pain*, 142.

[52] Austin Farrer addresses the same topic in a chapter entitled 'Animal Pain' in *Love Almighty and Ills Unlimited*, arguing that pain is a necessity for survival for all animals and useless pain could only be avoided if the natural systems that produce it had knowledge of the future. Farrer shares with Lewis the view that God's relations with other-than-human animals are mediated through the human: 'God loves his animal creatures by being God to them, that is, by natural providence and creative power; not by being a brother creature to them, as he does for mankind in the unique miracle of his incarnation. He provides them with brother-saviours, or sometimes human saviours, through the working of compassion, and not otherwise' (Austin M. Farrer, *Love Almighty and Ills Unlimited* (London: Collins, 1966), 104).

[53] Moltmann, *The Way of Jesus Christ*, 297.

text from Moltmann, together with Wesley's 'General Deliverance' sermon and Keith Ward's view that any sentient creature that suffers pain must find that pain transfigured by a greater joy, making theodicy one of the main reasons to believe in immortality.[54] Southgate provides three focal reasons for believing that non-human creatures find a place in a redeemed creation: a few 'profoundly enigmatic' biblical texts (Rom. 8, Col. 1, Eph. 1, Isa. 11, 65), the fact that in the Bible human beings are always considered in the context of other creatures, and the belief that our conviction of the goodness of God requires 'some sort of eschatological fulfilment for creatures'.[55] It is this latter concern for theodicy, however, that is Southgate's prime concern in the book and it is this argument that he explores in detail.

In response to these various attempts to respond to the suffering of non-human creatures in the context of the doctrine of redemption, we must first be aware of the importance of recognizing the reality of non-human suffering. Malebranche's option of denying the possibility of any non-human suffering may seem extreme, but the preference it represents for the coherence of a particular thought-world over attending properly to the lives of other animals is by no means unique. Many thinkers have distinguished between pain and suffering along the lines of Lewis above, and denied the significance of mere pain without self-consciousness. Others have pushed the philosophical objection that because we cannot have reliable knowledge about what it is like to have the experiences of non-human creatures we do not have reason to believe their suffering is morally relevant in a similar way to that of humans. In relation to this latter point, we should recognize that there is a natural extension of this position in the direction of a thoroughgoing solipsism that denies the reality of any experience beyond one's own.[56] Despite or irrespective of such philosophical scepticism, we are moved to respond to the suffering of other humans because we recognize that they are likely to be experiencing similar situations in a way that is similar to us, given their physiological similarity to us and the behaviours they exhibit. If I see someone trap her finger in a closing door, shout in pain, shake her hand and shed tears, I make the assumption that given she has a similar physiology to mine and that she is exhibiting the kind of behaviour I do when I am in pain, she is experiencing something like what I feel when I trap my finger in a door. If I saw my cat trap her paw in a door, screech, jump and then take refuge in a corner of the house, I also have grounds

---

[54] Cited in Southgate, *Groaning of Creation*, 78.

[55] Southgate, *Groaning of Creation*, 82.

[56] For an overview of the key arguments in relation to the pain suffered by non-human animals, see Donna Yarri, *The Ethics of Animal Experimentation*, ch. 3: 'Animal Pain', 57–84.

on the basis of similar physiology and similar behaviour to think that she is experiencing something like the pain I feel. Against Malebranche and against modern sceptics, we must be clear that pain is an experience that is unpleasant for all animals, human and non-human, and reject attempts to deny the reality or significance of non-human suffering.

To recognize the reality of the suffering of other animals, however, does not necessitate a theological response in the form of theodicy. There are important reasons to doubt that theodicy is a good starting point for theological thinking in general, quite apart from the question of how it pertains to other-than-human animals. In a reflection on the book of Job, Terry Tilley has argued that theodicies require 'silencing the voice of the sufferer' and place the theodicist in the company of Job's comforters, delivering answers to those plagued by questions.[57] Stanley Hauerwas discusses Tilley's article alongside Walter Brueggemann's judgement that theodicy is a legitimation of the way society is organized.[58] Hauerwas argues that the 'problem of evil' is a modern phenomenon and that until the seventeenth century Christians were not interested in explaining evil, but in how to persevere in practical action to relieve it.[59] The danger that theodicy may become a rationale for oppression is acute in the context of the suffering of non-human animals. In Chapter 5, I noted Southgate's defence of God's goodness in the face of the suffering inevitable in the evolutionary process, on the basis that this process was the 'only way' for God to produce 'the sort of beauty, diversity, sentience, and sophistication of creatures that the biosphere now contains'.[60] This theodicy risks rationalizing the suffering of non-human animals, making it an acceptable cost as part of an overall divine plan, rather than seeing in it a motivation for practical action, together with lament and protest. Once such a framework has been adopted, the desire to make God seem less tyrannical by admitting guilt and providing a collective settlement in which the injured parties receive compensation for their mistreatment is understandable, but it badly mistakes an appropriate Christian construal of the relationship between creator and creature, where creatures are called not to be inquisitors of their God but instead to offer thanksgiving and praise. God must be understood to be the redeemer of all creatures, human and other-than-human, because God has determined to be gracious and faithful to them in this sphere, as well as in their creation and reconciliation, not because they would otherwise have a legitimate cause of complaint.

---

[57] T. W. Tilley, 'God and the Silencing of Job', *Modern Theology* 5: 3 (1989), 267, cited in Stanley Hauerwas, *Naming the Silences: God, Medicine, and the Problem of Suffering* (Grand Rapids, MI: Eerdmans, 1990), 45.

[58] Hauerwas, *Naming the Silences*, 46.

[59] Hauerwas, *Naming the Silences*, 49–51.

[60] Southgate, *Groaning of Creation*, 16.

A Universal Restoration?

The focus in this chapter on the early modern accounts of Hildrop and Wesley should not be taken to suggest that there are not earlier Christian roots for the belief in the redemption of all creatures. The affirmation of the gathering up (*anakephalaiosis*) of all things in Christ in Ephesians 1.10 led Irenaeus in the second century to develop a doctrine of recapitulation in which Christ redeems the whole creation and restores the world to its primeval state, with creatures returning to obedience to human beings and to their first food provided by God.[61] In response to commentators seeking to interpret the wild animals in Isaiah's prophecies as different nations of human beings, Irenaeus comments 'nevertheless in the resurrection of the just [the words shall also apply] to those animals mentioned. For God is rich in all things.'[62] The statement in Peter's Pentecost sermon that Jesus would remain in heaven 'until the time of universal restoration [*apokatastasis*]' (Acts 3.21) inspired Origen to develop the related tradition in which all things are restored to their state in Paradise. Tom Greggs notes that this doctrine was rooted in Origen's doctrine of the participation of the rational soul in the Logos, but also makes clear that according to Origen's understanding of rationality, non-human creatures are not excluded from this participation.[63] Instead, Origen takes seriously the Psalmist's praise that God saves both humans and other animals (Ps. 36.6)[64] and concludes from Romans 8 that God will be all in all, and all creatures, 'since they are a part of all, may have God even in themselves, as he is in all things'.[65] The tradition of *apokatastasis* is taken up in the fourth century by Gregory of Nyssa, who

---

[61] Irenaeus, 'Against Heresies', bk 5, ch. 33, §4.

[62] Irenaeus, 'Against Heresies', bk 5, ch. 33, §1. For an overview of Irenaeus's view of recapitulation, see Eric Osborn, *Irenaeus of Lyons* (Cambridge: Cambridge University Press, 2001), Part III, 95–140. Osborn notes that for Irenaeus, 'Christ inaugurates for ever the renewal of all creation' (140). Ryan McLaughlin discusses Irenaeus's views of relationships between humans and non-human animals in Ryan McLaughlin, 'Evidencing the Eschaton: Progressive-Transformative Animal Welfare in the Church Fathers', *Modern Theology* 27: 1 (2010).

[63] Tom Greggs, 'Apokatastasis: Particularist Universalism in Origen (*c.* 185–*c.* 254)', in Gregory Macdonald ed. '*All Shall be Well*': *Explorations in Universalism and Christian Theology, From Origen to Moltmann* (Eugene, Oregon: Cascade Books, 2011); see also Greggs, *Barth, Origen and Universal Salvation*, 54–84.

[64] Origen, *Commentary on the Gospel of John*, The Fathers of the Church: A New Translation, vol. 80, ed. Ronard E. Heine (Washington, DC Catholic University of America Press, 1989), 1.22, quoted in Greggs, *Barth, Origen and Universal Salvation*, 74.

[65] Origen, *On First Principles: Together with an Introduction and Notes*, ed. G. W. Butterworth (Gloucester, MA: Peter Smith, 1973), 1.7.5, quoted in Greggs, 'Apokatastasis', 34–5. Mark Edwards makes clear that for Origen, *apokatastasis* is not merely a return to origins (Mark Julian Edwards, *Origen Against Plato*

also looks forward to the final harmony of all things.[66] The condemnation of various Origenist positions by the fifth ecumenical council in AD 553, where *apokatastasis* is mentioned, led to many being nervous of espousing it, but the church did not condemn *apokatastasis* as such and the position Gregory of Nyssa, for example, is never questioned.[67] The doctrines of *anakephalaiosis* and *apokatastasis* remain attractive to many theologians: Dietrich Bonhoeffer, for example, calls Irenaeus's position 'a magnificent and consumately consoling thought'.[68] Karl Barth judges it dangerous to count on or claim *apokatastasis*, but concludes 'we are surely commanded the more definitely to hope and pray for it as we may do already on this side of this final possibility'.[69]

The question of the orthodoxy of the doctrine of *apokatastasis* alerts us to the issue of the relationship between the claim that non-human creatures may be redeemed by God and the question of whether all human beings will participate in redemption. Clearly, many of the arguments that have been advanced in this chapter and earlier ones concerning the inclusive character of God's grace towards creatures could also be deployed in order to support a universalist view of human salvation. If Hildrop is right that God has reason to redeem what God has reason to create; if God's great works of creation, reconciliation and redemption are in one sense different aspects of the same act of grace; then it seems that all human beings, together with God's other creatures, will be swept up in God's redemption. In my view, this is not a problematic corollary to the redemption of non-human animals, but it seems that it is not necessary to defend universalism in a human context in order to make the case for the inclusion of non-human animals in redemption. We might say, for example, that one of the particular features of being a human creature is the capacity for a radical and rebellious rejection of one's identity

(Aldershot: Ashgate, 2002), 113), *contra* Colin Gunton's critique that Origen and Augustine see everything rolled back into God (Gunton, 'End of Causality', 80–1).

[66] See Morwenna Ludlow, *Universal Salvation: Eschatology in the Thought of Karl Rahner and Gregory of Nyssa* (Oxford: Oxford University Press, 2000).

[67] See Gregory MacDonald, 'Introduction', in *'All Shall be Well': Explorations in Universalism and Christian Theology, From Origen to Moltmann*, ed. Gregory MacDonald (Eugene, OR: Cascade Books, 2011), 4–10 and Greggs, 'Apokatastasis', 30. For a consideration of the issue in the context of Patristic eschatology, see Brian E. Daley, *The Hope of the Early Church: A Handbook of Patristic Eschatology* (Cambridge: Cambridge University Press, 1991).

[68] Dietrich Bonhoeffer, *Letters and Papers From Prison*, Dietrich Bonhoeffer Works, Vol. 8, (eds) Christian Gremmels, Eberhard Bethge, Renate Bethge and Ilse Tödt, trans. John W. de Gruchy (Minneapolis, MN: Fortress Press, 2010), 230. I discuss Bonhoeffer's thought in relation to non-human animals in Clough, 'Interpreting Human Life'.

[69] Barth, *CD* IV/3.1, 477–8.

as a creature of God. Taking into account the discussion of the previous chapter, this need not require that human beings are uniquely capable of sin, but we might propose that on a creaturely continuum, human beings are the only earthly creatures we believe to be capable of a response to God that would constitute grounds for their exclusion from the life of the new creation. If so, we could envisage a new creation in which all non-human creatures, but not all human ones, were able to participate. As noted above, this is not my view, but it is significant to note that one need not be convinced of human universalism in order to admit the possibility of the redemption of non-human creatures.

Beyond the independence of affirming universalism in a human context and affirming the inclusion of non-human creatures in redemption, we should also note that the motivation for Barth's reserve in endorsing *apokatastasis*, which is echoed by other theologians, is based on considerations that apply only in relation to universalism in a human context.[70] Barth explains the danger of expecting *apokatastasis* is that '[e]ven though theological consistency might seem to lead our thoughts and utterances most clearly in this direction, we must not arrogate to ourselves that which can be given and received only as a free gift'.[71] This worry about presuming upon God's grace for ourselves and for fellow human beings is not readily applicable beyond the sphere of the human. We might be guilty of the improper presumption about which Barth is concerned if we count on our own redemption on the basis of God's universal grace, or those human beings we are close to, or perhaps if we presume particular non-human companions will be present alongside us in the new creation. We do not risk such presumption, it seems to me, if led by the biblical and doctrinal traditions we have surveyed up to this point, we dare to hope or affirm that, just as God has been gracious to non-human creatures in their creation and reconciliation, so God will be faithful to them in redemption. This is finally a hope and belief on behalf of others, rather than one originating in our own interests, and to hope for God to be gracious to those beyond ourselves and those we love does not carry the spiritual dangers to which Barth and others are alert.

---

[70] MacDonald surveys the debate concerning the relationship between 'hopeful' and 'convinced' universalisms in MacDonald, 'Introduction', 11–13.

[71] Barth, *CD* IV/3.1, 477. See also Barth's discussion of the issue in Barth, *CD* II/2 (Edinburgh: T. & T. Clark, 1957), 295–6, 417–8. Greggs notes that a similar pastoral concern may have motivated Origen to avoid espousing universalism in his homiletic works (Greggs, 'Apokatastasis', 31).

Redemption in Practice

In this chapter we have seen that considering the place of non-human animals in God's work of redemption is not a novel concern. Rather, the hope that the whole of creation will be restored, liberated and redeemed is present in the Old and New Testaments and in patristic teaching, as well as being represented in more recent theological discussions. These points of reference can therefore be seen as congruent with the conclusion of the systematic theological argument I have developed in favour of understanding God's purposes in creation, reconciliation and redemption in continuity with one another. As Chapter 1 made clear, not all theologians have agreed that God is concerned about more than humanity in the act of creation, let alone in reconciliation and redemption, but arguments developed in that chapter and subsequent chapters demonstrate the theological unattractiveness and implausibility of a position restricting God's aims to the human sphere. Having now surveyed the actions of God towards creatures in creation, reconciliation and redemption, we are now able to glimpse the full and majestic extent of the ways in which God is gracious to God's animal creatures, human and other-than-human.

If any were tempted to consider the question of the redemption of non-human creatures an esoteric issue without connection to any important issues of practice, the discussion of the positions of Descartes and his followers on this question should be sufficient grounds to demonstrate the contrary. Resolute Cartesians reasoned that to attribute souls to non-human animals would make Christian doctrine of the afterlife implausible, proceeded to pronounce them mechanisms devoid of both soul and reason, and argued from that position that they were incapable of suffering and therefore the most extreme treatment of them by humans was of no moral concern. Wesley's argument, as we have seen, also connected the question of the redemption of non-human animals to Christian practice, with very different results. He argued that if we recognize that God will wipe the tears from the eyes of other-than-human animals and redeem them from death, sorrow and pain, we may be encouraged to imitate God's mercy and 'soften our hearts towards the meaner creatures, knowing that the Lord careth for them', that 'not one of them is forgotten in the sight of our Father who is in heaven' and therefore to 'habituate ourselves to look forward, beyond this present scene of bondage, to the happy time when they will be delivered therefrom, into the liberty of the children of God'.[72] There are other possible ways of configuring the relationship between answers to the question of the redemption of other animals and how we should treat them: if you took the view that non-human animals were outside God's redemptive purposes, you

---

[72] Wesley, *Sermons*, 131–2.

could suggest they should be treated especially kindly because they only have this mortal existence. Alternatively, if one viewed redemption as compensation for non-human animals, as discussed above, it might lessen one's concern for their ill-treatment in this life. What all four of these positions have in common, however, is that how broadly one conceives of the scope of God's redemption of creatures strongly influences ethical judgements concerning appropriate modes of relationship between human and non-human creatures. The ethical implications of Christian beliefs about other animals is the topic of the second volume of this work, but it is helpful here to note that the question this chapter has addressed is one of practical import, as well as theoretical interest. The same is the case of the topic of the following and final chapter, which enquires concerning the relationships between creatures in a redeemed creation.

Chapter 7

The Shape of Redeemed Living

The close connection between God's acts of creation, reconciliation and redemption means that eschatological doctrine is not pointless speculation concerning things we cannot know, but crucial tenets of faith with significance for the life of the Christian here and now. To have faith that bodies have a place in the new creation, for example, as Christians do in proclaiming the resurrection of the body, means rejecting Gnostic interpretations of the human condition as pure eternal spirit trapped in the messy fleshiness of an evil material and temporal order. This means in turn that the religious task cannot be construed as attempted escape from the world through ascetic practice, the mortification of the body or denying God's good work of creation. Christianity has been less clear, however, about whether and where other kinds of bodies – those of non-human animals – belong in the new creation, and it is this question that I take up in this final chapter. The previous chapter argued that we have grounds to hope for the redemption of non-human animals alongside human ones; the focus of this chapter is to reflect on the modes of existence of redeemed animal life, human and non-human.

In Jürgen Moltmann's extended argument for the importance of eschatology in Christian doctrine, *The Theology of Hope*, one of the methodological cautions he notes at the outset is the danger that we are merely indulging in 'dreams, speculations, longings and fears, which must all remain vague and indefinite because no one can verify them'.[1] Such a concern would seem amplified in relation to speculations about the lives of non-human animals in the new creation: a question after one lecture I gave on the topic asked about what would happen to all the excrement in a new creation with other animals. No doubt, reflection on such a question would provoke us to ponder a range of interesting theological questions concerning the materiality of the life beyond, but this topic struck me as one clearly belonging to a class where speculation was likely to deliver little in the way of reliable knowledge. For other

---

[1] Jürgen Moltmann, *Theology of Hope*, trans. Leitch, James W. (London: SCM Press, 1967), 17.

questions about the new creation, however, there seems both reliable grounds for knowledge and important reasons to maintain the claim. For example, the prophecy in Revelation accompanying the vision of the new Jerusalem declares that death, mourning, crying and pain will be no more (Rev. 21.4). Here is a fundamental statement of Christian hope for a life where the evils we currently experience are abolished, which is rooted in the Christian doctrine of God: we cannot contemplate a dwelling place where God is fully and finally present (v. 3) and these ills persist. About excrement, perhaps then, we cannot say, but about death, we can. For other questions, we must decide in each case whether there is a sufficient basis in the biblical witness or Christian doctrine to make it possible to address them. It is notable that Revelation 21.4 expresses its claims in negative form: we do not know what this life will be like, but we do know that it will not contain these evils. Expressing claims in negative form does not protect us from foolishness – in relation to the excrement question, for example, we could declare that there will be none of that in the new creation – but it may be a useful precaution against wilder claims.

Visions of Animal Redemption

There is no shortage of biblical texts that might provide a basis for reflection on the nature of redeemed animal life. First there is the harmony between the creatures in the Garden of Eden (Gen. 2), the renewal of this harmonious living on the ark (Gen. 7–8) and the covenant of God with all creatures that follows the flood (Gen. 9). The Psalms provide a vision of 'all flesh' coming before God in praise: hills, valleys, seas, floods, sea monsters, wild animals, cattle, creeping things and birds joining with human beings to worship (Pss 65–6, 98, 145, 148). Then there are the visions in Isaiah of wolves living with lambs, leopards lying with kids, bears with cows, lions eating straw, children playing near the nests of snakes, with no one hurt and nothing destroyed (Isa. 11.6–9 and 65.25–6). Daniel and his friends thrive on a vegetarian diet in the court of Nebuchadnezzar (Dan. 1.12–15) and Daniel is unharmed when Darius condemns him to be thrown to the lions. Paul's vision in Romans of a creation freed from its bondage to decay suggests that the redeemed life of animals must be an escape from the suffering and deterioration they experience in the present time (Rom. 8.19–23). The opening of the letters to the Colossians and Ephesians discussed in previous chapters proclaim Christ's work in reconciling and making peace between all things in heaven and earth, which suggests that in the new creation all creatures must live in peace with one another (Eph. 1.10; Col. 1.15–20). At the heart of the vision of heavenly worship in Revelation are a transformed lion, ox, eagle and human being leading the praises of the lamb *(Rev. 4.6–11; 5.11–14)*. Finally, as noted already, there is the vision of the new heaven and the new earth in Revelation 21.1–2, picturing a place where there will be no more tears, pain or death.

Isaiah's visions of peace between creatures are worth examining in a little more detail in the context of reflecting on what might constitute relationships between redeemed creatures in the new creation. The vision of the peaceable kingdom is a focal part of what it will mean for the righteousness of Yahweh to be realized on earth. In Chapter 11, Isaiah prophesies that a shoot will come out of the stump of Jesse on whom the Spirit of Yahweh rests (v. 1). Righteousness and faithfulness will characterize his rule: he will judge the poor and the meek with equity (vv. 4–5) and a new mode of existence between animal creatures will be inaugurated:

> The wolf shall live with the lamb,
> the leopard shall lie down with the kid,
> the calf and the fatling together,
> and a little child shall lead them.
> The cow and the bear shall graze,
> their young shall lie down together;
> and the lion shall eat straw like the ox.
> The nursing child shall play over the hole of the asp,
> and the weaned child shall put its hand on the adder's den.
> They will not hurt or destroy on all my holy mountain;
> for the earth will be full of the knowledge of the Lord
> as the waters cover the sea. (Isa. 11.6–9)

The vision is echoed in Second Isaiah where the prophet records God's declaration that 'I am about to create a new heaven and a new earth' and 'Jerusalem as a joy', where 'no more shall the sound of weeping be heard ... or the cry of distress' (Isa. 65.17–19). No longer will infants live but a few days; the people will 'build houses and inhabit them ... plant vineyards and eat their fruit' (v. 21). These blessings will extend to the animals, as well:

> The wolf and the lamb shall feed together,
> the lion shall eat straw like the ox;
> but the serpent – its food shall be dust!
> They shall not hurt or destroy on all my holy mountain, says the Lord.
> (Isa. 65.25–6)

These prophecies of the new creation to be established by God are taken up at the beginning of Revelation 21, making clear that this vision is recognized canonically as a fundamental source of Christian eschatological doctrine.[2]

The biblical visions of harmony between creatures as characteristic of their redemption are echoed in Christian accounts of the relationship between saints and non-human animals. Helen Waddell's *Beasts and Saints* is a remarkable collection of such stories, which collectively make clear the significance that was attributed to harmony between humans and other animals as character-izing holiness of life.[3] In these stories, animals usually considered wild behave tamely with the saints, as well as often exhibiting virtuous behaviour. One story tells of a hyena that brought its whelp to St Macarius, who saw it was blind and healed it. The next day the hyena brought the saint a sheepskin, but the saint believed it had come from the hyena's killing of a sheep, and told the hyena he would not accept it because it had come from violence. After being begged by the hyena to accept the gift, St Macarius said that he would only do so on the basis that the hyena promised never to kill another creature. The hyena 'bowed her head to the ground, and dropped on her knees, bending her paws, moving her head up and down, looking at her face as if promising him', so the saint accepted the skin, slept on it until he died, and the hyena came to him whenever it needed food.[4] Another story tells of St Kevin's care for a blackbird:

> At one Lenten season, St Kevin, as was his way, fled from the company of men to a certain solitude, and in a little hut that did but keep out the sun and the rain, gave himself earnestly to reading and to prayer, and his leisure to contemplation alone. And as he knelt in his accustomed fashion, with his hand outstretched through the window and lifted up to heaven, a blackbird settled on it, and busying herself as in her nest, laid in it an egg. And so moved was the saint that in all patience and gentleness he remained, neither closing nor withdrawing his hand: but until the young ones were fully hatched he held it out unwearied, shaping it for the purpose.[5]

---

[2] David Aune notes that Isaiah 65.17 is by no means the only Jewish text relating to the renewal of creation, noting 1 Enoch 91.16 in particular as a possible source for Rev. 21.1–2 (David E. Aune, *Revelation 17–22*, Word Biblical Commentary, vol. 52C (Dallas, TX: Word, 2002), 1116). Loren Stuckenbruck is clear, however, that Isaiah 65.17 and 66.22 were the sources for 1 Enoch 91.16, although he also notes the shared expectation of Jubilees 1.29, which looks forward to 'the time of the new creation when the heavens, the earth, and all their creatures will be renewed like the powers of the sky and like all the creatures of the earth' (Loren T. Stuckenbruck, *1 Enoch 91–108*, Commentaries on Early Jewish Literature (Berlin: Walter de Gruyter, 2007), 149).

[3] Helen Waddell, *Beasts and Saints* (London: Darton, Longman & Todd, 1995).

[4] Waddell, *Beasts and Saints*, 13–15.

[5] Waddell, *Beasts and Saints*, 137.

In other stories, sea otters minister to St Cuthbert by warming his feet after he had kept vigil in the sea up to his neck all night, and the ravens that he chastises for destroying his crops return in penance.[6] St Werburga of Chester miraculously restores to life a goose who has been killed by a greedy steward.[7] Such stories of the saints echo the biblical visions of harmony between creatures: the lives of saints recall an original harmony between creatures in the biblical narrative and anticipate the final peace between creatures proclaimed in biblical prophecy. Saints such as Kevin are unusually attuned to what it would mean to live in accordance with God's desire for peace between creatures; creatures such as St Macarius's hyena demonstrate an awareness of the sanctity of the lives of the saints they encounter.[8]

Peace between Creatures

Given the visions of harmony between creatures in biblical texts and later Christian traditions surveyed above, it may seem redundant to state that relations between creatures in the new creation will be peaceable. Isaiah's vision of peaceable relations between wolves and lambs, leopards and kids, bears and cows, babies and venomous snakes, and of lions turning to diets of straw, makes it absolutely clear that all creaturely enmity will be overcome in the new creation, and predator and prey will be reconciled to one another.[9] Not everyone has been happy to accept this peaceable vision, however: Christopher Southgate comments 'It is very hard to see how the leopardness of leopards could be fulfilled in eschatological coexistence with kids.'[10] Southgate uses the poem 'The Heaven of Animals' by James Dickey to imagine an alternative new creation to that of Isaiah, in which predators continue to be predators, but now with perfectly deadly claws and teeth, while their prey accept and comply with their destruction and then rise and walk again. Dickey comments that he was

---

[6] Waddell, *Beasts and Saints*, 60–6.

[7] Waddell, *Beasts and Saints*, 68–9.

[8] There is no shortage of similar stories of saints and other animals. Carolinne White's *Early Christian Lives* contains many similar accounts of peaceable relations between Christian and non-human animals, with other animals providing willing service to saints. See, for example Jerome's 'Life of Paul of Thebes' and 'Life of Malchus' (Carolinne White ed. *Early Christian Lives*, trans. Carolinne White (London: Penguin, 1998), 75–84, 119–128). I am grateful to Morwenna Ludlow for this reference.

[9] Irenaeus comments that the wheat in the new creation must be of exceptional quality such that its straw can serve as suitable food for lions (Irenaeus, 'Against Heresies', bk 5, ch. 33, §5).

[10] Southgate, *Groaning of Creation*, 86.

motivated to write the poem after watching the Disney film *The African Lion* repeatedly, and he tried to imagine a heaven in which each beast could have its own identity, 'that is, the lion would not really be a lion if, as the Bible says, the lion lies down with the lamb'. Dickey reports wondering 'what kind of heaven there could be in which the hunted would still be hunted and the hunters would still hunt.'[11] Dickey's poem is successful in portraying a heaven for predators, but is not as convincing in suggesting a heaven for their prey. Surely a heaven for animals preyed upon would be a new creation in the absence of their predators, rather than one in which being torn apart was no longer painful. Yet a new creation in which predator and prey were separated would be, on Dickey's account, no heaven for predators at all.

Dickey's heaven for predators, which Southgate favours over a vision of predators giving up their predatory ways, is clearly a stark departure from the peaceable visions of Eden, Isaiah, Romans and Revelation. Violence and destruction are not exiled, but transformed, in this new creation and, as a result, Dickey's imaginative account of heaven for predators must be rejected as incompatible with the Christian doctrine of redemption. For Southgate, Dickey's commitment to the biological integrity of predators is of a piece with his rejection of any originally peaceable creative intention of God as incompatible with evolutionary theory, as discussed in Chapter 5. This perspective has something in common with the ecological visions of Aldo Leopold in *A Sand County Almanac*, picked up by Holmes Rolston, where the death of individual creatures is of little concern once one gains an aesthetic appreciation for the systemic whole.[12] Southgate opposes key points of Rolston's account, but his acceptance of predation as God's original creative intent, continued into the new creation, ontologizes violence in the same way as these ecologies.[13]

Transferring Dickey's poem to a human context makes the defects in this account still clearer. There is no shortage of literary celebrations of a heroic warrior class of human beings, for whom developing skill in efficiently killing enemy human beings is their life's work. We could make arguments based in evolutionary biology for the necessity of such endeavour in the development of human culture as we know it. For such warrior types, unreconstructed in the new creation, it is clear that an existence oriented around living peaceably and

[11] Dickey's poem and his commentary on it are published in James Dickey, *Self-Interviews* (Garden City, NY: Doubleday & Company, 1970), 106–9. The poem is cited in Southgate, *Groaning of Creation*, 88–9.

[12] Rolston discusses the relative importance of individuals and biotic communities in Holmes Rolston, III, *Environmental Ethics: Duties to and Values in the Natural World* (Philadelphia, PA: Temple University Press, 1988), 179–86.

[13] See the discussion of Southgate's position in Chapter 5, above.

singing praises to God would be a very dubious benefit: instead we would need a happy hunting ground where soldiers continue to develop their murderous skills, although presumably by analogy with Dickey's poem their destructive success would no longer be painful or permanent for its victims. This is clearly, I hope, not a possible Christian vision of a new creation reigned over by the Prince of Peace (Isa. 9.6). Instead, it is a Christian expectation that such human lives require transformation in order to fit them for life under the reign of God, just as the lives of non-warriors will need to be purged of their manifold vices. The transformation required to fit human beings for life in the new creation is hard to imagine while still preserving personal identity, if the human life I know best is anything to go by. Yet biblical and later Christian traditions encourage us to entertain the audacious hope that even creatures like us could find a place in the peaceable kingdom. Surely if such transformations can be wrought in vicious human beings, it is a failure of imagination to consider that leopards cannot find their own perfection once released from the necessity of killing in order to survive. A Christian vision of redeemed creaturely life must be one in which predation is no longer a possibility for human or non-human creatures.[14]

In his insightful discussion of Thomas Aquinas's theology in the context of ecological questions, Willis Jenkins notes the danger that if we attribute moral evil to the natural practices of lions, tsunamis or parasites, we will have reason to despise the creatures we find inconvenient. Instead, he suggests, we need to learn from Aquinas the wonder of the particular mode of practice exhibited by each particular creature, including predators:

> When the lion roars, therefore, it voices its desire for God. But that misleads; rather, the lion's 'speech' is in the way it breeds and naps and runs. Perhaps jarringly, lions love God by stalking, pouncing upon, and tearing asunder their prey. Such are their natural operations, their ways of seeking divine goodness. The ravens call upon God by building nests and stealing owl eggs. The rivers clap their hands by falling over cataracts, spreading silt over flood plains, and broadening into fluvial deltas.[15]

---

[14] Southgate outlines the possibility of transformed human existence in Christ in a way that is discontinuous with the potential for transformation of other creatures (Southgate, *Groaning of Creation*, 92–115). He would therefore join me in rejecting the happy hunting ground for soldiers imagined here. Our difference here is therefore whether non-human creatures are in an entirely different situation than human ones: my argument is that if we can envision redeemed human creatures thriving in ways very different from our current patterns of life, we can envision similar redeemed non-human creaturely thriving.

[15] Jenkins, *Ecologies of Grace*, 120.

Later Jenkins argues that different creaturely practices would mean the creatures were no longer themselves: 'Were the wolf tamed or the lion pacified, it would no longer intelligibly be wolf or lion but something else, perhaps a new species or maybe just a simulcra of something lost' – indeed a bucolic lion, Jenkins concludes, would come under the heading of sin for Aquinas.[16] Elsewhere, Jenkins cites Aquinas's justification of the evil of predation on the basis of its effects in comparison with tyranny: 'there would be no life for the lion were there no animals for its prey, and no patience of martyrs were there no persecution for tyrants'.[17]

We do well to take careful note of the warning from Aquinas via Jenkins against assimilating the magnificent diversity of creaturely excellences into a single pattern. Instead they are right to insist that we should be open to the possibility of each creature praising its creator in its own particular and unsubstitutable way. The critical question remains, however, whether Jenkins is right to insist that creatures can only remain themselves insofar as they continue in the creaturely practices they exhibited in the created order as we know it, so that they can play no part in a peaceable kingdom. There are several reasons we should reject this view. First, the example of martyrs encourages us to make another human comparison. In this life, the existence of martyrs depends on the existence of tyrants, as Aquinas argues, but in the prophecy of Revelation the white-robed multitude of martyrs who have come through the great ordeal and washed their robes in the blood of the lamb (Rev. 7) cannot depend for their identity on the continued existence of their enemies, for God has vanquished them. The life-practices of the martyrs are transformed in the new creation – instead of suffering as a result of their witness to God, they live lives of blissful praise – yet they have not become a different species, but remain identifiable with the persons that they were. There seems no reason why the being of lions cannot also survive such a change of practice. Second, the logic of the Thomistic position rests on a static conception of creaturely living, whereas, as discussed in Chapter 3 as an objection to the Great Chain of Being, we now have to recognize that kinds of creatures change over time. In addition, recent scientific accounts of culture in a range of non-human contexts suggest that practices are not stable even within shifting species boundaries.[18]

---

[16] Jenkins, *Ecologies of Grace*, 144.

[17] Aquinas, *Summa Theologica*, 1.22.2, quoted in Jenkins, *Ecologies of Grace*, 146.

[18] There remains debate concerning exactly what culture means and how far divergent practices between different populations of conspecific non-human animals are comparable to what culture means in a human context: for an overview of the debate, see Kevin N. Laland and Bennett G. Galef (eds), *The Question of Animal Culture* (Cambridge, MA: Harvard University Press, 2009). There is no doubt, however,

On Aquinas's account, it seems we would have to classify the groups of orcas that hunt sea lions and other mammals as a different species than those that restrict their diet to fish.[19] Therefore, the idea that creatures that behave differently can no longer be recognized as themselves must be discarded, and we can retain Isaiah's vision of lions remaining lions after having turned to eating straw.[20]

As I write, the family cat, Mitsy, has climbed onto my desk and, having walked over my keyboard and interrupted my work, is now sitting in rapt attention watching through the window as pigeons, blackbirds, bullfinches and starlings flit across the garden in their busy late-spring preparations for nests, eggs and young. She passes hours in this way: birdwatching is one of her favourite activities. I am interested in the birds, too, although conscious that the nature of our interest is different, since Mitsy would catch and kill the birds if she could, as is manifest in her twitches and even growling noises when birds fly especially close to the window. Fortunately, from my point of view and that of the birds, she is a poor hunter and the birds she watches have very little to fear from her, even when glass does not separate her from them. If I speculate on the relationship between cats and birds in the new creation, Mitsy's birdwatching makes me wonder whether cats might retain their interest in birds but lose their desire to capture and consume them, with birds being receptive of the appreciative interest in them without having to be fearful of it being driven by any ulterior motive. It seems to me that for this cat, at least, there could be a perfect existence that consisted in the contemplation or even befriending of birds, without having to rely on killing them to survive, and it does not seem implausible to me that her lounging bigger relatives could also enjoy an existence in which they were freed from the burdens of having to kill to assure their continued existence.

---

that, in a range of species, particular groups of non-human animals have developed practices that are distinct from other groups of the same species, which is the relevant point here.

[19] See Southgate, *Groaning of Creation*, ix.

[20] I recognize that there is a powerful political reason for affirming that creatures are defined by their particular practices in an ecological context: it provides an under-girding for a theological affirmation of creatures as they are, and therefore for human actions to protect and sustain the particular creaturely modes of being that are far distant from our own. I am wholly sympathetic to the moral conclusion to this argument, but obviously theological arguments should not stand or fall on the basis of an evaluation of their consequential utility, and in any case I believe there are other good theological arguments for defending the particular modes of life of other species that do not depend on them being wholly defined by their practices.

Redemption of the Wilderness?

Beyond the question of how creatures now at enmity might live in peace in a redeemed state, a further question arises concerning their relationship to humanity. Given the modern romantic preference for unspoilt natural environments as the ideal, it is striking that the biblical ideal of Paradise portrayed in Genesis 2 is of a garden, and when Adam and Eve are disobedient to God, in Genesis 3, they are expelled from the garden to till the wild ground. Similarly, the image of the new creation in Revelation 21 is of a crystal city descending from heaven (21.10–11), with the river of the water of life and the tree of life within it (Rev. 22.1–2). These images suggest that ideal forms of nature are domesticated and ordered, rather than wild and untamed. The wilderness, in contrast, is the land through which Israel is forced to wander in search of the promised land (Exod. 13–40; Deut. 1–3) and the place where the consequences of God's wrath are evident (e.g. Hos. 2; Is. 34.8–17; Jer. 9.10–11). Ulrich Mausner summarizes J. Pedersen's discussion as follows: 'for the Israelite the inhabited and cultivated country is the land of blessing, while the desert is its exact opposite, the land of curse'.[21] It is true that the wilderness is often a place of encounter with God, of testing, and, as Mausner notes, a place Jesus seeks out for refuge, but it is a place that can only serve these functions because it is not the kind of place humans can flourish.[22]

As Roderick Nash observes in *Wilderness and the American Mind*, the concept of wilderness is fundamentally anthropocentric: characterized by the absence of human beings, the lack of resources that would support human life and the presence of threats to human living.[23] Nash notes the interesting etymology of the term: 'wild' may have originated in the Teutonic and Norse roots for 'will', thus indicating entities that are wilful, uncontrollable and unruly; while the root for the second part of the word is likely to be the Old

---

[21] Ulrich Mausner, *Christ in the Wilderness: The Wilderness Theme in the Second Gospel and Its Basis in the Biblical Tradition* (London: SCM Press, 1963), 37.

[22] Mausner, *Christ in the Wilderness*, 103–43. See also Susan P. Bratton, *Christianity Wilderness and Wildlife: The Original Desert Solitaire* (Cranbury, NJ: Associated University Presses, 1993), in which Bratton is critical of Roderick Nash's contention that Christianity is antagonistic to wilderness in Roderick Nash, *Wilderness and the American Mind*, 4th edn (New Haven, CT: Yale University Press, 2001); Robert Barry Leal, *Wilderness in the Bible: Toward a Theology of Wilderness* (New York: Peter Lang, 2004); Peter N. Carroll, *Puritanism and the Wilderness: The Intellectual Significance of the New England Frontier, 1629–1700* (New York; London: Columbia University Press, 1969); David Ross Williams, *Wilderness Lost: The Religious Origins of the American Mind* (Cranbury, NJ: Associated University Presses, 1987).

[23] Nash, *Wilderness and the American Mind*, 1–7.

English *déor,* meaning a beast. 'Wilderness' is therefore the place of those beasts that are beyond human control. The concept of wilderness, therefore, names a non-human space, a place where human beings are absent and unable to control events.

Given this biblical inheritance of wilderness as a threat to humanity and redemption as the exclusion of wildness, it is unsurprising that many accounts of redemption imply the abolition of wilderness. In Martin Luther's commentary on Genesis, he is particularly concerned with the relationship between Adam and the other animals before and after the fall. Before Adam sinned,

> His intellect was the clearest, his memory was the best, and his will was the most straightforward – all in the most beautiful tranquillity of mind, without any fear of death and without any anxiety. To these inner qualities came also those most beautiful and superb qualities of body and of all the limbs, qualities in which he surpassed all the remaining creatures. I am fully convinced that before Adam's sin his eyes were so sharp and clear that they surpassed those of the lynx and eagle. He was stronger than the lions and the bears, whose strength is very great; and he handled them the way we handle puppies.[24]

Beyond Adam's strength in this original condition, Luther is enthusiastic about the authority Adam and Eve exercised:

> Just as Adam and Eve acknowledged God as their Lord, so later no they themselves ruled over the other creatures in the air, in the water, and on the earth. Who could adequately describe this glory in words? I believe that Adam could command a lion with a single word, just as we give a command to a trained dog.[25]

After the fall, Luther laments that humans are subject to passions that are greater than those of cattle and are surpassed 'by the boars in their sense of hearing, by the eagles in their sense of sight, and by the lion in his strength'.[26] He affirms, however, that God will restore humanity as the image of God and one of the signs of this restoration will be the authority humans have once again, so that 'all the other creatures will be under our rule to a greater degree

[24] Luther, *Luther's Works,* I.62.
[25] Luther, *Luther's Works,* I.64.
[26] Luther, *Luther's Works,* I.62.

than they were in Adam's Paradise'.[27] For Luther, therefore, redemption means an end to wilderness, with all creatures brought under human authority.

In addressing the question of wilderness in the context of redemption, it is of course important to be attentive to the difference in context between the time during which Israel's concept of wilderness was formulated, the time of the New Testament, Luther's sixteenth-century environment, and the twenty-first century in which I write. Most pre-modern humans – in common with many poor modern ones – lived on the margins of areas that were threatening and dangerous to human life. They kept at bay the animals that sought to prey on them, their domesticated animals and their crops, only with difficulty and without complete success. It is unsurprising, then, that they dreamt of a life that was free of such threats to their existence and easy to forget the novelty of living a life in a developed nation where the major threats to life are from road traffic, obesity or other diseases caused by the side-effects of affluence. It is also easy to forget that it is only in the past few decades that the complete eradication of wilderness on earth, in the sense of environments not subject to the effects of human activity, has been a realistic possibility. Environmental pollution combined with anthropogenic climate change may already mean that there is no longer any environment on earth unaffected by human life. In this radically novel context, Luther's vision of all creaturely life brought under human authority seems much more like a curse than a blessing. In setting out an account of redemption that could apply to human and non-human creatures of all kinds, we clearly stand in need of a way of thinking about the redemption of the wilderness that honours the liberation of human beings from crying, suffering and death while allowing other animals a similar liberation.

It is clear that the argument above concerning peace between creatures rules out certain possible options at this point. One might, for example, judge that redemption of the wilderness might mean its restoration to some pre-human state, where non-human animals could thrive in an environment untouched by any human contamination. While preferable in many respects to the life other animals are currently subjected to through human impacts on their environments, this would still be an existence in which the rabbit feared death in the jaws of the fox and the lion feared starvation through failing to find a gazelle to kill. If we are to remain true to the kind of redemption that the Prince of Peace might bring, therefore, we cannot hope merely for environments characterized by the absence of human beings.

The rejection of restoration of the wilderness as its redemption does not mean, however, that we need to be thrust back into Luther's vision where all other animals have become tamed by human beings. In the terms of Chapter 1

---

[27] Luther, *Luther's Works*, I.62.

of this book, this would be a description of redeemed living where humans were the centre of all God's works and other creatures mere supporting players. If the end of creation is not the human, as Chapter 1 argued, then it will not end in creaturely relations where all other animals are made subservient to the human animal. If the argument in Chapter 3 is correct in proposing that the theologically distinctive human characteristic of bearing the image of God is best understood as a vocation to image God to the rest of creation, then, in a new creation where creatures live in the presence of God, it would seem that this vocation is no longer necessary. For now, humans should seek to live in a way that reflects God's gracious purposes to all creatures, on the grounds that they are a species uniquely capable of taking a view as to what might lead to the flourishing of other creatures; in the new creation, humans will be able to set aside this responsibility and join with other creatures in the praises of the lamb (Rev. 4.1–5.14).

Redemption of the wilderness, the place of wilful beasts, therefore, can neither be its return to some pristine non-human state, nor its domestication. Instead we must picture an existence for 'wild' animals where they continue to be wild, in the sense that they are the possessors of their own wills and direct their lives unconcerned by threats from humans or other animals. Perhaps we might think of the redeemed wilderness as a place where other-than-human animals delight in being themselves before their God, and where redeemed humans might delight in their modes of living without threatening or curtailing them. The wilderness could then continue to be the place of wild animals even in the presence of human beings, who would no longer be dependent on human absence for their flourishing. Perhaps the stories of saints living in the wilderness in harmony with the wild animals there can be taken as some kind of foreshadowing of this mode of redemption.

Redemption of Domesticated Animals?

The question of the redemption of wild animals provokes a further question about the redemption of the animals that humans have domesticated. In the previous chapter, I noted and gave reasons for rejecting C. S. Lewis's view that the only non-human animals for whom immortality was a possibility were those who might be resurrected as part of a human household. Once we have reoriented our view to recognize God's regard for other animals in their own right, however, what are we to make of the question of what will become of those animals who live alongside human beings in various kinds of relationship? For some, the question is straightforward: we can picture the liberation of fish from overcrowded fish farms to freedom in the renewing waters of the river of life. The birds that are caged in the zoo near my home will relish the chance to stretch their wings and soar or flutter in an endless expanse. The rats bred for laboratory experiments will escape their cages and flourish in warm nests with easy access to the tastiest morsels. For others, however, things are not so clear. Caged wolves would thrive in their return to the wild, but it is harder to conceive of a redeemed life for the dachshunds, poodles or chihuahuas who have been bred into shapes so distant from their original selves. A still harder case is that of the intensively reared chicken, who has been bred to achieve slaughter weight so quickly that its legs are not strong enough to support its body. Still harder, perhaps, are those creatures being genetically modified in harmful ways to make them more suitable for experimenting on, such as Harvard's 'OncoMouse': a mouse genetically manipulated to make it susceptible to various kinds of cancer.[28] In the realms of science fiction – but only just, one fears – is Margaret Atwood's dystopic vision of the future of chicken production in *Oryx and Crake*:

> 'This is the latest,' said Crake.
> What they were looking at was a large bulblike object that seemed to be covered with stippled whitish-yellow skin. Out of it came twenty thick fleshy tubes, and at the end of each tube another bulb was growing.
> 'What the hell is it?' said Jimmy.
> 'Those are chickens,' said Crake. 'Chicken parts. Just the breasts, on this one. They've got ones that specialize in drumsticks, too, twelve to a growth unit.'
> 'But there aren't any heads,' said Jimmy …
> 'That's the head in the middle,' said the woman. 'There's a mouth opening at the top, they dump the nutrients in there. No eyes or beak or anything, they don't need those.'
> 'This is horrible,' said Jimmy. The thing was a nightmare. It was like an animal-protein tuber.
> 'Picture the sea-anemone body plan,' said Crake. 'That helps.'
> 'But what's it thinking?' said Jimmy.
> The woman gave her jocular woodpecker yodel, and explained that they'd removed all the brain functions that had nothing to do with digestion, assimilation, and growth.'[29]

---

[28] See Donna Haraway, *Modest_Witness@Second_Millennium. Femaleman©_Meets_ Oncomouse: Feminism and Technoscience* (New York: Routledge, 1997), 79–85.

[29] Margaret Atwood, *Oryx and Crake* (New York: Anchor Books, 2004), 202–3.

Atwood's vision of 'NeoAgriculture' presents the extreme example of a human-created animal for which it is hard to conceive of a redeemed life, so fully has its life been assimilated to human interests. For other domesticated species, such as dogs for which breeding has not made life unsustainable, we may consider whether true redemption could include a life lived in companionship with humans, where perhaps former masters become just friends. Perhaps the redemption of the family cat, Mitsy, would be to leave humans far behind; perhaps she would choose to drop by to revel in being stroked from time to time. For Atwood's 'chickens', however, it seems that redemption would have to consist in the undoing of the manipulation human beings had wrought, which would mean the annihilation, rather than redemption, of the particular creaturely modes of being that human beings had been responsible for creating. To anticipate the ethics of the next volume of this work for a moment, we might judge that creatures for whom no redemption can be imagined should not be bred at all.

Redemption of Each?

The previous chapter argued that a Christian account of redemption would be incomplete if it excluded non-human creatures from its work. It is important to note, however, that including all kinds of creatures in redemption does not necessarily entail including each and every creature. Denis Edwards has identified five different ways in which theologians could give an account of the resurrection of non-human creatures: universal resurrection, as envisaged by Jürgen Moltmann, where every individual creature is restored to life; objective immortality, as set out by Alfred North Whitehead, where events and individuals achieve immortality through the effect they have on God; the Whiteheadian approach proposed by Jay McDaniel, with the supplement of a hope for subjective immortality; a material inscription, as outlined by Ernst

Conradie, where the existence of each being may be held and healed by God in a depth dimension of space-time; and Edwards's own approach, rooted in the life-giving Spirit, where resurrection will depend on the kind of creature involved.[30] In relation to Moltmann's universal resurrection, Edwards is concerned that the radically new creation it would require undermines the goodness of this creation and ecological commitments, and does not think bodily resurrection is the most appropriate form of resurrection for bacteria or a dinosaur. He judges that Whitehead's concept of objective resurrection is insufficiently Christological and relational, while finding merit in Conradie's approach. He believes the key features of an account of resurrection for non-human creatures are that it is shrouded in mystery; the participation of creatures in God is mediated by the Spirit; individual creatures find healing and fulfilment in Christ; redemption will be specific to each creature;[31] and some individual creatures may find redemption in the memory and life of the Trinity and Communion of Saints.[32]

While Edwards identifies a range of crucial aspects of Christian doctrine in this area, not least his emphasis on the particular roles that the Holy Spirit and Jesus Christ play in the redemption of non-human creatures, my judgement is that it is a mistake to doubt whether some creatures will be resurrected on the basis that this would require too great a discontinuity between the world as we know it and the new creation. Edwards is right to recognize a potential risk in Christian eschatological accounts that stress discontinuity: at the extreme, if one believed that the earth will be destroyed by fire at any moment and only a few fortunate human beings saved through being teleported away before the calamity, it would be hard to find the motivation to develop sustained theological attention to the

---

[30] Denis Edwards, 'Every Sparrow that Falls to the Ground: The Cost of Evolution and the Christ Event', *Ecotheology* 11: 1 (2006), 115–21, discussed in Southgate, *Groaning of Creation*, 87. The four sources Edwards draws on are: Jürgen Moltmann, *The Coming of God: Christian Eschatology* (London: SCM Press, 1996), 265; Alfred North Whitehead, *Process and Reality: An Essay in Cosmology* (New York: Harper & Row, 1957), 526–33; Jay McDaniel, *Of God and Pelicans: A Theology of Reverence for Life* (Louisville, KY: Westminster John Knox Press, 1989), 47–8; Ernst Conradie, 'Resurrection, Finitude and Ecology', in Ted Peters, Robert John Russell and Michael Walker (eds), *Resurrection: Theological and Scientific Assessments* (Grand Rapids, MI: Eerdmans, 2002), 292. Edwards categorizes McDaniel's approach with that of Whitehead, so numbers only three approaches in addition to his own.

[31] This is the point Jay McDaniel makes in considering what it might mean for a pelican chick to experience redemption: 'The hope is not that all creatures share in the same kind of fulfillment beyond death. Rather it is that all creatures share in that kind of fulfillment appropriate to their own interests and needs. What a pelican chick might know as a fulfillment of needs would have its own kind of harmony and intensity, one quite different from what we humans might know. If there is a pelican heaven, it is a *pelican* heaven' (McDaniel, *God and Pelicans*, 45 (italics in original)).

[32] Edwards, 'Every Sparrow', 117–19.

well-being of creatures within the created order. It is a mistake, however, to be so concerned about this risk that one scales back one's expectations about the kind of redemption God may bring about. It seems that because Edwards finds it hard to see how humans and dinosaurs could co-exist a world similar to the one we know, dinosaurs must be relegated to some secondary kind of resurrection, where they are remembered by God rather than able to live their own redeemed lives. As I noted above in relation to the possibility of peaceful relations between creatures, this risks underestimating the kind of transformation human beings will need to participate in redeemed creaturely life: if the new creation will be so transformed that human beings can live happily in peace with one another, the change necessary to allow dinosaurs and bacteria bodily resurrection seem of little consequence. It seems to me that a diplodocus or pterodactyl might have just as much to gain from a life set free from bondage to decay as I do. We must, of course, respect Edwards's point about the final mystery of the redemption God will bring, but if we are to hope for the promised redemption of all things in Christ, it seems to me that we should hope for a place for each creature within God's unending graciousness, rather than invent distinctions in advance in order to make sure an omnipotent and bounteous God can manage an appropriate relationship between this world and the next.[33]

Redemption, Future and Present

Christian understandings of redemption do not concern only hopes for the future, but also entail action in the present. Jesus's teaching about the kingdom of heaven in Matthew's gospel make this clear: because the kingdom of heaven has come near (4.17), the righteousness of his followers must exceed that of the scribes and Pharisees (5.20), those who wish to enter must do the will of the Father (7.21), those who seek it must give up everything for it (13.44–5) and those who wait must be wise in their preparations like the bridesmaids who took oil for their lamps (25.1–4). Jürgen Moltmann's *Theology of Hope* made clear the practical implications of the Christian hope he described: 'The coming

---

[33] An additional reason for maintaining the subjective immortality of all creatures would be the theodicy-driven concern common to John Wesley, Jürgen Moltmann, Keith Ward and Christopher Southgate, that each creature needed compensation from God in the next life for unhappiness in this one. Any kind of objective immortality would seem insufficient to make it up to creatures that had done badly in this life. As discussed in the section 'Redemption as Compensation?' of the previous chapter; however, I judge that there are important reasons to avoid the position that creatures need compensation for hardships they suffer in this life, so I do not consider this to be a useful support for the subjective immortality of non-human animals.

lordship of the risen Christ cannot be merely hoped for and awaited. This hope and expectation also sets its stamp on life, action and suffering in the history of society. Hence mission means not merely propagation of faith and hope, but also historic transformation of life.'[34] In his later work *The Coming of God*, he rejects accounts that transpose eschatology into time, such as those of Albert Schweitzer and Oscar Cullmann, together with accounts that transpose eschatology into eternity, such as those of Karl Barth, Paul Althaus and Rudolf Bultmann. Instead, he argues, we need an eschatology focussed on the advent of God, who is coming towards the world from its future.[35] Kathryn Tanner identifies Moltmann's position as the most influential example of future-oriented eschatology, but believes its optimism about the future is becoming harder to sustain.[36] Instead, she defends the practical relevance of a de-temporalized eschatology, where Christians believe not in a better future for the world, but in eternal life in Christ in the present.[37] Where future-oriented eschatologies rule out complacency about the world as it is by a transcendent future, she argues that complacency can be also challenged by faith in a transcendent present, 'by present life in God as the source of goods that the world one lives in fails to match'.[38] Christians are then liberated from the demand that their actions will succeed in making the world a better place, because one is obligated to act instead 'simply because this is the only way of living that makes sense in light of one's life in God'.[39]

While it is important to note these options for the further specification of Christian eschatology, it is also important to recognize that we need not choose between future-oriented and de-temporalized eschatologies in order to make sense of the redeemed life of animals described in this chapter and its relevance to present Christian practice. For both Moltmann and Tanner, a vision of what the reconciliation and redemption of all things by God in Christ through the Spirit might mean for relationships between humans and other animals will cause Christians to be motivated to act in whatever ways they can to witness to redeemed patterns of creaturely relations. For both, the doctrine of redemption is not reducible to a set of beliefs about some future state, but is an understanding of what God is doing in the world and of how God intended and intends creaturely relations to be ordered.

If the argument of this final part of the book is correct, it makes no more sense to exclude God's other-than-human animals from redemption, than it does to exclude

---

[34] Moltmann, *Theology of Hope*, 329–30.

[35] Moltmann, *Coming of God*, 6–23.

[36] Kathryn Tanner, 'Eschatology and Ethics', in Gilbert Meilander and William Werpehowski (eds), *The Oxford Handbook of Theological Ethics* (Oxford: Oxford University Press, 2005), 44–6.

[37] Tanner, 'Eschatology and Ethics', 47–52.

[38] Tanner, 'Eschatology and Ethics', 52.

[39] Tanner, 'Eschatology and Ethics', 54.

them from God's great works of creation and reconciliation. Those theological accounts that have attempted to make redemption a exclusively human enterprise seem in this context to be oddly partial, preoccupied with the human condition, inattentive to the breadth of biblical witness and – for no good theological reasons – neglectful of the other creatures that God had reason to make part of the astonishing diversity of creation. The Christian hope must therefore be that the bodies of other-than-human animals are not disposable parts of the current world order, but will be resurrected with human bodies in the new creation. Such a vision of the redeemed bodies of animals – human and other-than-human – should encourage Christians to appreciate that their relationships with other animals in the present is a particular and pressing concern, and therefore requires the ethical reflection that will be the topic of the second volume of this work.

CONCLUSION

This volume has aimed to answer the question of where animals – human and other-than-human – belong in Christian theology. Before surveying the ground that has been covered in response to that question, however, it is worth reflecting on the prior point *that* animals belong in Christian theology. While the discussion up to this point demonstrates that there is no shortage of theological material with relevance to animals, it is nonetheless the case that very few theologians have ever made animals the subject of their concern for anything other than brief and passing references. Whether or not this was understandable or justifiable in the past, it is not so in the present and in the future. The Bible makes clear that other-than-human animals have a place in the purposes of their creator, that they are providentially sustained by God and respond to God in praise. If they were extra-terrestrial creatures with which humans had no interaction, it might be defensible to ignore them in relation to other more immediate concerns, but we live alongside these other animal creatures, employ them for our own purposes with little regard for their well-being, and threaten their environments through our activities, making species extinct through thoughtless neglect or deliberate action. Christian theologians therefore have a responsibility to be attentive to where other animals belong in their theological work, to resist the simplistic and inaccurate received formulations of human exceptionalism that manifest an inexcusable ignorance of the lives of other creatures and to seek new ways of representing the relations of our animal neighbours with God and with ourselves.

Part I of this volume enquired after the place of animals within the Christian doctrine of creation. It acknowledged that some theologians have believed that God created the Universe for the benefit of human beings, but noted the absence of support for such a position in the Bible and the theological dangers of assuming the activity of God is so wholly identifiable with humanity. Better grounded theological accounts celebrate God's graciousness to human beings in the context of the gracious bestowal of being on all God's creatures (Chapter 1). The basic theological declaration of the transcendence of God leads to the recognition of solidarity among all that is not God, the creatures God has made. Amidst this creaturely solidarity human beings find themselves in particular relationship with those creatures most like them: their fellow animals. The Bible frequently treats humans and other animals together as creatures with the breath of life or creatures with flesh, often the common beneficiaries of God's blessing and the common subjects of God's judgement. Animal creatures are the recipients of divine address and are able to respond to God's command in ways unlike others of God's creatures (Chapter 2). The Bible and the Christian tradition have also treated the question of distinguishing between animal creatures: between those of the water, the air and the land; between those that are clean and unclean; between those that are high up and low down in a Great Chain of Being; between those that are domesticated and those that are wild; between those identified as bearers of God's image and those that are not. Many of the ways of distinguishing between animals that have become routine in theological and philosophical discussion, however, particularly as they are used to define the human/non-human boundary, are ill-informed and represent inadequate and unsustainable theological positions that should be abandoned. Instead, we need ways of attending to other animals that are alert to the particularities of their existence and responsive to it (Chapter 3).

Part II addressed the place of animals in the Christian doctrine of reconciliation. The incarnation should not be misread as a privileging of a particular species, any more than it was a privileging of a particular gender, geographical area or period of time. Instead, New Testament Christologies confess Christ as the reconciler of all things, the one who takes on creaturely flesh and takes up the cause of God's creatures. A worked example of rethinking the structure with this broad definition of the creature in mind demonstrated that the coherence of Christian theology was not put at risk in such a rethinking: indeed, the symmetry between creation and incarnation this perspective makes clear seems rather to secure the relationship between creation and incarnation evident in the prologue to John's gospel (Chapter 4). All animals stand in need of the reconciliation and liberation Christ's work of atonement establishes and a reading of Genesis 6 in the context of recent observation of the behaviour of particular non-human species suggests that it does not make sense to restrict the attribution of sin to human animals. The interpretation of the crucifixion of Christ as an animal sacrifice makes clear that the association between atonement and non-human animals is almost as old as the church (Chapter 5).

Part III considered where animals belong in the context of the Christian account of redemption. While many theologians have judged that human beings are the unique possessors of an eternal soul, Hildrop's insight that what

God creates God has a reason to redeem and the universal restoration expected by certain of the Church Fathers suggest that singling the human species out for redemption would be an odd conclusion to God's project in creation, even if the arguments of some theologians that certain creatures deserve redemption as compensation from God are rejected (Chapter 6). There then follows the challenge of suggesting what the contours of redeemed animal life might be, without overstepping appropriate boundaries of necessary human ignorance. Here we can affirm that redemption will mean peace between creatures and an end to suffering and death, and that this means an end to cycles of predation and the consequent transformation of creatures such as lions and human beings who are inextricably caught up in patterns of destruction in the present world (Chapter 7).

In addressing this comparatively new area, I am aware that the work completed in this volume is of the most provisional and preliminary sort. At best, the preceding reflections have begun to survey the areas where theological thinking about animals is required, to lay boundary markers and note particular points of interest. Further work will be necessary to correct some of the sightings I have taken and to triangulate landmarks in relation to more frequently visited locations. At many points I have taken particular paths aware of possible alternative routes that may well look more attractive to those who next come this way. In some places it has seemed possible to me to build structures on foundations that appear stable, but in others the ground beneath my feet seems less secure and the results of my labours correspondingly more transient. At no point, of course, have I had the benefit of the view of the angels that will be ours only at the last. It is my hope, therefore, that this sketch map will encourage other pioneers to undertake more careful and detailed cartographies.

The end of this volume marks the end of this initial project in thinking about animals in the context of systematic theology, but if Barth is right that dogmatics 'has the problem of ethics in view from the very first, and it cannot legitimately lose sight of it',[1] we must recognize that the doctrinal conclusions of this volume necessarily point beyond themselves to a second task of interpreting the implications of these positions for questions of Christian practice. The scope and diversity of human practices in relation to our fellow animal creatures fall under the judgement of God and Christians therefore need to reconsider what account they can give of their actions. Given that God did not merely establish the world for our own convenience, but wills the flourishing of all God's creatures, we must ask what this might this mean for the appropri-

---

[1] Karl Barth, *Church Dogmatics*, vol. III/4, ed. G. W. Bromiley and T. F. Torrance, trans. A. T. MacKay et al. (Edinburgh: T. & T. Clark, 1961), 3.

ateness of Christian uses of other animals for food, clothing, labour, research, entertainment, companions and for our responsibilities to non-human animals that live beyond relationships of domestication. This will be the topic of the second volume of this work: *On Animals: II. Theological Ethics.*

Bibliography

Adams, Carol J. and Marjorie Procter-Smith, 'Taking Life or "Taking on Life"? Table Talk and Animals', in *Ecofeminism and the Sacred*, Carol J. Adams ed. 295–310. New York: Continuum, 1993.

Adams, Robert M., 'Thisness and Primitive Identity', *Journal of Philosophy* 76: 1 (1979), 5–26.

Adani, Christoph, 'What is Complexity?', *BioEssays* 24: 12 (2002), 1085–94.

Agamben, Giorgio, *The Open: Man and Animal*, trans. K. Attell. Stanford, CA: Stanford University Press, 2004.

Alberigo, G. and Norman P. Tanner (eds), *Decrees of the Ecumenical Councils Vol. 1: Nicaea I to Lateran V*. London: Sheed & Ward, 1990.

Algra, Keimpe, 'Stoic Theology', in Brad Inwood ed. *The Cambridge Companion to the Stoics*, 153–78. Cambridge: Cambridge University Press, 2003.

Anselm, 'Cur Deus Homo', in Thomas Williams ed. *Anselm: Basic Writings*, 237–326. Indianapolis, IN: Hackett, 2007.

Aquinas, Saint Thomas, *Summa Contra Gentiles*, trans. English Dominican Fathers. London: Burns Oates & Washbourne, 1923.

Aquinas, Thomas, *Summa Theologica*, trans. Fathers of the English Dominican Province. London: Blackfriars, 1963.

Aristotle, *Parts of Animals*, Loeb Classical Library, trans. A. L. Peck. London; Cambridge, MA: William Heinemann; Harvard University Press, 1937.

—*Generation of Animals*, Loeb Classical Library, trans. A. L. Peck. London; Cambridge, MA: William Heinemann; Harvard University Press, 1943.

—*Historia Animalium*, Loeb Classical Library, trans. A. L. Peck. London; Cambridge, MA: William Heinemann; Harvard University Press, 1965.

Ashcraft, Richard, 'Hobbes's Natural Man: A Study in Ideology Formation', *The Journal of Politics* 33: 4 (1971), 1076–117.

Athanasius, *Contra Gentes and de Incarnatione*, ed. and trans. Robert W. Thompson. Oxford: Clarendon, 1971.

Atwood, Margaret, *Oryx and Crake*. New York: Anchor Books, 2004.

Augustine, *The Literal Meaning of Genesis*, Ancient Christian Writers, trans. John Hammond Taylor, SJ. New York; Mahwah, NJ: Paulist Press, 1982.

—*The Trinity (de Trinitate)*, The Works of Saint Augustine: A Translation for the 21st Century, ed. John E. Rotelle, trans. Edmund Hill, O.P. Hyde Park, NY: New City Press, 1991.

—'A Treatise on the Soul and its Origin', in *A Select Library of Nicene and Post-Nicene Fathers of the Christian Church. First Series*, vol. 5, Philip Schaff ed. 315–71. Edinburgh: T & T Clark, 1994.

—*The City of God Against the Pagans*, trans. R. W. Dyson. Cambridge: Cambridge University Press, 1998.

—*On Genesis: On Genesis: A Refutation of the Manichees, Unfinished Literal Commentary on Genesis, the Literal Meaning of Genesis*, The Works of Saint Augustine, ed. John E. Rotelle, trans. Edmund Hill, O.P. New York: New City Press, 2002.

Aune, David E., *Revelation 17–22*, Word Biblical Commentary, vol. 52C. Dallas, TX: Word, 2002.

Bacon, Francis, 'The Natural and Experimental History for the Foundation of Philosophy: Or Phenomena of the Universe: Which is the Third Part of the Instauratio Magna', in *The Works of Francis Bacon*, vol. 5, James Spedding, Robert Leslie Ellis and Douglas Denon Heath (eds), 131–34. London: Longman & Co., 1858.

—*The Essays*, ed. John Pitcher. London: Penguin, 1985.

—*The New Organon*, Cambridge Texts in the History of Philosophy, eds Lisa Jardine and Michael Silverthorne. Cambridge: Cambridge University Press, 2000.

Baker, Gordon and Katherine J. Morris, *Descartes' Dualism*. London: Routledge, 1996.

Barilan, Y. Michael, 'The Vision of Vegetarianism and Peace: Rabbi Kook on the Ethical Treatment of Animals', *History of the Human Sciences* 17: 4 (2004), 69–101.

Barnes, Jonathan, 'Metaphysics', in Jonathan Barnes ed. *The Cambridge Companion to Aristotle*, 66–108. Cambridge: Cambridge University Press, 1995.

Barrett, C. K., *The Gospel According to John, 2nd edn*. London: SPCK, 1978.

Barth, Karl, *Church Dogmatics*, 13 vols, ed. G. W. Bromiley and T. F. Torrance. Edinburgh: T. & T. Clark, 1956–75.

Barth, Markus, *Ephesians: Introduction, Translation and Commentary on Chapters 1–3*, The Anchor Bible, vol. 34, (eds) William Foxwell Albright and David Nowell Freedman. Garden City, NY: Doubleday & Company, 1974.

Barth, Markus, and Helmut Blanke, *Colossians: A New Translation with Introduction and Commentary*, The Anchor Bible, vol. 34B, (eds) William

Foxwell Albright and David Nowell Freedman, trans. Astrid B. Beck. New York: Doubleday, 1994.

Bartholomew I, *Cosmic Grace, Humble Prayer: The Ecological Vision of the Green Patriarch Bartholomew I*, ed. John Chryssavgis. Grand Rapids, MI: Eerdmans, 2003.

Basil, Saint, 'On the Hexaemeron', in *Exegetic Homilies*, 3–150, trans. Sister Agnes Clare Way. C.D.P. Washington, DC: Catholic University of America, 1963.

Bauckham, Richard, 'Jesus and the Wild Animals (Mark 1:13): A Christological Image for an Ecological Age', in Joel B. Green and Max Turner (eds), *Jesus of Nazareth: Lord and Christ (Essays on the Historical Jesus and New Testament Christology)*, 3–21. Grand Rapids, MI: Eerdmans, 1994.

—'Joining Creation's Praise of God', *Ecotheology* 7 (2002), 45–59.

—'Reading the Sermon on the Mount in an Age of Ecological Catastrophe', *Studies in Christian Ethics* 22: 1 (2009), 76–88.

Bekoff, Marc, *Minding Animals: Awareness, Emotions, and Heart*. New York: Oxford University Press, 2002.

—*Animal Passions and Beastly Virtues: Reflections on Redecorating Nature*. Philadelphia, PA: Temple University Press, 2006.

Bekoff, Marc and Paul W. Sherman, 'Reflections on Animal Selves', in *Animal Passions and Beastly Virtues: Reflections on Redecorating Nature*, 66–76. Philadelphia, PA: Temple University Press, 2006.

Bennett, Jonathan, *Rationality: An Essay Towards an Analysis*. Indianapolis, IN: Hackett, 1989.

Bergjan, Silke-Petra, 'Celsus the Epicurean? The Interpretation of an Argument in Origen, Contra Celsum', *Harvard Theological Review* 94: 2 (2001), 179–204.

Berkman, John, 'Towards a Thomistic Theology of Animality', in Celia Deane-Drummond and David Clough (eds), *Creaturely Theology: On God, Humans and Other Animals*, 21–40. London: SCM, 2009.

Best, Ernest, *A Critical and Exegetical Commentary on Ephesians*, International Critical Commentary. Edinburgh: T & T Clark, 1998.

Bluhm, H. S., 'The Significance of Luther's Earliest Extant Sermon', *The Harvard Theological Review* 37: 2 (1944), 175–84.

Bonhoeffer, Dietrich, *Letters and Papers From Prison*, Dietrich Bonhoeffer Works, Vol. 8, (eds) Christian Gremmels, Eberhard Bethge, Renate Bethge and Ilse Tödt, trans. John W. de Gruchy. Minneapolis, MN: Fortress Press, 2010.

Borges, Jorge Luis, 'The Analytical Language of John Wilkins', in *Other Inquisitions, 1937–52*, Tans. Ruth L. C. Simms, Austin, TX: University of Texas Press, 1964.

Bougeant, Guillaume Hyacinthe, *Amusement Philosophique sur le Langage des Bêtes*. La Haye: Chez A. van Dole, 1739.

Boyle, T. C., *When the Killing's Done*. London: Bloomsbury, 2011.

Brakke, David, 'Review of Rethinking "Gnosticism": An Argument for Dismantling a Dubious Category', *Church History* 67 (1):1 (1998), 119–21.

Bratton, Susan P., *Christianity Wilderness and Wildlife: The Original Desert Solitaire*. Cranbury, NJ: Associated University Presses, 1993.

Briggs, Richard, 'Humans in the Image of God and Other Things Genesis Does Not Make Clear', *Journal of Theological Interpretation* 4: 1 (2010), 111–26.

Brown, Stuart C., *Philosophy of Religion: An Introduction with Readings*. London: Routledge, 2001.

Browne, Peter, *The Procedure, Extent, and Limits of Human Understanding*. London: William Innys, 1729.

Bruce, F. F., *The Gospel of John*. Grand Rapids, MI: Eerdmans, 1983.

—*The Epistles to the Colossians, to Philemon, and to the Ephesians*, The New International Commentary on the New Testament. Grand Rapids, MI: Eerdmans, 1984.

Brueggemann, Walter, *Genesis*. Louisville, KY: John Knox Press, 1982.

Bultmann, Rudolf, *The Gospel of John: A Commentary*, (eds) R. W. N. Hoare and J. K. Riches, trans. G. R. Beasley-Murray. Oxford: Blackwell, 1971.

Callicott, J. Baird (ed) *Companion to a Sand County Almanac*. Madison, WI: University of Wisconsin, 1987.

Calvin, John, *The Gospel According to John*, Calvin's Commentaries, (eds) T. F. Torrance and D. W. Torrance, trans. T. H. L. Parker. Edinburgh; London: Oliver and Boyd, 1959.

—*Genesis*, ed. and trans. John King. Edinburgh: Banner of Truth Trust, 1965.

—*Institutes of the Christian Religion*, trans. Henry Beveridge. Grand Rapids, MI: Eerdmans, 1989.

Campbell, Neil A. and Jane B. Reece, *Biology*, 7th edn. San Francisco, CA: Benjamin Cummings, 2005.

Canlis, J, 'Being Made Human: The Significance of Creation for Irenaeus' Doctrine of Participation', *Scottish Journal of Theology* 58: 4 (2005), 434–54.

Carroll, Peter N., *Puritanism and the Wilderness: The Intellectual Significance of the New England Frontier, 1629–1700*. New York; London: Columbia University Press, 1969.

Cavalieri, Paola and Peter Singer (eds), *The Great Ape Project: Equality Beyond Humanity*. New York: St Martin's Press, 1993.

Chadwick, Henry, 'Origen, Celsus and the Stoa', *Journal of Theological Studies* 48 (1947), 34–49.

Chomsky, Noam, *Language and Mind*. New York: Harcourt Brace Jovanovitch, 1968.

Christianson, Eric S., *Ecclesiastes Through the Centuries*. Oxford: Blackwell, 2007.

Chrysostom, John, Saint, *Homilies on Genesis*, Fathers of the Christian Church, trans. Robert C. Hill. Washington, DC: Catholic University of America, 1986.

Cicero, Marcus Tullius, *De Natura Deorum; Academica*, Loeb Classical Library, trans. H. Rackham. London: William Heinemann, 1933.

Clair, Colin, *Unnatural History: An Illustrated Bestiary*. London; New York; Toronto: Abelard-Schuman, 1967.

Clough, David, *Ethics in Crisis: Interpreting Barth's Ethics*. Aldershot: Ashgate, 2005.

—'All God's Creatures: Reading Genesis on Human and Non-Human Animals', in Stephen Barton and David Wilkinson (eds), *Reading Genesis After Darwin*. Oxford: Oxford University Press, 2009.

—'The Anxiety of the Human Animal: Martin Luther on Non-Human Animals and Human Animality', in *Creaturely Theology: On God, Humans and Other Animals*, Celia Deane-Drummond and David Clough (eds), 41–60. London: SCM, 2009.

—'Interpreting Human Life by Looking the Other Way: Bonhoeffer on Human Beings and Other Animals', in Ralf K. Wüstenberg, Stefan Heuser and Esther Hornung (eds) *Bonhoeffer and the Biosicences: An Initial Exploration*, International Bonhoeffer Interpretations, 51–74. Frankfurt am Main: Peter Lang, 2010.

Coad, Dominic, 'Creation's Praise of God: An Ecological Theology of Non-Human and Human Being'. PhD thesis. University of Exeter, 2010.

Cohen, Noah J, *Sa`ar Ba`aley Hayim: The Prevention of Cruelty to Animals: Its Bases, Development and Legislation in Hebrew Literature*. Jerusalem: Feldheim Publishers, 1976.

Colish, Marcia L., *Stoicism in Christian Latin Thought Through the Sixth Century*, The Stoic Tradition From Antiquity to the Early Middle Ages. Leiden: E. J. Brill, 1985.

Compassion in World Farming, *Global Warning: Climate Change and Farm Animal Welfare*. Godalming, Surrey: Compassion in World Farming, 2008.

Conradie, Ernst, 'Resurrection, Finitude and Ecology', in Ted Peters, Robert John Russell and Michael Welker (eds), *Resurrection: Theological and Scientific Assessments*, 277–96. Grand Rapids, MI: Eerdmans, 2002.

Conway Morris, S., *The Crucible of Creation: The Burgess Shale and the Rise of Animals*. Oxford; New York: Oxford University Press, 1998.

Cottingham, John, '"A Brute to the Brutes?" Descartes' Treatment of Animals', *Philosophy* 53 (1978), 551–61.

Crisp, Oliver D., 'Multiple Incarnations', in Martin Stone ed. *Reason, Faith and*

History: Philosophical Essays for Paul Helm, 219–38. Aldershot; Burlington, VT: Ashgate, 2008.

Cunningham, David, 'The Way of All Flesh', in Celia Deane-Drummond and David Clough (eds), *Creaturely Theology: On God, Humans and Other Animals*, 100–17. London: SCM, 2009.

Daley, Brian E., *The Hope of the Early Church: A Handbook of Patristic Eschatology*. Cambridge: Cambridge University Press, 1991.

Davies, Brian, *The Thought of Thomas Aquinas*. Oxford: Oxford University Press, 1992.

Davis, Ellen, *Proverbs, Ecclesiastes, and the Song of Songs*. Louisville, KY: Westminster John Knox, 2000.

de Waal, Frans, *Good Natured: The Origins of Right and Wrong in Humans and Other Animals*. Cambridge, MA: Harvard University Press, 1996.

—*Chimpanzee Politics: Power and Sex Among Apes*. Baltimore, NJ: Johns Hopkins University Press, 1998.

Deane-Drummond, Celia, *The Ethics of Nature*, New Dimensions to Religious Ethics. Malden, MA; Oxford: Blackwell, 2004.

—'Are Animals Moral? Taking Soundings Through Vice, Virtue, Conscience and *Imago Dei*', in Celia Deane-Drummond and David Clough (eds), *Creaturely Theology: On God, Humans and Other Animals*, 190–210. London: SCM, 2009.

—*Christ and Evolution: Wonder and Wisdom*. London: SCM, 2009.

Deane-Drummond, Celia, and David Clough (eds), *Creaturely Theology: On God, Humans and Other Animals*. London: SCM, 2009.

DeGrazia, David, *Taking Animals Seriously: Mental Life and Moral Status*. Cambridge: Cambridge University Press, 1996.

Demant, V. A., *Christian Polity*. London: Faber and Faber, 1936.

Derrida, Jacques and David Wills, 'The Animal That Therefore I Am (More to Follow)', *Critical Inquiry* 28: 2 (2002), 369–418.

Descartes, René, *Discourse on Method and Other Writings*, trans. Frank Edmund Sutcliffe. Harmondsworth: Penguin, 1968.

—*The Philosophical Writings of Descartes*, vol. III, *The Correspondence*, trans. John Cottingham et al. Cambridge: Cambridge University Press, 1991.

Dickey, James, *Self-Interviews*. Garden City, NY: Doubleday & Company, 1970.

Dillman, A., *Genesis Critically and Exegetically Expounded*. Edinburgh: T & T Clark, 1897.

Dinzelbacher, Peter, 'Animal Trials: A Multidisciplinary Approach', *Journal of Interdisciplinary History* 32: 3 (2002), 405–21.

Dostoyevsky, Fyodor, *The Brothers Karamazov*, trans. Richard Pevear and Larissa Volokhonsky. New York: Farrar, Strauss and Giroux, 1990.

duBois, Page, *Centaurs and Amazons: Women and the Pre-History of the Great Chain of Being*. Ann Arbor, MI: University of Michigan Press, 1982.

Dunn, James D. G., *Christology in the Making: A New Testament Inquiry Into the Origins of the Doctrine of the Incarnation, 2nd edn*. London: SCM, 1989.

Dupré, John, 'Are Whales Fish?', in Douglas L. Medin and Scott Atran (eds), *Folkbiology*, 461–76. Cambridge, MA: MIT, 1999.

—*Humans and Other Animals*. Oxford: Clarendon, 2002.

Edwards, Denis, 'Every Sparrow That Falls to the Ground: The Cost of Evolution and the Christ Event', *Ecotheology* 11: 1 (2006), 103–23.

Edwards, Mark Julian, *Origen Against Plato*. Aldershot: Ashgate, 2002.

Evans, E. P., *The Criminal Prosecution and Capital Punishment of Animals*. London: William Heinemann, 1906.

Farrer, Austin M., *Love Almighty and Ills Unlimited*. London: Collins, 1966.

Fee, Gordon D., *The First Epistle to the Corinthians*, The New International Commentary on the New Testament. Grand Rapids, MI: Eerdmans, 1987.

Fergusson, David A. S., *The Cosmos and the Creator: An Introduction to the Theology of Creation*. London: SPCK, 1998.

Feuerbach, Ludwig, *The Essence of Christianity*, trans. George Eliot. New York: Prometheus Books, 1989.

Fisher, Christopher L. and David Fergusson, 'Karl Rahner and the Extra-Terrestrial Intelligence Question', *Heythrop Journal* 47: 2 (2006), 275–90.

Foucault, Michel, *The Order of Things: An Archaeology of the Human Sciences*. London; New York: Routledge, 2002.

Francis of Assisi, St, *The Little Flowers of Saint Francis*, trans. L. Sherley-Price. Harmondsworth: Penguin, 1959.

Fudge, Erica, *Animal*. London: Reaktion, 2002.

Galloway, Allan D., *The Cosmic Christ*. Nisbet & Co., 1951.

Glacken, Clarence J., *Traces on the Rhodian Shore: Nature and Culture in Western Thought From Ancient Times to the End of the Eighteenth Century*. Berkeley, CA: University of California Press, 1967.

Goldingay, John, *Psalms*, Baker Commentary on the Old Testament, vol. 3. Grand Rapids, MI: Baker Academic, 2008.

Goodall, Jane, 'Infant Killing and Cannibalism in Free-Living Chimpanzees', *Folia Primatologica* 28:4 (1977), 259–89.

—*Beyond Innocence: An Autobiography in Letters: The Later Years*, ed. Dale Peterson. Boston, MA, New York: Houghton Mifflin, 2001.

Goodman, Morris, Lawrence I. Grossman and Derek E. Wildman, 'Moving Primate Genomics Beyond the Chimpanzee Genome', *Trends in Genetics* 21: 9 (2005), 511–17.

Goodwin, Brian, *How the Leopard Changed its Spots: The Evolution of Complexity*. New York: Charles Scribner's Sons, 1994.

Grant, Robert M., 'Review of Rethinking "Gnosticism": An Argument for Dismantling a Dubious Category', *The Journal of Religion* 81 (1):1 (2001), 645–47.

Grant, Robert McQueen, *Early Christians and Animals*. London: Routledge, 1999.

Greggs, Tom, *Barth, Origen, and Universal Salvation: Restoring Particularity*. Oxford: Oxford University Press, 2009.

—'Apokatastasis: Particularist Universalism in Origen (*c.* 185–*c.* 254)', in *'All Shall be Well': Explorations in Universalism and Christian Theology, From Origen to Moltmann*, Gregory Macdonald ed. 29–46. Eugene, OR: Cascade Books, 2011.

Gregory of Nyssa, 'On the Making of Man', in *A Select Library of Nicene and Post-Nicene Fathers of the Christian Church. Second Series*, vol. 5, Philip Schaff ed. Edinburgh: T & T Clark, 1997.

Gregory the Great, *Saint Gregory the Great: Dialogues*, Fathers of the Church, vol. 39, trans. O. J. Zimmerman. Washington, DC: Catholic University of America, 1959.

Grene, Marjorie Glicksman and David J. Depew, *The Philosophy of Biology*. Cambridge: Cambridge University Press, 2004.

Grumett, David, 'Christ the Lamb of God and the Christian Doctrine of God', paper presented at the Annual Conference of the American Academy of Religion, Atlanta, GA (30 October, 2010).

Grumett, David and Rachel Muers, *Theology on the Menu: Asceticism, Meat and Christian Diet*. Abingdon: Routledge, 2010.

Gunton, Colin, *The One, the Three and the Many: God, Creation and the Culture of Modernity*. Cambridge: Cambridge University Press, 1993.

Gunton, Colin E., 'The Doctrine of Creation', in *The Cambridge Companion to Christian Doctrine*, Colin E. Gunton ed. Cambridge; New York: Cambridge University Press, 1997.

—*The Triune Creator: A Historical and Systematic Study*. Edinburgh: Edinburgh University Press, 1998.

—'The End of Causality? The Reformers and Their Predecessors', in Colin E. Gunton ed. *The Doctrine of Creation: Essays in Dogmatics, History and Philosophy*, 63–82. London: T & T Clark, 2004.

Gustafson, James M., *Ethics From a Theocentric Perspective*, vol. 2. Chicago, IL: University of Chicago, 1984.

Haeckel, Ernst, *The History of Creation, or the Development of the Earth and its Inhabitants by the Action of Natural Causes*, trans. E. Ray Lankester. London: Kegan Paul, Trench, 1883.

Hamilton, Victor P., *The Book of Genesis, Chapters 1–17*, NICOT Series, ed. R. K. Harrison. Grand Rapids, MI: Eerdmans, 1990.

Haraway, Donna, *Modest_Witness@Second_Millennium. Femaleman©_Meets_ Oncomouse: Feminism and Technoscience*. New York: Routledge, 1997.

—*The Companion Species Manifesto: Dogs, People, and Significant Otherness*. Chicago, IL: Prickly Paradigm Press, 2003.

Harrison, Peter, 'The Virtues of Animals in Seventeenth-Century Thought', *Journal of the History of Ideas* 59: 3 (1998), 463–84.

Hatton, Peter T. H., *Contradiction in the Book of Proverbs: The Deep Waters of Counsel*, Society for Old Testament Study Series. Aldershot: Ashgate, 2008.

Hauerwas, Stanley, *Naming the Silences: God, Medicine, and the Problem of Suffering*. Grand Rapids, MI: Eerdmans, 1990.

Hausfater, Glenn and Sarah Blaffer Hrdy, 'Comparative and Evolutionary Perspectives on Infanticide: An Overview', in Glenn Hausfater and Sarah Blaffer Hrdy (eds), *Infanticide: Comparative and Evolutionary Perspectives*, xiii–xxxv. Piscataway, NJ: Transaction Publishers, 2008.

Hausfater, Glenn and Sarah Blaffer Hrdy (eds), *Infanticide: Comparative and Evolutionary Perspectives*. Piscataway: NJ: Transaction Publishers, 2008.

Hayward, Tim, 'Anthropocentrism: A Misunderstood Problem', *Environmental Values* 6: 1 (1997), 49–63.

Henry, Matthew, *An Exposition of the Old and New Testament*. London: Samuel Bagster, 1811.

Hepplethwaite, Brian, 'The Impossibility of Multiple Incarnations', Theology 104 (2001): 323–334.

Herman, Louis M., Stan A. Kuczaj and Mark D. Holder, 'Responses to Anomalous Gestural Sequences by a Language-Trained Dolphin: Evidence for Processing of Semantic Relations and Syntactic Information', *Journal of Experimental Psychology: General* 122: 2 (1993), 184–94.

Hiebert, Theodore, *The Yahwist's Landscape: Nature and Religion in Early Israel*. New York: Oxford University Press, 1996.

Higton, Mike, *Christian Doctrine*, SCM Core Texts. London: SCM, 2008.

Hildrop, John, *Free Thoughts Upon the Brute Creation, or, an Examination of Father Bougeant's Philosophical Amusement, &c.: In Two Letters to a Lady*. London: R. Minors, 1742.

Hopkins, Gerard Manley, *Poems of Gerard Manley Hopkins*, 4th edn, eds. W. H. Gardner and N. H. Mackenzie. London: Oxford University Press, 1970.

Horrell, David and Dominic Coad, '"The Stones Would Cry Out" (Luke 19.40): A Lukan Contribution to a Hermeneutics of Creation's Praise', *Scottish Journal of Theology* 64 (2010), 29–44.

Horrell, David, Cherryl Hunt and Christopher Southgate, *Greening Paul: Rereading the Apostle in a Time of Ecological Crisis*. Waco, TX: Baylor University Press, 2010.

Hrdy, Sarah Blaffer, 'Infanticide as a Primate Reproductive Strategy', *American Scientist* 65: 1 (1977), 40–49.

Huff, Peter A., 'Calvin and the Beasts: Animals in John Calvin's Theological Discourse', *Journal of the Evangelical Theology Society* 42: 1 (1999), 67–75.

Hunt, Cherryl, David Horrell and Christopher Southgate, 'An Environmental Mantra? Ecological Interest in Romans 8:19–23 and a Modest Proposal for its Narrative Interpretation', *Journal of Theological Studies* 59: 2 (2008), 546–79.

Hurley, Susan and Matthew Nudds (eds), *Rational Animals?* Oxford: Oxford University Press, 2006.

Inoue, Sana and Tetsuro Matsuzawa, 'Working Memory of Numerals in Chimpanzees', *Current Biology* 17: 23 (2007), R1004–5.

Irenaeus, 'Against Heresies', in. Cleveland Coxe, James Donaldson and Alexander Roberts (eds), *The Ante-Nicene Fathers: Translations of the Writings of the Fathers Down to AD 325*, vol. 1, A 315–567. Edinburgh: T & T Clark, 1997.

Jack, Jordynn, 'A Pedagogy of Sight: Microscopic Vision in Robert Hooke's Micrographia', *Quarterly Journal of Speech* 95: 2 (2009), 192–209.

Jenkins, Willis, *Ecologies of Grace: Environmental Ethics and Christian Theology*. New York: Oxford University Press, 2008.

Jenson, Robert W., 'Aspects of a Doctrine of Creation', in Colin E. Gunton ed. *The Doctrine of Creation: Essays in Dogmatics, History and Philosophy*, 17–28. London: T & T Clark, 2004.

John of the Cross, St, *The Complete Works*, ed. and trans. A. E. Peers. Wheathampstead: Anthony Clarke, 1974.

Jolley, Nicholas, *Locke: His Philosophical Thought*. Oxford: Oxford University Press, 1999.

Justin Martyr, 'First Apology', in A. Cleveland Coxe, James Donaldson and Alexander Roberts (eds), *The Ante-Nicene Fathers: Translations of the Writings of the Fathers Down to AD 325*, 1, vol. 1, 163–87. Edinburgh: T & T Clark, 1997.

Justin Martyr, St, *Dialogue With Trypho*, ed. Michael Slusser, trans. Thomas B. Falls and Thomas P. Halton. Washington, DC: Catholic University of America Press, 2003.

Keener, Craig S., *The Gospel of John: A Commentary*. Peabody, MA: Hendrickson Publishers, 2003.

Kelbie, Paul, 'Campaign Wins Reprieve for Uist Hedgehogs', *The Independent*, 20 February, 2007.

Kendrick, Keith M., 'Sheep Don't Forget a Face', *Nature* 414: 4860 (2001), 165–66.

Kirby, William, *On the History, Habits and Instincts of Animals*, The Bridgewater

Treatises on the Power and Wisdom of God as Manifested in the Creation, vol. VII. London: Pickering, 1835.

Kirby, William, 1759–1850, *On the Power, Wisdom and Goodness of God as Manifested in the Creation of Animals and in Their History, Habits and Instincts*, Bridgewater Treatises, vol. VII. London: W. Pickering, 1835.

Klein, Jan and Naoyuki Takahata, *Where Do We Come From? The Molecular Evidence for Human Descent*. Berlin; Heidelberg; New York: Springer, 2002.

Lactantius, *Divine Institutes*, eds and trans. Anthony Bowen and Peter Garnsey. Liverpool: Liverpool University Press, 2003.

Laland, Kevin N. and Bennett G. Galef (eds), *The Question of Animal Culture*. Cambridge, MA: Harvard University Press, 2009.

Leakey, Richard and Roger Letwin, *Origins Reconsidered: In Search of What Makes Us Human*. New York: Anchor Books, 1992.

Leal, Robert Barry, *Wilderness in the Bible: Toward a Theology of Wilderness*. New York: Peter Lang, 2004.

Lee, Sang Hyun, 'Edwards on God and Nature: Resources for Contemporary Theology', in Sang Hyan Lee and Allen C. Guelzo (eds), *Edwards in Our Time: Jonathan Edwards and the Shaping of American Religion*, 15–44. Grand Rapids, MI: Eerdmans, 1999.

Leiber, Justin, 'Descartes: The Smear and Related Misconstruals', *Journal for the Theory of Social Behaviour* 41: 4 (2011).

Leopold, Aldo, *A Sand County Almanac and Sketches Here and There*. Oxford: Oxford University Press, 1949.

Lewis, C. S., *The Problem of Pain*. New York: Oxford University Press, 2002.

Lightfoot, R. H., *St John's Gospel: A Commentary*, ed. C. F. Evans. Oxford: Clarendon, 1956.

Lindsay, Mark R., *Barth, Israel, and Jesus: Karl Barth's Theology of Israel*. Aldershot: Ashgate, 2007.

Linzey, Andrew. 'The Neglected Creature: The Doctrine of the Non-Human Creation and its Relationship With the Human Creation in the Thought of Karl Barth'. PhD thesis. University of London, 1986.

—*Christianity and the Rights of Animals*. London: SPCK, 1987.

—*Animal Theology*. London: SCM Press, 1994.

—*Animals and Trinitarian Doctrine: A Study of the Theology of Karl Barth*. Lampeter: Mellen, 1996.

—*Animal Gospel: Christian Faith as Though Animals Mattered*. London: Hodder & Stoughton, 1998.

—'So Near and Yet So Far: Animal Theology and Ecological Theology', in Roger S. Gottlieb ed. *The Oxford Handbook of Religion and Ecology*, 348–61. Oxford: Oxford University Press, 2007.

Linzey, Andrew and Dorothy Yamamoto (eds), *Animals on the Agenda: Questions About Animals for Theology and Ethics*. London: SCM Press, 1998.

Lloyd, Michael, 'Are Animals Fallen?', in Andrew Linzey and Dorothy Yamamoto (eds), *Animals on the Agenda: Questions About Animals for Theology and Ethics*, 147–60. London: SCM Press, 1998.

Locke, John, 'Mr. Locke's Reply to the Bishop of Worcester's Answer to His Second Letter', in *Works of John Locke*, vol. IV, 191–498. London: Thomas Tegg et al., 1823.

Lohse, Eduard, *A Commentary on the Epistles to the Colossians and to Philemon*, Hermeneia – a Critical and Historical Commentary on the Bible, ed. Helmut Koester. Philadelphia, PA: Fortress Press, 1971.

Louth, Andrew, 'The Cosmic Vision of Saint Maximus the Confessor', in Philip Clayton and Arthur Peacocke (eds), *In Whom We Live and Move and Have Our Being: Pantheistic Reflections on God's Presence in a Scientific World*, 184–96. Grand Rapids, MI; Cambridge: Eerdmans, 2004.

Lovejoy, Arthur O., *The Great Chain of Being: A Study of the History of an Idea*. Cambridge, MA: Harvard University Press, 1942.

Lovelock, James E., *The Revenge of Gaia: Earth's Climate Crisis and the Fate of Humanity*. New York: Basic Books, 2006.

Ludlow, Morwenna, *Universal Salvation: Eschatology in the Thought of Karl Rahner and Gregory of Nyssa*. Oxford: Oxford University Press, 2000.

—'Power and Dominion: Patristic Interpretations of Genesis 1', in David Horrell, Cherryl Hunt, Christopher Southgate and Francesca Stavrakopoulou (eds), *Ecological Hermeneutics: Biblical, Historical and Theological Perspectives*, 140–54. London: T & T Clark, 2010.

Luther, Martin, *Luther's Works*, (eds) Helmut T. Lehmann and Jaroslav Pelikan. Philadelphia, PA: Muhlenberg Press, 1958.

Lyons, J. A., S.J., *The Cosmic Christ in Origen and Teilhard de Chardin*. Oxford: Oxford University Press, 1982.

MacDonald, Gregory, 'Introduction', in Gregory MacDonald ed. *'All Shall be Well': Explorations in Universalism and Christian Theology, From Origen to Moltmann*, 1–25. Eugene, OR: Cascade Books, 2011.

Macdonald, Nathan, 'Review of J. Richard Middleton, *the Liberating Image: The Imago Dei in Genesis 1*', *Review of Biblical Literature* (2005), http://www.bookreviews.org

Mahoney, Edward P., 'Lovejoy and the Hierarchy of Being', *Journal of the History of Ideas* 48: 2 (1987), 211–30.

Maimonides, Moses, *The Guide of the Perplexed*, trans. Shlomo Pines. Chicago, IL: University of Chicago Press, 1963.

Malebranche, Nicolas, *The Search After Truth*, Cambridge Texts in the History of Philosophy, eds. Thomas M. Lennon and Paul J. Olscamp. Cambridge: Cambridge University Press, 1997.

Maloney, George A., S.J., *The Cosmic Christ From Paul to Teilhard*. New York: Sheed & Ward, 1968.

Marrow, James H., *Passion Iconography in Northern European Art of the Late Middle Ages and Early Renaissance: A Study of the Transformation of Sacred Metaphor Into Descriptive Narrative*. Kortrijk, Belgium: Van Ghemmert Publishing Company, 1979.

Marx, Karl, *Early Writings*, Penguin Classics, trans. Rodney Livingstone and Gregor Benton. London: Penguin Books,

Matthews, Gareth B., 'Animals and the Unity of Psychology', *Philosophy* 53: 206 (1978), 437–54.

Mausner, Ulrich, *Christ in the Wilderness: The Wilderness Theme in the Second Gospel and its Basis in the Biblical Tradition*. London: SCM Press, 1963.

Maximus the Confessor, *Ambigua 41*, (Patrologia Graeca 91:80a).

—Paul M. Blowers and Robert Louis Wilken (eds), *On the Cosmic Mystery of Jesus Christ: Selected Writings From Maximus the Confessor*. Crestwood, NY: St Vladimir's Seminary Press, 2003.

May, Gerhard, *Creatio Ex Nihilo: The Doctrine of 'Creation Out of Nothing' in Early Christian Thought*, trans. A. S. Worrall. Edinburgh: T & T Clark, 1994.

McDaniel, Jay, *Of God and Pelicans: A Theology of Reverence for Life*. Louisville, KY: Westminster John Knox Press, 1989.

McFadyen, Alistair, *Bound to Sin: Abuse, Holocaust and the Christian Doctrine of Sin*. Cambridge: Cambridge University Press, 2000.

McIntosh, Adam, 'Human and Animal Relations in the Theology of Karl Barth', *Pacifica* 22: 1 (2009), 20–35.

McKeown, John, 'What Are the Main Elements in an Old Testament Anthropology?' (2006) (unpublished paper).

—'An Ecologically Motivated Critique of Modern Natalist and Cornucopian Reception of Genesis 1:28a, "be Fruitful and Multiply", and Other Biblical "Fertility" Texts, as a Mandate for Unlimited Reproduction and Population Growth'. PhD thesis. University of Chester, 2011.

McKinion, Steven A. and Thomas C. Oden (eds), *Isaiah 1–39*, Ancient Christian Commentary on Scripture, vol. X. Downers Grove, IL: IVP, 2004.

McLaughlin, Ryan, 'Evidencing the Eschaton: Progressive-Transformative Animal Welfare in the Church Fathers', *Modern Theology* 27: 1 (2010), 121–46.

Messer, Neil, 'Natural Evil After Darwin', in Michael Northcott and R. J. Berry (eds), *Theology After Darwin*, 139–54. Milton Keynes: Paternoster, 2009.

Middleton, J. Richard, *The Liberating Image: The Imago Dei in Genesis 1.* Grand Rapids, MI: Brazos, 2005.

Minucius Felix, 'The Octavius of Minucius Felix', in A. Cleveland Coxe, James Donaldson and Alexander Roberts (eds), *The Ante-Nicene Fathers: Translations of the Writings of the Fathers Down to AD 325*, vol. 4, 167–98. Edinburgh: T & T Clark, 1997.

Moltmann, Jürgen, *Theology of Hope*, trans. James W. Leitch. London: SCM Press, 1967.

—*The Way of Jesus Christ: Christology in Messianic Dimensions*. San Francisco, CA: Harper, 1990.

—*The Coming of God: Christian Eschatology*. London: SCM Press, 1996.

Muddiman, John, *The Epistle to the Ephesians*, Black's New Testament Commentaries. London; New York: Continuum, 2001.

Naess, Arne, 'The Shallow and the Deep, Long-Range Ecology Movement', *Inquiry* 16 (1973), 95–100.

Nagel, Thomas, 'What is it Like to be a Bat?', *Philosophical Review* 83: 4 (1974), 435–50.

Nash, Roderick, *Wilderness and the American Mind*, 4th edn. New Haven, CT: Yale University Press, 2001.

Niebuhr, Reinhold, *The Nature and Destiny of Man: A Christian Interpretation*, Library of Theological Ethics. Louisville, KY: Westminster John Knox Press, 1996.

Nietzsche, Friedrich Wilhelm, *The Genealogy of Morals: A Polemic*, The Complete Works of Friedrich Nietzsche, vol. 13, ed. Oscar Levy, trans. Horace B. Samuel. Edinburgh; London: T. N. Foulis, 1910.

—*Human, All Too Human (1878)*. Cambridge; New York: Cambridge University Press, 2007.

Norton, Bryan G., 'Environmental Ethics and Weak Anthropocentrism', *Environmental Ethics* 6 (1984), 133–48.

Origen, *Origen: Contra Celsum*, trans. Henry Chadwick. Cambridge: Cambridge University Press, 1965.

—*Origen: On First Principles: Being Koetschau's Text of the de Principiis Into English, Together With an Introduction and Notes*, ed. G. W. Butterworth. Gloucester, MA: Peter Smith, 1973.

—*Commentary on the Gospel of John*, The Fathers of the Church: A New Translation, vol. 80, ed. Ronard E. Heine. Washington, DC: Catholic University of America Press, 1989.

Osborn, Eric, *Irenaeus of Lyons*. Cambridge: Cambridge University Press, 2001.

Osborne, Catherine, *Dumb Beasts and Dead Philosophers: Humanity and the Humane in Ancient Philosophy and Literature*. Oxford: Clarendon, 2007.

Paley, William, *Natural Theology, or, Evidences of the Existence and Attributes of the Deity: Collected From the Appearances of Nature*. London: C. J. G. and F. Rivington, 1830.

Pannenberg, Wolfhart, *Anthropology in Theological Perspective*. Edinburgh: T. & T. Clark, 1985.

—*Systematic Theology*, trans. Geoffrey W. Bromiley. Edinburgh: T & T Clark, 1994.

Patterson, F. and E. Linden, *The Education of Koko*. New York: Holt, Rinehart & Winston, 1981.

Patton, Kimberley C., 'Animal Sacrifice: Metaphysics of the Sublimated Victim', in Paul Waldau and Kimberley C. Patton (eds), *A Communion of Subjects: Animals in Religion, Science, and Ethics*, 391–405. New York: Columbia University Press, 2006.

Peacocke, Arthur, 'Biological Evolution – A Positive Theological Appraisal', in Robert John Russell, William R. Stoeger and Francisco J. Ayala (eds), *Evolutionary and Molecular Biology: Scientific Perspectives on Divine Action*, 357–76. Vatican City State; Berkeley, CA: Vatican Observatory and Center for Theology and the Natural Sciences, 1998.

Peacocke, Arthur Robert, *Theology for a Scientific Age: Being and Becoming – Natural, Divine, and Human*, Enlarged edn. Minneapolis, MN: Fortress Press, 1993.

Peck, A. L., 'Introduction', in *Historia Animalium*, Loeb Classical Library, trans. A. L. Peck, v–lxi. London; Cambridge, MA: William Heinemann; Harvard University Press, 1965.

Pellegrin, Pierre, *Aristotle's Classification of Animals: Biology and the Conceptual Unity of the Aristotelian Corpus*, trans. Anthony Preus. Berkeley, CA: University of California Press, 1986.

Pepperberg, Irene M., *The Alex Studies: Cognitive and Communicative Abilities of Grey Parrots*. Cambridge, MA: Harvard University, 2000.

Petropoulou, M.-Z. 'Animal Sacrifice in Greek Religion, Judaism, and Early Christianity in the Period 100 BC–AD 200'. D.Phil. thesis. University of Oxford, 2004.

Pettersen, Alvyn, *Athanasius*. London: Geoffrey Chapman, 1995.

Philo, *Philo Suppl. I*, Loeb Classical Library, trans. F. H. Colson and G. H. Whitaker. London: Heinemann, 1929.

Philo of Alexandria, *Philonis Alexandrini de Animalibus*, Studies in Hellenistic Judaism, ed. Abraham Terian, trans. Abraham Terian. Chico, CA: Scholars Press, 1981.

—*On the Creation of the Cosmos According to Moses*, ed. David T. Runia. Leiden: Brill, 2001.

Plaskow, Judith, *Sex, Sin and Grace: Women's Experience and the Theologies of Reinhold Niebuhr and Paul Tillich*. Lanham, MY: University Press of America, 1980.

Plato, *Timaeus*, trans. Donald J. Zeyl. Indianapolis, IN: Hackett, 2000.

Polkinghorne, John, *Reason and Reality*. London: SPCK, 1991.

Preece, Rod, *Animals and Nature: Cultural Myths, Cultural Realities*. Vancouver: UBC Press, 1999.

Preece, Rod and David Fraser, 'The Status of Animals in Biblical and Christian Thought: A Study in Colliding Values', *Society and Animals* 8: 1 (2000), 245–63.

Reinders, Hans S., *Receiving the Gift of Friendship: Profound Disability, Theological Anthropology, and Ethics*. Grand Rapids, MI: Eerdmans, 2008.

Renehan, Robert, 'The Greek Anthropocentric View of Man', *Harvard Studies in Classical Philology* 85 (1981), 239–59.

Ridley, Mark, *Evolution, 3rd edn*. Malden, MA; Oxford: Blackwell, 2004.

Roberts, Richard H., *Religion, Theology and the Human Sciences*. Cambridge; New York: Cambridge University Press, 2002.

Robinson, John A. T., *The Body: A Study in Pauline Theology*, Studies in Biblical Theology. London: SCM, 1952.

Rogerson, J. W., 'What Was the Meaning of Animal Sacrifice?', in Andrew Linzey and Dorothy Yamamoto (eds), *Animals on the Agenda: Questions About Animals for Theology and Ethics*, 8–17. London: SCM, 1998.

Rolston, Holmes, III, *Environmental Ethics: Duties to and Values in the Natural World*. Philadelphia, PA: Temple University Press, 1988.

Rosenfield, Leonara Cohen, *From Beast-Machine to Man-Machine*. New York: Oxford University Press, 1941.

Ross, David, *Aristotle, 6th edn*. London: Routledge, 1995.

Runia, David, *Philo in Early Christian Literature*. Assen; Minneapolis, MN: Van Gorcum; Fortress, 1993.

Sandmel, Samuel, *Philo of Alexandria: An Introduction*. Oxford: Oxford University Press, 1979.

Santmire, H. Paul. 'Creation and Nature: A Study of the Doctrine of Nature With Special Attention to Karl Barth's Doctrine of Creation'. ThD thesis. Harvard University, 1966.

—*The Travail of Nature: The Ambiguous Ecological Promise of Christian Theology*. Minneapolis, MN: Fortress Press, 1985.

—'Partnership With Nature According to the Scriptures: Beyond the Theology of Stewardship', in R. J. Berry ed. *Environmental Stewardship: Critical Perspectives, Past and Present*, 253–72. London; New York: T & T Clark, 2006.

Schäfer, Alexander O. F. M., 'The Position and Function of Man in the Created World, Part I', *Franciscan Studies* 20 (1960), 261–316.

Schmidz, David, 'Are All Species Equal?', *Journal of Applied Philosophy* 15: 1 (1998), 57–67.

Schnackenburg, Rudolf, *The Gospel According to John*, vol. 1, trans. Kevin Smyth. New York: Herder & Herder, 1968.

Schochet, Elijah Judah, *Animal Life in Jewish Tradition: Attitudes and Relationships*. New York: KTAV, 1984.

Schwartz, Eilon, 'Mastery and Stewardship, Wonder and Connectedness', in Hava Tirosh-Samuelson ed. *Judaism and Ecology: Created World and Revealed Word*, Religions of the World and Ecology, 93–106. Cambridge, MA; London: Harvard University Press, 2002.

Schweitzer, Eduard, *The Letter to the Colossians: A Commentary*, trans. Andrew Chester. London: SPCK, 1982.

Schwöbel, Christoph, 'God, Creation and the Christian Community', in Colin E. Gunton ed. *The Doctrine of Creation: Essays in Dogmatics, History and Philosophy*, 149–76. London: T & T Clark, 2004.

Scott, Peter, 'Thinking Like an Animal: Theological Materialism for a Changing Climate', *Studies in Christian Ethics* 24: 1 (2011), 50–66.

Singer, Peter ed. *In Defence of Animals*. Oxford: Blackwell, 1985.

—'All Animals Are Equal', in Tom Regan and Peter Singer (eds), *Animal Rights and Human Obligations*, 73–86. Eaglewood Cliffs, NJ: Prentice Hall, 1989.

—*Animal Liberation, 2nd edn*. London: Pimlico, 1995.

—'All Animals Are Equal', in James Rachels ed. *The Right Thing to Do: Basic Readings in Moral Philosophy*, Boston, MA: McGraw-Hill, 1999.

—*Practical Ethics, 3rd edn*. Cambridge: Cambridge University Press, 2011.

Sittler, Joseph, 'Called to Unity', *Ecumenical Review* 14: 2 (1962), 177–87.

—*Evocations of Grace: The Writings of Joseph Sittler on Ecology, Theology and Ethics*, eds. Steven Bouma-Prediga and Peter Bakken. Grand Rapids, MI: Eerdmans, 2000.

Skinner, John, *A Critical and Exegetical Commentary on Genesis*, International Critical Commentary. Edinburgh: T & T Clark, 1910.

Sly, Dorothy I., *Philo's Alexandria*. London; New York: Routledge, 1996.

Solomon, Norman, 'Judaism and the Environment', in *Judaism and Ecology*, World Religions and Ecology, vol. World religions and ecology, Aubrey Rose ed. 19–53. London: Cassell, 1992.

Sorabji, Richard, *Animal Minds and Human Morals: The Origins of the Western Debate*. Ithaca, NY: Cornell University Press, 1993.

—'Body and Soul in Aristotle', in Michael Durrant ed. *Aristotle's de Anima in Focus*, 162–96. London; New York: Routledge, 1993.

Southgate, Christopher, *The Groaning of Creation: God, Evolution, and the Problem of Evil*. Louisville, KY; London: Westminster John Knox, 2008.

—'Reading Genesis, John, and Job: A Christian Response to Darwinism', *Zygon* 46: 2 (2011), 370–95.

Steeves, H. Peter, 'The Familiar Other and Feral Selves: Life At the Human/ Animal Boundary', in Angela N. H. Creager and William Chester Jordan (eds), *The Animal-Human Boundary: Historical Perspectives*, 228–64. Rochester, NY: University of Rochester Press, 2002.

Steiner, Gary, *Anthropocentrism and Its Discontents: The Moral Status of Animals in the History of Western Philosophy*. Pittsburgh, PA: University of Pittsburg Press, 2005.

Strecker, Ulrike, Chrisitan G. Meyer, Christian Sturmbauer and Horst Wilkens, 'Genetic Divergence and Speciation in an Extremely Young Species Flock in Mexico Formed by the Genus Cyprinodon (Cyprinodontidae, Teleostei)', *Molecular Phylogenetics and Evolution* 6: 1 (1996), 143–49.

Stuckenbruck, Loren T., *1 Enoch 91–108*, Commentaries on Early Jewish Literature. Berlin: Walter de Gruyter, 2007.

Tanner, Kathryn, 'Creation and Providence', in John Webster ed. *The Cambridge Companion to Karl Barth*, 111–26. Cambridge: Cambridge University Press, 2000.

—'Eschatology and Ethics', in *The Oxford Handbook of Theological Ethics*, 41–56. Oxford: Oxford University Press, 2005.

—*Christ the Key*. Cambridge: Cambridge University Press, 2010.

Tappert, Theodore G. ed. *The Book of Concord: The Confessions of the Evangelical Lutheran Church*. Philadelphia, PA: Fortress Press, 1959.

Taylor, Jeremy, *Not a Chimp: The Hunt to Find the Genes That Make Us Human*. Oxford: Oxford University Press, 2009.

Teilhard de Chardin, Pierre, *The Phenomenon of Man*, trans. Bernard Wall. New York: Collins, 1959.

Thomas, Keith, *Man and the Natural World: Changing Attitudes in England 1500–1800*. London; New York: Penguin, 1984.

Ticciati, Susannah, *Job and the Disruption of Identity: Reading Beyond Barth*. London; New York: T & T Clark, 2005.

Tilley, T. W., 'God and the Silencing of Job', *Modern Theology* 5: 3 (1989), 257–70.

Tillich, Paul, *Systematic Theology*, 3 vols. Chicago, IL: University of Chicago, 1957.

Torrance, Thomas Forsyth, *Divine and Contingent Order*. Oxford: Oxford University Press, 1981.

Toulmin, George Hoggart, *The Antiquity and Duration of the World*. Boston, MA: J. P. Mendum, 1854.

Twain, Mark and Baender, Paul ed. *What is Man? And Other Philosophical Writings*. Berkeley and Los Angeles, CA: University of California Press, 1997.

van Huyssteen, J. Wentzel, *Alone in the World: Human Uniqueness in Science and Theology*. Grand Rapids, MI: Eerdmans, 2006.

VanDrunen, David, 'Natural Law in Noahic Accent: A Covenantal Conception of Natural Law Drawn From Genesis 9', *Journal of the Society of Christian Ethics* 30: 2 (2010), 131–49.

Villarreal, Luis P., *Viruses and the Evolution of Life*. Washington, DC: ASM Press, 2005.

Vischer, Lukas, 'Listening to Creation Groaning: A Survey of Main Themes of Creation Theology', in Lukas Vischer ed. *Listening to Creation Groaning: Report and Papers From a Consultation on Creation Theology Organised by the European Christian Environmental Network at the John Knox International Reformed Center From March 28 to April 1 2004*, 11–31. Geneva: Centre International Reforme John Knox, 2004.

von Balthasar, Hans Urs, *Origen: Spirit and Fire: A Thematic Anthology of His Writings*, trans. Robert J. Daly. Edinburgh: T & T Clark, 1984.

von Rad, Gerhard, *Genesis*. London: SCM, 1972.

Waddell, Helen, *Beasts and Saints*. London: Darton, Longman & Todd, 1995.

Wasserman, E. A., 'Comparative Cognition: Beginning the Second Century of the Study of Animal Intelligence', *Psychological Bulletin* 113: 2 (1993), 211–28.

Watson, Francis, 'In the Beginning: Irenaeus, Creation, and the Environment', in *Ecological Hermeneutics: Biblical, Historical and Theological Perspectives*, 127–39. London; New York: T & T Clark International, 2008.

Webb, Stephen H., *On God and Dogs: A Christian Theology of Compassion for Animals*. New York; Oxford: Oxford University Press, 1998.

Weir, Alex A. S., Jackie Chappell and Alex Kacelnik, 'Shaping of Hooks in New Caledonian Crows', *Science* 297: 5583 (2002), 981.

Wenham, Gordon J., *Genesis*, Word Bible Commentary. Waco, TX: Word, 1994.

Wesley, John, *Sermons on Several Occasions*, vol. V. New York: Ezekiel Cooper and John Wilson, 1806.

—*A Survey of the Wisdom of God in the Creation: Or, a Compendium of Natural Philosophy, Containing an Abridgement of That Beautiful Work, the Contemplation of Nature By Mr. Bonnet, of Geneva, Also, an Extract From Mr Deuten's 'Inquiry Into the Origin of the Discoveries Attributed to the Ancients*. New York: N. Bangs and T. Mason, 1823.

Westermann, Claus, *Genesis 1–11: A Commentary*, trans. John J. Scullion, S.J. London: SPCK, 1974.

White, Carolinne ed. *Early Christian Lives*, trans. Carolinne White. London: Penguin, 1998.

Whitehead, Alfred North, *Process and Reality: An Essay in Cosmology*. New York: Harper & Row, 1957.

Whitehead, Hal, *Sperm Whales: Social Evolution in the Ocean*. Chicago, IL: University of Chicago, 2003.

Wilkins, John S., *Defining Species: A Sourcebook From Antiquity to Today*. New York: Peter Lang, 2009.

Williams, David Ross, *Wilderness Lost: The Religious Origins of the American Mind*. Cranbury, NJ: Associated University Presses, 1987.

Williams, Michael Allen, *Rethinking 'Gnosticism': An Argument for Dismantling a Dubious Category*. Princeton, NJ: Princeton University Press, 1999.

Daniel J. Wilson, 'Lovejoy's the Great Chain of Being After Fifty Years', *Journal of the History of Ideas* 41: 2 (1980).

Wilson, R. McLachlan, *A Critical and Exegetical Commentary on Colossians and Philemon*, International Critical Commentary. London; New York: T & T Clark International, 2005.

Wingren, Gustaf, *Man and the Incarnation: A Study in the Biblical Theology of Irenaeus*. Edinburgh and London: Oliver and Boyd, 1959.

Winick, Charles, *The Dictionary of Anthropology*. New York: Philosophical Library, 1956.

Yarri, Donna, *The Ethics of Animal Experimentation: A Critical Analysis and Constructive Christian Proposal*. Oxford: Oxford University Press, 2005.

INDEX OF BIBLICAL REFERENCES

Note: 'n.' indicates a reference in a footnote.

Old Testament

New Testament

INDEX OF AUTHORS AND SUBJECTS

Made in the USA
Middletown, DE
20 January 2017